The Unquestionable Right To Be Free

Black Theology from South Africa

EDITED BY: **Itumeleng J Mosala and Buti Tlhagale**

ORBIS BOOKS

Maryknoll, New York 10545

This book is dedicated to
the memory of four-year-old
Mitah Ngubeni

Second Printing, February 1990

The Catholic Foreign Mission Society of America (Maryknoll) recruits and trains people for overseas missionary service. Through Orbis Books Maryknoll aims to foster the international dialogue that is essential to mission. The books published, however, reflect the opinions of their authors and are not meant to represent the official position of the society.

First published in South Africa by Skotaville Publishers (Incorporated Association not for Gain), 307 Hampstead House, 46 Biccard Street, P.O. Box 32483, Braamfontein 2017

Copyright © 1986 by the Institute for Contextual Theology
Published in the United States of America, with slight revisions, by Orbis Books
Manufactured in the United States of America

CONTENTS

EDITORIAL NOTE

It is more than a decade since the first Black Theology book by black South African theologians was published in South Africa. The banning of that book by the South African government remains a living testimony of the political and economic repression that black South Africans struggle under and against. What cannot be wished away, however, is the fact that the appearance of that book heralded the dawn of a new kind of black militancy: The struggle for the liberation of the oppressed and exploited black people was to be waged at all levels of the social formation. Christianity and the Christian church had up till that time served as the ideological tool for the softening up of black people and as a means by which black culture had been undermined. The emergence of Black Theology, however, spelt the dawn of a new awareness of the relation between western capitalist culture and Christianity. Black people were, as of that time, to draw the liberation struggle to the very centre of capitalist ideology, namely, the Christian theological realm.

It is important to remember that Black Theology did not drop from the sky, it was not created *ex nihilo*. It was, on the contrary, the product of concrete struggles that were being waged by black people in the late 1960s and early 1970s. These struggles were themselves a more contemporary expression of the historic struggles of black people against colonialism and capitalism.

The essays contained in this anthology address the South African black struggle at an important conjuncture in the development of late monopoly capitalism and its effects on peripheral capitalisms. Since the late 1960s we have been witnessing a worldwide capitalist crisis. There are, *inter alia*, two key characteristics of this crisis that have been part of the material conditions underlying the origins of Black Theology and the specifically black autonomous character of the struggle for liberation. These are, first, change from growth to stagnation in the dynamics of the economic substructure of western capitalism. As every thinking person can observe, the unbridled quest for profits has always inevitably led to an overproduction crisis. This overproduction of goods is, however, accompanied by the concomitant impoverishment and immiserization of the producers of these goods, namely, the workers. This is so because under conditions of an overproduction crisis, capitalism's priority is not the welfare of human beings but the maintenance of profit rates. Thus a reduction of the costs of production, especially the cost of employing workers, becomes one of its major priorities.

Secondly, 'the ruling class is aggressively using racism and sexism as weapons to divide the working class, prevent it from developing unified opposition to capitalist policies' (Marlene Dixon, *The Future of Women,* 1983, pp. 177f.). The development of *volkskapitalisme* in particular, but with an unprecedented impetus from international capital in the 1960s, required, as a condition of its valorization, the super exploitation of blacks and women and the political repression over opposition formations.

There is also a campaign mounted by the ruling class factions to promote federal and/or consociational constitutional models — an outrageous manoeuvre aimed at entrenching and consolidating the present apartheid structures with minimum adjustments.

There are, however, signs of hope. The growing militancy of the young black people who have virtually brought the entire educational system to a standstill and even rendered the black townships 'ungovernable' almost warrants the failure of the machinations of the dominant groups. The emergence of the massive Congress of South African Trade Unions (1985) equally promises more resistance from the working class as the rhetoric of a socialist alternative begins to take root.

The emergence of the United Democratic Front (1983) and its call for 'unity in the struggle through which all democrats regardless of race, religion or colour shall take part together' (*Race Relations Survey 1983*, p. 58) are bound to pose themselves as a challenge to the strategy of the Black Consciousness Movement that excludes white people in the struggle for liberation. This challenge is also posed by the newly formed Congress of South African Trade Unions that embraces the principle of non-racialism (*Sowetan* 2.12.85). There is of course no evidence that any significant number of white workers are interested in creating a new South Africa where colour will cease to be a determining factor.

These developments are bound to catch up with Black Theology. Furthermore it is becoming increasingly imperative to give content to and to distinguish between strategies and the ultimate goal of the liberation struggle. Black Theology needs to address this question.

Most essays in this book tend to be historical. Bonganjalo Goba, Takatso Mofokeng, Mokgethi Motlhabi and Lebamang Sebidi address the emergence and discursive expressions of Black Theology under the conditions of black suffering in the late sixties and early seventies in South Africa. The rest of the essays focus on the adjustments, developments and refinements which have taken place since then. The single most important feature of this publication on Black Theology and the black struggle in South Africa is the inclusion in it of two papers on Black Feminist Theology. It is the hope of many progressive black theologians that these two contributions herald a future of greater developments in the same direction. The editors of this book would like to extend their gratitude to the Institute for Contextual Theology for providing the financial, administrative and moral support that made the eventual publication of a Black Theology book in South Africa possible.

In particular our thanks are due to the director of ICT, the Rev. Frank Chikane, a selfless Christian activist and committed subject of the black struggle for liberation. We would also like to thank Mrs. Frances Chappelle, an American African of Berkeley, California, for patiently typing the manuscript from drafts that were often difficult to wade through.

It is our hope that this book will serve not only as a source of inspiration for countless black Christians who care, but also as an important text in the seminaries and faculties of theology, especially in the black institutions. We make no pretense to be writing for a white audience although we would hope a reading of this book in the white context could foster something of that *metanoia* that white missionaries came to Africa preaching to black people.

To enable the readers and especially the academic teachers to determine quickly which essay to read or prescribe for a particular purpose we have provided an abstract at the beginning of each essay.

Itumeleng Jerry Mosala, *Berkeley, California, 1985;*
Buti Tlhagale, *Soweto, 1985.*

INTRODUCTION

Almost fifteen years have passed since Black Theology was adopted as an approach to theological reflection by blacks in South Africa. Originating in America in the late 1960s, this kind of theology was imported to South Africa in the early 1970s by the Black Theology Project of the University Christian Movement. It was popularized through seminars, conferences and consultations, culminating in the publication of a book titled *Essays on Black Theology* (1972).[1] That book was subsequently published under different titles in various overseas editions, including British and American editions.

Some people may object to the suggestion that Black Theology originated in the 1960s and that black South African theologians imported it from America. It is not the task of an introduction, however, to engage in long discussions to defend a point. For this I would refer the reader to the book edited by James Cone and Gayraud Wilmore, *Black Theology: A Documentary History, 1966 – 1979,*[2] and to the essays referred to above. Suffice it to say that the first scholarly book on Black Theology was written by a black American, James Cone.[3] This was in 1969.

With the appearance of *Essays on Black Theology,* and because of the mood in this country at that time, many people thought that black theologians had begun to discover the true relevance of the Christian faith by reflecting seriously on their situation in the light of the gospel. Indeed, this was a beginning of relevant theologizing for South African blacks. The essays confirmed this. Most of the early attempts on Black Theology in this country were, however, of an introductory nature. They mostly attempted a definition of Black Theology: what made it necessary, what it sought to do, how it differed from white theology, etc., rather than dwelt upon its content in the sense of engaging fully in actual reflection and interpretation of the word of God in the South African situation.

Few of the theologians who engaged in Black Theology at that stage had an academic background in theology. Most were professional ministers of religion or students for the ministry. The latter tended to be polemic in their approach, inspired by black theologians like Cone and Cleage. This approach was 'iconoclastic' in nature rather than constructive. This was perhaps understandable at the beginning, and it was to be hoped that in due course the situation would reverse itself. Amidst all this fighting-talk were at least a few attempts at constructive work. Dr. Manas Buthelezi, now Lutheran bishop of Johannesburg, was to become the leading exponent of Black Theology. Similar construction was also attempted by Dr. Basil

Moore, a white theologian whose organization was originally responsible for engaging black theologians in this kind of theological reflection.

Essays on Black Theology was banned by the government within a month of its publication. This followed the banning of two people who were mostly responsible for importing Cone's books and some of his ideas into South Africa and for organizing reflection sessions on Black Theology. One of these was Dr. Basil Moore, already mentioned. The other one was the Reverend Sabelo Ntwasa, who was still a seminary intern at the time. By the time the book was banned there was already confusion regarding what organizational form the work of Black Theology would take in the future. It was 1972. The government had recently also banned eight leaders of the South African Students Organization (SASO) and the Black People's Convention (BPC) and an equal number of leaders of the white National Union of South African Students (NUSAS). This was followed by the appointment of a commission of enquiry, known as the Schlebusch Commission, to look into the activities of four organizations. These were the Christian Institute of South Africa, NUSAS, the Wilgespruit Fellowship Centre, and the University Christian Movement (UCM).

Convinced that the commission of enquiry would end with a decision by the government to ban it, the UCM decided to dissolve itself in advance. In so doing it left three of its projects, one of which was the Black Theology Project, to decide on their future structures as separate, independent entities. The Black Theology Project joined forces with SASO and the Black Community Programmes[4] to determine means of future support and continued existence. It was agreed that the project should remain independent from any existing organizations, be they church or secular. Instead, it was — in the spirit of self-reliance — to seek the sponsorship of all sympathetic black organizations at the time to enable it to continue its work.

A conference was held at Pietermaritzburg where most of these organizations, including the African Independent Churches Association (AICA) and the Interdenominational African Ministers Association of South Africa (IDAMASA), two black church and clergy organizations, were represented. While the general mood of the conference was sympathetic and morally supportive, the organizations were financially non-committal. This was equally true of the Black Community Programmes, which had provided funds for the conference. This was the beginning of the end. In fact, after that conference the Black Theology Project as an organization remained in existence only long enough for the conference report to be prepared and submitted. While the main cause of this decline was financial, it seems

ix

that the theological spirit was also beginning to wane and interest was being turned to other activities. Indeed, Black Theology at the time had received its support chiefly from students rather than from church leadership. Hence it was understandable that with students' change of focus, it would inevitably be affected. IDAMASA was, on the other hand, unhappy that the project was at the time headed by a person who was not an ordained minister.[5]

After the disintegration of the Black Theology Project several individual clergy and interested parties began publishing occasional articles in church periodicals and journals. Few of these were scholarly papers, still continuing in the early mood of polemic against white approaches to theology and 'mainline' church government. This approach continued until the appearance of the first major scholarly publication on South African Black Theology, by Allan Boesak.[6] Organizationally, Black Theology activity was a thing of the past. It had been abruptly terminated for lack of proper support, a permanent constituency, and continuing interest from the very structures that it sought to serve and make relevant.

Belatedly, however, the seminaries developed interest in it and began to think of ways in which it could be fitted in theological studies syllabi. Because the only South African publication on Black Theology had been banned, however, the only literature available was American books and a few surviving articles by South African black theologians. Books on African traditional religions were also brought in for attempted interpretation *a la* Black Theology. Black seminary lecturers found themselves called upon to turn into experts in interpreting biblical and theological texts in the black theological sense, even though most of them were themselves late-comers in the field of Black Theology. Most of them had never taken it seriously, contending that theology was neither black nor white. Two of Cone's early books were soon banned by the government.The time would come when Boesak's *Farewell to Innocence* (1977) would be considered the major text on Black Theology in seminaries.

We may thus speak of two stages in Black Theology in this country so far. The first, it has been suggested, was polemic and definitional (introductory), with some passing allusions to method. The second I will call quasi-academic, more with reference to the attempts that were made to adopt the approach at seminaries than to Boesak's book, which was the first major academic work on the subject in this country. Because of the lull that has followed these early attempts at Black Theology in South Africa, I have elsewhere referred to them as phase I of Black Theology and recommended the embarking on phase II.[7]

The essays in this volume may be regarded as a new beginning in engaging in black theological reflection. For this we have the Institute for Contextual Theology to thank. The institute has several task forces, of which the Black Theology Task Force is one. The essays in this volume issued from two conferences, in 1983 and 1984, organized by the institute through its Black Theology Task Force. The papers may not be too far removed in their approach from the original attempts at Black Theology. This is true particularly of the approach which often begins with a description of the historical, social, political or economic situation of blacks in this country before attempting a theological analysis or critique of it. This approach tends to juxtapose the situation described with its theological interpretation, often failing to do justice to the latter.

Should this necessarily be the approach of Black Theology or is there perhaps need for integrating the two activities: descriptive analysis of the situation and its theological interpretation in the course of the examination? Dr. Bonganjalo Goba, one of the early pioneers of Black Theology, is fond of speaking of the need for a hodogenic method of Black Theology in actual theologizing from the onset, while at the same time appealing to actual experience of the *sitz im leben* of black South Africans. This, he contends, is more meaningful than beginning by giving readers the impression that they were reading an essay on the history of black protest or resistance in this country rather than one on theology.

On the other hand, however, these papers are different from those in *Essays on Black Theology* in at least two respects. First, the majority are not 'compositions' but they rather attempt to be academic in approach. Almost half the papers in the original volume were of a compositional type. Second, some of the essays take Marxist analysis seriously. In this way they introduce into Black Theology an element which has long characterized Latin American Liberation Theology Early attempts on Black Theology in this country, like its American counterpart, had neglected Marxist analysis. They were suspicious of the idea of a class analysis, which, in their opinion, seemed to have the effect of blurring the race issue — the main cause of oppression in South Africa and America! Recent writings on the subject in the U.S. show that even black theologians there have begun to take Marxist analysis seriously.[8] This is partly as the result of dialogue with Latin American theologians and other minority theologians in the U.S., which began with a conference on 'Theology in the Americas'. To what extent such an analysis will continue to be employed in practice in this country is a matter of speculation best left in time.

The interjection of Marxist analysis introduces an element in method. To this extent and to the extent that there will be progress in black theological reflection once more, we may say that phase II of Black Theology in this country has begun. No doubt, there were allusions to method in phase I, as already admitted. This was not, however, a primary concern. With a few exceptions, it was subservient to polemics and definition posing as actual theological engagement. The method discussed broadly in the context of polemics seemed to display a vague grasp of the full import of the relationship between situational realities and the mission of the Bible. Few of its advocates were sufficiently equipped academically to apply it in practice, though this might well be done 'instinctively' in actual preaching and pastoral duties. Its emphasis also tended to be on biblical theology rather than constructive (systematic) theology, Christian ethics, practical theology, and other theological disciplines. For phase II to be fully realized, more concentration will have to be given to attempts at searching for and clarifying a method and the content upon which it will have to act.

Although most of the current contributors are trained in various theological disciplines, they have not necessarily written on fields of their specialties. They rather responded to the topics they were given to write and speak on. Another element of phase II will, hopefully, be to encourage theologians to write more and more on their specific fields of specialization. This will bring a variety of perspectives to the theological exercise, which can only be for its further enrichment. In addition to these perspectives, we must also determine what Black Theology can learn and what influence on it may be derived from African traditional religions, the African Independent Churches, black history and the liberation struggle in South Africa, as well as what can be learned from the African heritage as a whole and from American Black Theology. To use Goba's favourite expression, phase II of Black Theology must include the 'drawing up of an agenda' as one of its primary tasks. 'In the beginning was the Word...' May this word rediscover new and lasting expression in Black Theology as a relevant theology of the oppressed.

Mokgethi Motlhabi

NOTES

1. *Essays on Black Theology* (Johannesburg: UCM, 1972) was to have been edited by Sabelo Ntwasa. Because of a government ban served on Ntwasa, however, Mokgethi Motlhabi's name was substituted. Motlhabi became acting director of the Black Theology Project after Ntwasa. British edition: *Black Theology: The South African Voice*, ed. Basil Moore (London: Hurst, 1973); U.S. edition: *The Challenge of Black Theology in South Africa*, ed. Basil Moore (Atlanta: John Knox Press, 1974).

2. James H. Cone and Gayraud Wilmore, eds., *Black Theology: A Documentary History, 1966–1979* (Maryknoll, N.Y.: Orbis Books, 1979).

3. James Cone, *Black Theology and Black Power* (New York: Seabury Press, 1969).

4. A project of SPROCAS, which was jointly sponsored by the Christian Institute and the South African Council of Churches.

5. This may have been simply a concern of a few individuals within the ministers' association.

6. Allan Boesak, *Farewell to Innocence* (Maryknoll, N.Y.: Orbis Books, 1977).

7. This phrase was suggested to me by the book edited by Calvin E. Bruce and William R. Jones, *Black Theology: Phase II* (Lewisburg, Pa.: Bucknell University Press, 1978).

8. See, for instance, Cone's *For My People: Black Theology and the Black Church* (Johannesburg: Skotaville Publishers, and Maryknoll, N.Y.: Orbis Books, 1985).

FOREWORD

The Institute for Contextual Theology (ICT) convened a meeting of a number of well-known black theologians at the beginning of 1983 to brainstorm on the position of Black Theology in Southern Africa after what was perceived as a long period of silence. This meeting noted that there had been no formal intellectual exercise of reflecting on Black Theology since 1972 (beside the 1975 Mazenod conference) although it was accepted that a very small number of black theologians continued 'doing' Black Theology by preaching and living it in their pastoral practice. The ICT meeting was undertaken with the oppressed and exploited masses of Southern Africa in their struggles for liberation.

Review of the History of Black Theology
In reviewing the history of Black Theology in Southern Africa this task force of black theologians shared their memories and experiences about the beginnings and the development of Black Theology in Southern Africa. They discussed how the University Christian Movement (UCM) pioneered the Black Theology Project in 1971 through its director of theological concerns, Basil Moore.

The first seminar on Black Theology in South Africa was organized by the first director of the project, Sabelo Ntwasa, and it was held at Wilgespruit Fellowship Centre in 1970. Various other seminars and ministers' caucuses were held to propagate Black Theology throughout Southern Africa. Some of the papers read at those seminars were published in a book entitled *Essays on Black Theology*. The book was later published in America after it was banned in South Africa. It appeared with the title *The Challenge of Black Theology in South Africa*.

The second and last conference was held at Mazenod in Lesotho in 1975, and it was organized by Smangaliso Mkhatshwa. After that there was a period of inactivity in this regard until the 1983 meeting of the task force. This group of black theologians therefore agreed to 'revisit' Black Theology in the form of a conference to review the state and relevance of Black Theology in our present situation.

The conference took place at Wilgespruit Fellowship Centre from 16-18 August 1983 with about fifty theologians attending. The theologians consisted of 'lay' people, ministers, seminarians and lecturers in theology. Because of the many unanswered questions raised at the conference a follow-up conference was held at St. Francis Xavier, in Cape Town, from 10-14 September 1984 to consider researched material on these issues.

The Political Praxis of the 1983 Conference

The political praxis within which the conference was launched was of particular significance. In the early seventies when this project was launched the philosophy of Black Consciousness was the 'sole' internal rallying or mobilizing factor for most blacks in the country who were involved in the struggle. At that time Black Consciousness was seen as a uniting force and did not openly indulge in the ideological divisions of the past. But the 1983 conference was launched during a period of 'historical shifts in political praxis', a time when ideological divisions and conflicts were rife in the black communities.

Those who were directly involved with the Black Consciousness Movement in the mid-seventies testify to the fact that there was already a sign of deep-seated differences within the movement (SASO, BPC, etc.) as early as 1975/76, even before the bannings of 1977. The conflict intensified after the formation of the Azanian People's Organization (AZAPO) in 1978 and of the Congress of South African Students (COSAS) followed by the formation of the Azanian Students Organization (AZASO). AZAPO upheld Black Consciousness with a new emphasis on the 'black worker' whilst both student organizations adopted the 'progressive' non-racial position (as it is called) subscribing to the Freedom Charter.

Although the division on the surface seemed to be between the Black Consciousness Movement and the progressive democrats, a division based on a play between the class and race models or the combination of these models in trying to understand the South African society, it seems that the real divisive matter was the attitudes of these groupings to the historical liberation movements, the African National Congress (ANC) and the Pan-African Congress (PAC), which were banned in the early sixties.

Because of these ideological tensions the Wilgespruit conference became a combustion chamber. The phraseology of the conference theme, 'Black Theology Revisited', itself made some suspect that there was a conspiracy to dispose of Black Theology. Some of the questions raised seemed so heretical, from the traditional position of Black Theology, that the very foundation of Black Theology seemed to be threatened. The final statement of this 1983 seminar reflects some of these tensions.

Resolution

At the 1984 conference it was accepted that what happens in the black struggle affects the process of theologizing about that struggle. Our present historical praxis therefore must affect Black Theology itself. Whilst agreeing that Black Theology is a theology of the oppressed and exploited black people, the conference recognized the divergences and convergences in the premises from which black theologians theologize. It was agreed therefore that a way be opened to allow creative black theological reflection and action irrespective of ideological differences, to avoid a paralysis in the movement of black theological ideas.

Black Theology, as a theology of the oppressed and exploited black masses must, therefore, rally these divergent ideological approaches to give them a purpose and a goal. This purpose must be evaluated in terms of liberation, justice and peace.

Frank Chikane

ABBREVIATIONS

AICA	African Independent Churches Association
AJA	*American Journal of Archaeology*
A.M.E.	African Methodist Episcopal Church
ANC	African National Congress
APO	African People's Organization
AZAPO	Azanian People's Organization
AZASO	Azanian Students Organization
BPC	Black People's Convention
COSAS	Congress of South African Students
ICT	Institute for Contextual Theology
ICU	Industrial and Commercial Workers Union
IDAMASA	Interdenominational African Ministers Association of South Africa
JSOT	*Journal for the Study of the Old Testament*
JTSA	*Journal of Theology for Southern Africa*
NFC	National Forum Committee
NRC	Natives Representative Council
NUSAS	National Union of South African Students
PAC	Pan-African Congress
PEQ	*Palestine Exploration Quarterly*
SASO	South African Students Organization
S.Ts.	Sotho-Tswana
TNC	Transvaal Native Congress
UCM	University Christian Movement
UDF	United Democratic Front
VTSupp	*Vetus Testamentum, Supplements*
Z.	Zulu

CONTRIBUTORS

BONITA BENNETT
A youth worker in the Anglican Students Fellowship of the Church of the Province of South Africa.

FRANK CHIKANE
General Secretary of the Institute for Contextual Theology.

BONGANJALO GOBA
A minister of the Congregational Church and Senior Lecturer at the University of South Africa.

SHUN GOVENDER
A minister of the black Dutch Reformed Church and Secretary General of the Belydende Kring.

JULIAN KUNNIE
A Lutheran minister from Durban currently pursuing a doctoral programme in Black Theology at the Graduate Theological Union in Berkeley, California.

SIMON MAIMELA
A minister of the black Dutch Reformed Church and Lecturer in Black Theology at the University of Botswana.

BERNADETTE MOSALA
Director of the South African Council of Churches division of Home and Family Life.

ITUMELENG JERRY MOSALA
A minister of the Methodist Church of South Africa and Lecturer in Old Testament and Black Theology at the University of Cape Town.

MOKGETHI MOTLHABI
Director of the Educational Opportunities Council and part-time Lecturer at the University of South Africa.

JOHN B. NGUBANE
Roman Catholic Priest and Lecturer at Cedara Seminary in Pietermaritzburg.

LEBAMANG SEBIDI
Director of Adult Education at the Funda Centre, Soweto.

BUTI TLHAGALE
Priest at Our Lady of Mercy, Soweto.

Chapter 1

The Dynamics of the Black Struggle and Its Implications for Black Theology
LEBAMANG SEBIDI

Editors' Abstract

Four historical phases of the black struggle in South Africa are discernible. The Khoisan phase represents the initial clash of economic and cultural interests between the indigenous people and the white settlers. The latter used their military might to dispossess the Khoisan of their land and cattle. The tribalistic phase refers to the armed clash between the African people in the Eastern Cape and the encroaching white colonial forces. This phase also ended in the landlessness of black people and their conversion into dependent wage labourers. The nationalistic phase points to the era of black national unity formed in 1912 following the formation of the all-white Union of South Africa in 1910. The politics of black nationalism from 1912 to 1960 were the politics of moderation, integration and constitutional reforms. The Black Consciousness phase 'represents an almost total break with white liberal tutelage... The black man was to be on his own because...the black struggle for genuine liberation could only be waged on the basis of black units, black solidarity'. Since the banning of Black Consciousness organizations in 1977 the black community has been ideologically divided between those who see race as a determinative category of understanding and those who see class as a fundamental factor in analysis of South Africa. Needless to say the relevance or otherwise of Black Theology is deeply affected by these ideological debates. But there is a neglected dialectic realization that 'theory must have historical and empirical rootage. Reality fathers theory, and not the other way round'. Taken separately, each of the two ideological perspectives is inadequate. But 'it is not in what both camps uphold, but in what both camps tend to reject or de-emphasize that the fault lies'. The relevance of Black Theology is determined by the nature of the reality of South Africa: A double bondage of racial oppression and economic exploitation. In the past 117 years 'blackness' has been a symbol of economic and class exploitation.

Introduction
In 1984 the struggle or conflict that this paper is focusing on entered
into its three hundred and thirty-secondth year. That struggle, that
conflict, which began in 1652, has been a long and arduous conflict.
And far from being a merely exciting academic head-trip, or a fitting
topic for some highfalutin, cerebral palaver, this protracted struggle,
in all its stark reality and immediacy, has already claimed thousands
of human lives, particularly black human lives. The sixty-seven that
were left stone dead at the 1960 Sharpeville massacre[1] were but a long
distant echo of the 1921 Bulhoek slaughter, where one hundred and
sixty-three black Israelites were gratuitously mowed down by the
sputtering rifle and machine-gun power of the South African police
and the defence force unit.[2] This struggle has always been dead serious.

The aim of this paper is, first of all, to give a brief historical survey
of this struggle. This survey will then serve as a kind of backdrop
against which an analysis of the nature of this three-century saga will
be attempted. An analysis, any analysis, is a process of understanding. Its goal is knowledge. But, unless one belonged to that Greek
school of philosophers who believed in the pursuit of knowledge for
its own sake, the knowledge that accrues to one through the process
of analysis is subservient to an evolution of practical solutions of life's
problems. Analysis is akin to diagnosis in medical practice. The goal
of diagnosis is prescription. In political parlance, the terms 'analysis'
and 'strategy' are, broadly speaking, a rendition of diagnosis and
prescription. A strategy or prescription which is not based on a sound
analysis or diagnosis is at best 'dangerous whistling in the dark'.
Analysis is important. This old Jewish proverb can hardly be bettered
on this score:

> If you don't know where you
> are going (diagnosis), any road
> will take you there (strategy).

The paper will then attempt to show that since the early 1970s the
South African problematic has been subjected to two conflicting
kinds of analysis. It will be seen that the dividing line between these
two analytic paradigms approximates the line that cleaves black opposition in this country into two seemingly irreconcilable ideological
camps. This is the so-called race/class debate.

The discussion of this debate will then be followed by an attempt at
assessing or weighing the validity or non-validity of Black Theology
in the light of the aforementioned debate. Finally a personal assess-

ment will be made of the debate in question and of the status of Black Theology in the maelstrom of this debate.

The Struggle: A Panoramic View of Some Historical Landmarks

The conflict between the natives of this country and Europeans, emigrant non-Africans, may be divided into four broad historical periods — phases of the struggle:

> ★The Khoisan phase
> ★The Tribalistic phase
> ★The Nationalistic phase, and
> ★The Black Consciousness phase.

We shall briefly look at each of these historical phases in turn.

The Khoisan Phase: Seventeenth Century

The term 'Khoisan' is used in recent scholarship to refer, collectively, to the so-called 'Hottentots' and 'Bushmen'. The pejorative overtones traditionally associated with these latter terms are avoided by substituting 'Khoi' (or 'Khoikhoi') for Hottentots and 'San' for Bushmen.[3]

When the first permanent European settlement was put up at the Cape in 1652, it was the Khoisan group of South Africans which was destined to deal with this new, portentous encounter. As we all know, the elements of that encounter are the stock-in-trade of every primary school history book. But what is often not given sufficient emphasis and clarity is the fact that in the minds and eyes of the native Khoisan, the setting up of that Cape settlement was no more and no less than a blatant invasion of their native land by curly-haired and blue-eyed, white-skinned foreigners. And against this foreign invasion, the Khoisan were prepared to put up a fight. They resisted the usurpation of their land by means of at least two recorded wars. Richard Elphick captures the core of that Khoisan resentment and determination to fight as he writes:

> As soon as the freeburghers put their hand to the plough the Peninsular Khoikhoi realised that the European presence at the Cape would be permanent and most probably expansive. The Khoikhoi resented not only the loss of exceptional pastures near Table Mountain, but also the way the new farms blocked their access to watering areas on the Cape Peninsula.[4]

It is a matter of no little significance that the Khoikhoi were themselves pastoral farmers who kept cattle and sheep and who, therefore, harboured a keen interest in the land, water and pasturage. The

Cape settlement community and the freeburghers also shared the selfsame interest. It is therefore the frontiers of trade and agrarian expansion that quickly brought about a bitter conflict of interests: Khoikhoi interests vs white settler interests. As intimated above, contrary to popular South African history the Khoikhoi resisted: in 1659, led by a courageous and determined man by the name of Doman, the Khoi furiously attacked the seven-year-old foreign settlement, destroying its food supplies, its farms, and its livestock. This was the first Khoikhoi-Dutch War. The indigenous people were defending their land, water and pasture against incipient colonial expansion.[5] The second Khoikhoi-Dutch War was led by the famous Gonnema and this war was waged intermittently between 1673 and 1677 when Gonnema and his followers were finally brought to heel in the obviously unequal conflict.

From this time onwards both the Khoi and the San were gradually, but inexorably incorporated into white society as farmhands, herders and kitchen servants. By the middle of the 1800s, these fascinating people, who lived so close to 'Mother Nature', were completely defeated and subjected to white rule.[6]

There are two points that one would wish to make here, namely, that the Khoisan did not willingly submit to their systematic incorporation into foreign, white rule; and that the Khoisan economic base — land and cattle — was the bone of contention between these indigenous people and the white foreigners, right from the onset.

This then was the seventeenth-century phase of the black struggle for the land, water, and pasturage. The scene of the struggle was mainly in the northwestern Cape.

The Tribalistic Phase: Eighteenth Century and Early Nineteenth Century

The dramatic events of the second phase of the black struggle were enacted mainly in the eastern frontier. The protagonists in conflict, this time round, were the so-called Bantu and the eastern vanguard of the white settler community in the Cape. The earliest recorded skirmish between Bantu and Boer was in 1702 — exactly one half century after the arrival of the Dromedaris, Rijger and Goedehoop at the Cape in 1652.[7]

It is this longish time-span between the arrival of white foreigners at the Cape (1652) and their first contact with the indigenous Bantu (1702) which has provided a basis for the popularization of the thesis that:

> ...the Bantu-speakers arrived as immigrants on the high-
> veld of the trans-Vaal at about the same time as the white
> men first settled in Table Bay.[8]

But recent scholarship is diametrically opposed to this thesis. Ra-
dio-carbon dating, for instance, bears testimony to the fact that there
were negroid iron age settlements in the Transvaal as early as the fifth
century A.D.[9] And if this is true, it means that the Bantu have a
head-start of centuries in their occupancy and possession of this
southern tip of Africa, relative to white occupancy and arrival. And
as regards that particular region called the Cape, the historian W. M.
MacMillan, writing in his book entitled *Bantu, Boer, and Briton,* has
this to say:

> Undoubtedly the tribes were in effective occupation down
> to the Fish River long before the Europeans. Williams, of
> the L.M.S., the first missionary to the 'kaffirs', took up
> residence at the "great place" of the paramount chief,
> Gaika, in 1816. The "great place" of a chief is not an
> outpost, and Williams' grave remains to show that Gaika
> was within three miles of the later Fort Beaufort, very near
> the Fish River. Even the outposts still further west in the
> Zuurveld must have been fairly strongly held.[10]

The Bantu were here long before the turn of the seventeenth century. Now, as in the case of the Khoi, the Bantu were pastoralists,
with a keen interest in cattle and sheep. But over and above this, they
were almost like the Boers in that they tilled the soil and were, therefore, less nomadic than the Khoi and San. It is these characteristics of
their economy — pastoral and agricultural — that were destined to
initiate and fan some of the fiercest conflicts between Bantu and Boer
on the eastern frontier, starting from the latter part of the eighteenth
century.

The eight or so wars that characterized this second phase of the
struggle came down in liberal history as the 'Kaffir Wars'. The first of
these was in 1779 and the last in 1879 — a *hundred year war* between
several clans of the black vanguard, Xhosas, in the eastern Cape,
ancestors of a Mandela, Biko, Pityana and a Ntwasa, on the one
hand, and the white settler communities, on the other hand. More
often than not when there is talk about this period, the impression is
given that the basic reason for this hundred year conflict was the fact
that the Xhosas were bellicose savages, filled with lust for colonial
cattle and an irrational desire to spill white Christian blood with their

metal assegais — in short, it was an inevitable clash of two cultures, one superior and civilized, the other inferior and barbaric. The historian C.W. de Kiewiet provides us with a different version of this ferocious saga. In this book entitled *A History of South Africa: Social and Economic,* he writes that:

> for the most part the wars were not caused by the inborn
> quarrelsomeness of savage and war-like tribes, but by the
> keen competition of two groups, with very similar agricul-
> tural and pastoral habits, for the possession of the most
> fertile and best-watered stretches of land.[11]

Again as was the case in the first phase, in this second phase the land was indisputably the issue. The indigenous people were dispossessed, sometimes by violent force of arms, at other times by sheer 'non-violent' chicanery. Either way, the bone of contention was the land. Says de Kiewiet:

> Land was bought with harness, guns, and cases of brandy.
> It was acquired by the process of turning a permission to
> graze into the right to occupy.[12]

These sordid deals were made possible because of the natives' different philosophy or understanding of ownership. In the white settlers' minds, ownership was more important and more decisive than *'use';* whereas for the African natives it was *'use'* that formed the basis of their relationship towards their communally-owned land.

> The notion that a signature or the gift of a spavined horse
> gave a white man the right to hold land to the exclusion of
> all others was foreign to the native mind. Even more for-
> eign was the notion that land where all men's beasts had
> grazed without let could be reserved for the herds of a
> single individual.[13]

However, be that as it may, the dispossession of the people's land and livestock went on unabated. The 1878 routing of the British forces by King Cetshwayo's Zulu army at Isandhlwana and the 1906 Bambata Rebellion were but late nineteenth- and early twentieth-century echoes, in the interior of the land, of the tumultuous hundred years war in the Cape eastern frontier.

The Sand River Convention (1852) and the Bloemfontein Convention (1854) recognized and ratified the sovereignty of the Boers both in the Transvaal and Orange Free State. This meant that the Boers in these newly 'established' republics would deal with their 'kaffirs' in the way they saw fit. So could the English in the Cape and Natal. What all this meant was that by the turn of the twentieth century there was relatively little independence left among the indigenous people of this country. Their socio-political structures and their economic base had been overrun by the ruthless and insatiable white settlers' hunger for land and labour. Describing the whites' exploitation of the natives and their resources, de Kiewiet writes:

> In the land in which they [natives] lived the free resources of soil, water, and grass had been expropriated or diminished. These resources represented the capital upon which tribal life had been based. Without these resources of soil, water and grass the natives were obliged to do labour for those who now controlled them. Acquisition of land by Europeans was quite frequently a method of annexing labour as well. Since the earliest days it was frequent practice for farmers to buy land, not for the land's own sake, but in order to command the labour of the natives upon it. It was a process that deliberately extinguished native property in the land and their security of tenure upon it, so that they were helpless before the power that private ownership conferred on the whites.[14]

The land had been foundational to the lives of the indigenous people. When they lost the land, they lost their independence and the ability to shape and determine their destiny.

The natives lost the land, but not without struggling valiantly to keep it. This is what we would refer to as the tribalistic phase of the struggle. It was characterized by the individual African tribes struggling to hold onto their land, each tribe labouring under the illusion that it could win that struggle on an individual, tribal basis. The beginning of the twentieth century saw almost every tribe or clan in South Africa virtually incorporated into the socio-political and economic system of the white settlers. The conquest was all but complete at the turn of the present century.

The Nationalistic Phase: End of the Nineteenth Century – Beginning of the Twentieth

By the mid-nineteenth century the delineation of South Africa into the four provinces was already a *de facto* reality: the two Boer Republics in the north — the Transvaal and Orange Free State — and the two southern British provinces — Natal and the Cape. Each of these provinces dealt with its 'native problem' in the way it saw fit. The natives, in turn, generally responded to this provincial handling severally and fragmentally, in a haphazard, un-coordinated manner. Individual, small tribes still believed in 'bargaining' with the white conquerors in the hope of getting a better deal for their individual communities. It is for this reason that very often when there was a military clash between a given tribe or clan and the white settler commandos, the latter invariably found it quite easy to enlist the help of the 'good, loyal' natives against the recalcitrant 'black rebels'. This is exactly what happened in the 1906 Bambata Rebellion: not only the native police (Nonqai), but also native 'soldiers' recruited from 'loyal tribes' made it extremely difficult for Bambata and his courageous followers to mount an effective resistance.[15]

This fragmented response to white settler encroachment was a characteristic feature of both the first and second phases of the struggle for the land.

The tail-end of the 1800s and the beginning of the 1900s in South · Africa were clearly marked by the defiant stand of the two northern Boer Republics — the Transvaal and Orange Free State — against any imperial interference in their affairs and attempts at annexation to the two southern British colonies, Natal and the Cape. At this stage South Africa's 'native policy' was in a fragmented state. For instance, the Cape Colony during this period operated a *non-racial,* qualified franchise, property and education being the only qualificatory factors. It is on record that by the 1880s there were well over 12 000 Africans on the common voters roll in the Cape, having considerable influence in at least five constituencies in the eastern Cape. In 1886 they made up 47% of the electorate in these five constituencies.[16] This so-called 'Cape tradition' came to be idealized by many African leaders as a system which offered '...a new method of political adjustment, an alternative to the wars of resistance'.[17] This idealization of the Cape liberal tradition was made to look even more attractive by what was at the time obtaining in Natal and the two Boer Republics — up north.

Natal had evolved its own brand of native policy. Despite Natal's non-racial constitution, less than a dozen Africans appeared on the common voters roll. Clever administrative devices ensured that this was so.[18]

In the independent republics of the Transvaal and Orange Free State the constitutional stand was simple and straightforward. There was to be no equality between Bantu and Boer, either in church or in state. The extension of the franchise to the Bantu in these two republics was a matter that could never be contemplated.

Thus both Natal and the two Boer Republics offered an unattractive alternative to the slightly lenient and partially open Cape liberal tradition. The extension of this tradition to the rest of the country became the *raison d'etre* of the black struggles of this period and for many years after.

This was the cry of the Transvaal Native Congress (TNC) founded in 1905. Comparable organizations in the Orange Free State and Natal also hankered after the Cape tradition. Furthermore, as Denoon states, the African People's Organization (APO) established in 1903 in the Cape aimed at fighting for the maintenance of the much valued Cape liberal tradition.[19]

It is in this context of the idealization of the Cape liberal tradition that one can understand why the bulk of the indigenous people of this country had their sympathies, and often, active support, on the side of the British imperial armies in the 1899-1902 Anglo-Boer War. As T.R.H. Davenport so aptly notes, 'white authority held real power in South Africa'.[20] But the natives, no doubt naively, had come during this time period to believe in and rely on what Peter Walshe refers to as '...the sense of common justice and love of freedom so innate in the British character'.[21] And so, in this sense, British victory over the Boers would represent, in the eyes and minds of the Bantu, the extension of the Cape liberal tradition, which was the only non-violent and constitutional way to the total incorporation of every South African in a unified socio-political and economic structure of their fatherland.

In this context, the Treaty of Vereeniging, which was signed by Boer and Briton in 1902, came as a world-shattering disillusionment to the Africans. In the incisive words of de Kiewiet: 'Downing Street had surrendered to the frontier'.[22] Native policy and political unity of the four provinces were the two issues that clamoured for immediate attention at the Vereeniging peace treaty. Britain, for fear of fragmenting white unity, left the decision on the enfranchisement of the natives in the hands of those who thought the very notion of native enfranchisement anathema.

> For Britain to have insisted upon a higher place for the natives was to offend the white communities, especially Natal and the Republics, in their deepest convictions. Humanity and liberty became opposites which for long years had paralysed action.[23]

It was the British failure to uphold and defend the well-appreciated

Cape liberal tradition, the non-racial albeit qualified franchise, which prompted African leaders, in the four provinces, into realizing that 'white unity' had to be met with 'supra-tribal African unity'. This crucial awakening was long in coming.

As it is now known, the 1902 Vereeniging peace treaty was but a prelude to the 1910 exclusive white union of South Africa. The impending white union gave rise to the *Native Convention,* which met in Bloemfontein in 1909 to discuss the burning problems spawned by the exclusion of blacks from the union talks. Writes Edward Roux:

> This was the first occasion on which politically minded
> Africans came together from all corners of South Africa to
> discuss common problems. To this meeting came Walter
> Rubusana from the Cape, John Dube from Natal, M. Mat-
> sisi and J. Makgothi from the Orange Free State. In addi-
> tion, were delegates from the Transvaal and from
> Bechuanaland.[24]

The mild and sycophantic requests that were issued by this 1909 Native Convention were hardly heeded by the British Crown or the architects of the union. The white union of South Africa became a constitutional reality in 1910.

It was only at the end of 1911 that a more permanent form of African political opposition to the union began to take shape. One of the moving spirits behind this historic move was one Pixley ka Isaka Seme. On October 24, 1911, Pixley made this impassioned plea to the blacks of South Africa:

> The demon of racialism, the aberrations of Xhosa-Fingo
> feud, the animosity that exists between the Zulus and the
> Tongas, between the Basuto and every other Native must
> be buried and forgotten... We are one people. These divi-
> sions, these jealousies, are the cause of all our woes and of
> all our backwardness and ignorance today.[25]

Pixley advocated the immediate formation of a South African native congress and suggested an agenda for an inaugural meeting. So on 8 January 1912, several delegates assembled in Bloemfontein. This was considered by many as the triumph of supra-tribalism and the birth of a South African *black nationalism.*

The executive of this all-important congress consisted of eleven members, who clearly represented the ideals of the elite of the African people. Of the eleven, four were ministers of religion, three were lawyers, one, Solomon Plaatje, was a newspaper editor, whilst Makgatho and Pelem were teachers and Mapikela a building contractor.[26] It was therefore not surprising that the general characteristic of this first group of leaders was political moderation. The fact that the newly formed union government was invited by the conveners of this first permanent African National Congress to send its representative to open the inaugural meeting of congress is sufficient indication of congress' political moderation and unwillingness to anger unnecessarily the powers that ruled over the country with a large store of armaments and control of most of South Africa's resources.[27]

The leaders and delegates of this Bloemfontein Conference were anything but hot-headed trade unionists or fire-eating political radicals. Their demands were simple and straightforward. In his key-note address to the conference, Pixley ka Isaka Seme intoned:

> The white people of this country have formed what is known as the union of South Africa — a union in which we have no voice in the making of laws and no part in their administration. We have called you therefore to this Conference so that we can together devise ways and means of forming one national unity and defending our rights and privileges.[28]

Mobilization at a national level, creating a supra-tribal organization, was obviously a means towards the attainment of what they considered to be their 'constitutional rights' — that is, 'equality of opportunity within the economic life and political institutions of the wider society'.[29] The ideal was always the Cape qualified but non-racial franchise, which they had so fervently hoped at the end of the Anglo-Boer War would be extended throughout South Africa as the foundation for the creation of a just and harmonious South African polity.

In contrast, therefore, to the first two phases of the struggle, where arrows, spears, assegais and shields were used in an extra-constitutional or extra-parliamentary effort to win back the land — this third phase tended to concentrate on non-military strategies and tactics in an attempt to win 'constitutional rights'. This is, obviously, a crucial distinction. Peter Walshe seems to confirm this shift in strategies, tactics and principles, when he writes:

> In his letter accepting the presidency, Dube [the Rev. John Dube, first ANC president, elected in absentia] set out to clarify the objectives of Congress and his own

hopes. The eighth of January (1912) had been a day her-
alding the renaissance of the native races. Although the
first-born sons of Africa, they were now the last-born children and citizens of the glorious British Empire. In the
excitement of this awakening to political life, the emphasis
was nevertheless to be on prudence, restraint, and dutiful
respect for the rulers God had placed over them. The
motto, he suggested, was *festina lente*.[30]

Thus the period between 1912 and 1960 was, on the whole, marked
by the sometimes powerful, at other times intermittent and hesitant
activities of the ANC. We used the qualificatory phrase 'on the
whole' because in 1919 another powerful African organization, called
the Industrial and Commercial Workers Union (ICU), led by men
like Clement Kadalie and George Champion, emerged to share the
stage with the ANC. But by the end of the 1920s, ICU was a spent
force.

The period between 1912 and 1960 would not come to a close
before a very significant split between the ANC and the Pan-African-
ists within the ANC became a formal reality. The Pan-African Congress (PAC), led by stalwarts like Robert Sobukwe, Potlako Leballo,
and Peter Raboroko, was formed in 1959. Many people believe that
the formation, in 1943, of the Congress Youth League foreshadowed
this 1959 split.

Three things stand out clearly in this phase of the struggle:
* Africans made a valiant attempt to struggle as a 'nation' instead of
  on the basis of tribal or clannish fragmentation.
* These first South African nationalists operated within the parameters of a completely conquered and dispossessed people. At this
  stage, conquest and dispossession were a *fait accompli*. Hence their
  integrationist demands. The overthrow of the state was furthest
  from their minds and hearts. They merely pleaded for the end of
  their collective exclusion from the system. Their perspective on the
  land had shifted considerably compared to what it was in the two
  previous phases: the Khoisan and the tribalistic.
* For almost half a century the ANC refused to let the flickering
  flames of the black struggle die. At the end of the sixties this torch
  was handed over to younger hands.

The Black Consciousness Phase: End of the Sixties Onwards
Ideologically this fourth phase — the Black Consciousness phase of
the struggle — represents an almost total break with white liberal
tutelage. The classic definition of Black Consciousness as, in Lodge's

words, 'an attitude of mind, a way of life', puts this movement at the philosophic and introspective level.[31] It was a hefty attempt at severing what one may call, for lack of a better term, the 'psychological umbilical cord' that held the black man tied to the slow-moving liberal band-wagon. The black man was to be on his own because, the Black Consciousness ideologues reasoned, the black struggle for genuine liberation could only be waged on the basis of black unity, black solidarity.

The Black Consciousness philosophy made itself felt through organizations like SASO, BPC and many others. For instance, the BPC constitution declared that membership of BPC 'shall be open to blacks only'. It continued to say 'unless inconsistent with the context, "black" shall be interpreted as meaning Africans, Indians and Coloureds'.[32] Here was a clear rejection of the integrationist and multi-racialist approach adopted by the ANC in the forty-eight years of its struggle for black freedom. This shift was no doubt significant. But it remains to be seen whether it was a shift at the level of principles (ideology) or merely at the level of strategies and tactics. These levels will be discussed below.

It is about time we brought this sketchy but necessary historical overview to a close, and went on to the analysis of that enormous political terrain.

The Anatomy of Rival Visions

That there is a struggle, a conflict, in South Africa, nobody can deny. The existence of this conflict has been amply evidenced by what we have, perhaps artificially, referred to as the four phases of the black struggle in this country. Conflict, red-hot and acrimonious, exists in this country and stares every South African in the face. The controversy is rather about *how one can best characterize and analyze the exact nature of this conflict.* And it is important to realize that this controversy is not spawned by South Africans' puerile and inane desire to indulge in mere academic palaver or logic chopping. No, South Africans are engaged in this debate because they suddenly realize that there must be something disastrously wrong for a people to struggle along for well over three hundred years and yet have very little to show by way of tangible and lasting results at the end of that gruesome period. There must be something very ineffectual with regard to the way they go about the struggle, their chosen strategies and tactics, and, perhaps, this lack of effectiveness may be due to poor, careless and inaccurate analysis of their problem. Strategies and tactics, it must be remembered, are derivatives. Good, effective strategies, like good, effective medical prescriptions, are those which are based on painstaking and accurate social analysis, diagnosis, in medical parlance.

This controversy about how best one can understand the root causes of the South African socio-political problems, analyze them and gain deeper insights into the present situation, and thereby be in a position to evolve correct and effective strategies for change in South Africa's apartheid society, gained particular ascendancy in the beginning of the 1970s, probably occasioned by the publication of the *Oxford History of South Africa* in 1971, which epitomized the liberal interpretation and analysis of South African society. The attack on the liberal interpretation of South African history came fast and furious. For instance, Harrison M. Wright says that:

> In 1972 alone four influential reviews [of the *Oxford History of South Africa*] by four South African historians living abroad — Martin Legassick, Shula Marks, Stanley Trapido, and Anthony Atmore — directly challenged the assumptions, the interpretations, and the social values of the liberal historians.[33]

Indeed, ever since that time the two opposing kinds of socio-political analysis, which can be roughly termed the Liberal and the Radical paradigms, have openly fought it out in the country's debating arenas. And as it was stated earlier on in this paper, this controversy between these two paradigms split black opposition into two seemingly irreconcilable and mutually exclusive camps. The now well known obstreperous race-class debate had begun in earnest. Furious and unremitting it was.

There were those who were fully persuaded that race provided them with an adequate explanatory key to the understanding of the peculiarities inherent in the South African scene, while others rejected this approach and opted, just as strongly, for the adoption of a class analysis of the South African situation. The basic problem, the class-analysts intoned, was not so much who should sit on the 'park benches', but who should enjoy the largest share of the 'goodies'. The controversy, as we know, often presented its participants with an either/or, clear-cut dichotomy between these two opposing views, with the protagonists on each side refusing to accept even the slightest possibility of a *tertium quid*.

The Two Paradigms in Silhouette
In this section we shall give a general outline of each of the two paradigms and see how the insights yielded by each position would

apply to our four phases of the black struggle. This is crucial because a good paradigm ought to be always open to empirical correction.

The Race-Analysts' Position

What do the race-analysts say in general? For them the basic ingredient in the South African three hundred year conflict is 'race'. The primacy of *racial ideology* or politico-racial factors, they say, should be obvious to any unbiased analyst of the South African problematic. This is their point of departure. And it is this which leads them to reject what they term the non-racial myth of proletarian unity between South Africa's black workers and white workers. The basic polarization is not between 'classes' but between groups that are segmented on the basis of pigmentation. Pigmentocracy, therefore, is the name of the South African game. The whole wide world knows that. Interests are polarized on the basis of race, not class or economics. It is for this reason that the high-priest and architect of racism in South Africa, Dr. H.F. Verwoerd, could feelingly argue that he personally would rather that South Africa be white and poor than rich and mixed.[34] The proponents of the race-analysis approach point to such sentiments as being affirmations of the primacy of 'race' in South Africa's social formation. For them 'race' is the unmistakable criterion of differential incorporation into the South African social system. And it is this differential incorporation which determines what size of the economic cake one is entitled to; it is not the size of the economic cake that determines the nature of this incorporation; otherwise financial heavy-weights like our own E.T. Tshabalala, Habakuk Shikwane, Sam Motsuenyane, etc., would be enjoying full franchise and parliamentary rights on the same level with South Africa's white oligarchy. They do not. The South African situation, therefore, seems to indicate that it is rather the ideology of 'class consciousness' — and not that of 'race-consciousness' — which is false, erroneous, twisted consciousness, an inverted image of the South African reality. Race is still a valid analytical concept to use for the understanding of South Africa's core problems, this approach argues.

The protagonists of the race-analysis approach do not see how the struggle of the people, at least at this stage, could be anything but a nationalistic struggle. They point to the obvious fact that in this country the so-called 'non-whites' are oppressed, excluded, discriminated against as a black nation, and not as a class. And, therefore, the proper response to this blatant and obvious national oppression is some form of 'nationalism'—not 'classism'. Nationalism at this present stage is still the only rallying cry which has the potential to rouse the oppressed African masses to join the struggle and substitute genuine democracy for an oppressive pigmentocracy.

Another point, the situation in South Africa has an unmistakable colonial character. Some would like to describe it as 'internal colonialism'. However, this designation does not alter the basic picture. The basic picture is colonial: a white settler community lording it over a black indigenous community. Colonialism is by definition *collective exploitation and oppression* of a whole people — not classes of people — as a totality. Such an oppression gives rise, not to a *class consciousness*, but to a *national or race consciousness*. Thus national oppression not only transcends class, but it also turns it into an irrelevant, strategically weak variable in the people's struggle.

Ours is therefore a fundamentally black versus white struggle, the race-analysts argue. The 1922 Rand miners' strike is regarded, within this paradigm, as a classic example of lack of 'natural' homogeneity between the interests of white workers and those of black workers. In this 1922 strike white workers unequivocally perceived their interests as being antagonistic to the interests of black workers. White labour and white capital would finally forge a perfect alliance against the subordinate black workers. The predominant factor here was not the so-called 'objective material conditions' or 'one's relationship to the forces of production', but the ideological force of racism.

This failure of working class solidarity between members of different races is regarded by race-analysts as being decisive in carrying on the struggle solely on the basis of black solidarity. There is no other realistic formula for change in South Africa, they argue.

The following words are an inference drawn from the above analysis:

> What blacks are doing is merely to respond to a situation in which they find themselves the objects of white racism...We are collectively segregated against — what can be more logical than for us to respond as a group? When workers come together under the auspices of a trade union to strive for the betterment of their conditions, nobody expresses surprise in the Western world. It is the done thing. Nobody accuses them of separatist tendencies. Teachers fight their battles, garbage men do the same, nobody acts as a trustee for another. Somehow, however, when blacks want to do their thing the liberal establishment seems to detect an anomaly...The liberals do not understand that the days of the Noble Savage are gone; that blacks do not need a go-between in this struggle for their

own emancipation.[35]

Let the blacks do their thing, from an exclusively black vantage point. This is the clarion cry of this camp.

The Class-Analysts' Position

Class-analysts inveigh against what they see as the superficiality of the race analysis of the South African situation. They feel that race analysis arbitrarily isolates the South African struggle not only from struggles against world capitalist exploitation, but also from liberating currents that have been a long-standing feature along the borders of this country. To de-internationalize the struggle in South Africa is to cling to a truncated, myopic view of that struggle. It is to be inexcusably unrealistic about the people's struggle.

South Africa, they argue, is part of the oppressive and exploitative capitalist world. This country is not peripheral to Reaganomics. It is part of the heart-beat of that monster. Reagan's 'constructive engagement' approach and the heavy presence of international corporations, IBM, Siemens, Mobil, etc., in our economy are sufficient evidence of the fact that the profile of the *real enemy* is much broader than that which is suggested within the race-analysis purview. And if the real enemy is broader, perhaps, by the same token, the victims' profile should be broadened to include people who are, prima facie, excluded in the narrow profile provided by the race-analysis picture.

Race-analysts are reminded, over and over again, that the international subsidiaries' operations in this country are part and parcel of the oppressive and exploitative machinery that grinds workers, regardless of their colour, for what the workers can produce to feed the already over-fed, affluent, capitalist minority. Now, to employ colour or race as a primary criterion in a liberatory struggle is, automatically, to alienate black South Africans, many of whom are workers, from the rest of the worker world. Given the existential set-up in South Africa today, it would be naive in the extreme to imagine that the struggle could be successfully waged internally without a massive dose of external cooperation from the non-black workers of the world. This is not merely to reject the criterion of 'race' for the sake of an ephemeral, passing theory, but it is an attempt to put aside the superficiality of a political-racial analysis in favour of an approach that ferrets out the causal-rootage of the South African conflict.

Racism, they say, lacks an independent explanatory power of analysis. Racial prejudice is either inborn or acquired. If it is inborn or innate, then there is very little that one can do about it. Such

inborn-ness of racism would certainly call for acquiescence, not militant involvement on the part of the victims. But the very history of
South Africa furnishes us with ample evidence that racism is not an
innate factor in man: the origin of the so-called Cape Coloured, the
de-classification of, first, the Japanese, and, then, the Chinese, the
existence of legislation to prohibit 'mixed' sexual relations and mar-
riages, etc. All these phenomena point to the fact that there is nothing inherent in man which naturally orients him antipathetically to
members of other races who manifest different skin-coloration. Racism is not innate. Thanks to God this is so, because if it were innate, it
would never be eradicated!

So racism does exist. But it exists as a social, not natural, construct.
It is a socially acquired habit, the source or origin of which is something other than itself. White people do not discriminate against
black people simply because, innately, they do not like 'blackness' in
colour. Such a theory would easily break down in the face of the
numerous experiences such as those at Sun City, Swaziland Spa,
Lesotho Hilton, etc. Racism is an acquired habit, and because it is
acquired, it can be de-learned through force of circumstances. Radical analysis often locates these circumstances in the *'competition-for-
scarce-resources'*. This is the pulse-beat of the South African conflict:
economic interests. Racism is, therefore, a function of capitalist exploitation and serves to legitimate the status of those who own the
means of production and the position of their functionaries. As such
'race' is not a peculiarly South African problem.

South African blacks are oppressed not primarily because they
show a different skin-colour, but because, basically, their economic
interests are antithetical to those who are the economically dominant
class. So whilst the conflict manifests itself in forms that are racial, its
origin is decidedly non-racial. Its origin is a collective attempt to
protect group-interests: the land, water, pasture, and later the mines,
manufacturing industry, and commerce. It is, therefore, not race-re-
lations that one should study and focus on, but class-relations. In
short, the 'face' of the problem is racial, but its essence is non-racial.
Genovese summed it up neatly:

> ...race relations are at bottom a class question into which
> the race question intrudes — and gives it a special force
> and form, but does not constitute its essence.

To assess the explanatory power of race as a tool of social analysis,
it might help to look at the treatment of whites by other whites in

other countries, e.g. the Jews in Nazi Germany. It was not the colour of their skin, the shape of their noses, or the texture of their hair that was the central motive behind the inhuman treatment meted out to them — but the position the Jews held in Germany's economy at the time.

For the class-analysis approach racial conflicts are simply epiphenomena of much deeper conflicts — class conflicts. And classes are by definition determined by their relationship to the means of production. Economic — not racial — criteria are used in this analytic approach. The basic, structural polarization is not between black and white, but between labour and capital. It is this latter polarization that has international repercussions or implications: workers are workers, everywhere. Capitalists are capitalists, everywhere. Their colour or race is peripheral and incidental to these pivotal categories, labour and capital. This stand, class-analysts argue, is both theoretically and pragmatically correct. It is a stand fraught with ideological, strategic and tactical implications for the struggle of the oppressed masses in this country.

According to this analysis, a nationalist liberation movement, which is easily countenanced by a race-analysis approach, is by definition a bourgeois movement. It is bourgeois because, as in the South African case, every black man, simply by reason of his blackness, would belong to the movement, regardless of his class position. The fact that he may be a rabid, exploitative capitalist would not seriously affect his participation in the national liberation movement. It is rather the wrong kind of colour or race that would throw one right out of the liberation movement. For instance, in a national liberation movement an E.T. Tshabalala and a Joseph Mavi can march cheek by jowl, shoulder to shoulder, completely oblivious of their deeply polarized interests. Such a movement cannot but be bourgeois — and somehow reactionary.

It is this sort of *reductio ad absurdum* which clearly shows the inadequacies and oversimplifications of the race-analysis approach.

Thus whilst class-analysts would not be averse towards 'working together with progressive whites in the liberation struggle', the race-analysts would be wary of 'collaboration with whites — whether progressive or reactionary'. By reason of the racial category to which they belong, they are basically part of the 'problem', and not the 'solution', in this country.

The two paradigms are painfully at daggers drawn.

What then would be the respective views of these paradigms vis-à-vis Black Theology?

Black Theology in Search of a Base

It is perhaps about time we saw how Black Theology, that wave-raising phenomenon of the late sixties and early seventies, relates to our two conflicting paradigms: race and class analyses.

Now, since the concept of Black Theology has found entry into so many books and documents the world over, our discussion of it will be very brief. In fact, our primary interest here is simply to map out the relationship Black Theology might have with the two warring analyses sketched above.

Let us start the discussion with a citation from one of the unpublished articles by James H. Cone, who is easily one of the foremost proponents of Black Theology. In one of his most blistering attacks against people who challenge the validity and Christian status of Black Theology and who argue that theology must be 'colourless', Cone had this to say:

> [They say] theology is colourless! Such judgements are typical of those who have not experienced the concreteness of human *suffering expressed through colour*, or whose own comfort has so long accepted a theology which is colourless only if one is talking about 'white' as the absence of colour.
>
> To ignore Black Theology is the easy way out... But what is more interesting, though not surprising, is the white response that theology does not come in colours. They who are responsible for colour being the vehicle of dehumanization are now telling us that theology is raceless, that it is 'universal' (international). This seems a bit late after nearly 400 years of silence on this issue.
>
> Black Theologians wonder why we did not hear the same word when people were being enslaved in the name of God and democracy precisely on the basis of colour? We wonder where were these colourless theologians when people were being lynched because of the colour of their skin?...To criticize the theology of the victims because it centres on that aspect that best defines the limits of their existence seems to miss the point entirely.[36]

There seems to be no doubt that central to the concerns of Black Theology stands the category of 'blackness'. This type of theology has taken up the role of uncovering, in a systematic way, the structures and forms of the black experience. In short, it aims at investigating anew 'the problem of the colour-line'.[37] Black Theology hates to trifle with the social phenomenon of colour. It takes colour seriously because it regards colour as being tragically co-terminous with the 400 years of slavery in the Deep South and the 330 years of blatant discrimination in this southern tip of Africa. In these regions, 'blackness' connotes man-imposed suffering. This category of 'blackness' needs to be put in theological perspective and expressed in God-oriented terms. The beginning and end of this exercise is the beginning and end of Black Theology.

This is in essence the theology of black victims, whose faces have been ground to the dust by a specific group of victimizers, fair-skinned victimizers.

Such a theology finds its natural home or base in an analytic approach which diagnoses South Africa's problems as being first and foremost rooted in 'racism'. Within the race-analysis paradigm, therefore, Black Theology is merely a systematic religious manifestation of a state of oppression experienced primarily in racial/colour terms. 'Blackness' is the vehicle through which this oppression is wielded. Liberation or salvation, outside this specific category of 'blackness', becomes an obscene irrelevancy. Black Theology is a theology of liberation from this specific category of suffering. To introduce 'class' into this process of liberation is to intrude dilatory dynamics that would hamper the natural momentum of the national liberation movement. This would have the effect of diluting the struggle to a considerable degree.

The fad of class analysis divides the real opposition in this country and dampens the militancy of the oppressed masses. Therefore, in our situation of racial oppression, it is argued, a theology that concerns itself with class oppression will be to that extent chasing after a chimera, at worst, or a marginal issue, at best. Such a theology would be anaemic for lack of a natural source or base.

In short, race-analysts are the natural proponents of Black Theology. For them, if the reasons that gave rise to black theologizing in the late sixties and early seventies were valid and impelling, the situation today has not changed one iota. Blacks, not as individuals, but collectively, are still catching hell from a specifically white system that is systematically rigged against them. This is something that cannot be easily overlooked and forgotten by the average black man in this country. The struggle of the races is still on, and, if the recent hair-raising and mind-boggling events in the Vaal triangle are anything to go by, this struggle is not about to grind to a halt.

Black Theology is the religious manifestation of this conflict.

Class-analysts turn round to reject Black Theology as a theology which is based, not only on a superficial, but also erroneous reading of the South African situation. Whilst colour enjoys high visibility and biting pervasiveness in South Africa, they argue, it must be read not as the cause but as the effect of a much deeper structural malady in society. Therefore, to base one's theologizing on an epiphenomenon of a social sickness is to run the risk of being incurably shallow in one's theological task. Black Theology operates at the level of 'mopping up water' from a room, whilst the tap is left completely uninterfered with. Needless to say, this is the classical exercise in futility. It is Liberation Theology, in the Latin American style, that one should opt for, because whilst Liberation Theology does not minimize the 'nuisance value' of the water (if we be allowed to carry on with our metaphor), it throws its whole weight behind the attempt to close the tap.

It is in fact Black Theology that fragments real, effective opposition to oppression and exploitation by refusing to forge meaningful links with other 'oppressed classes' of the world. This unfortunate refusal, apart from being Christianly suspect, narrows the parameters of the struggle by its ideological exclusivity. Thus the prime *locus theologicus* of Black Theology, namely, race/colour, is rejected by this paradigm as inadequate, shallow and misdirected. Talk of something as being only skin-deep! You are talking about the insights of Black Theology.

What should provide a point of departure for a truly liberatory theology is the *economic dependency* of economic exploitation, not racial oppression. A theology that treats the labour-capital polarity as secondary can only be half-heartedly liberatory. The history of the ANC at least up to the 1960s has amply proved this point.

In short, there is no room for Black Theology qua black in the inn of the class-analysts. On the contrary, it is theologians like Gustavo Gutierrez, Miguez Bonino, etc., and not a James Cone or a Manas Buthelezi, who are expressive of the class-analysis theological point of departure and basic concerns. In this paradigm the *locus theologicus* is *economic dependency,* not racial oppression. In this sense, therefore, Liberation Theology finds its natural home or base in the class-analysis camp. Thus the controversy between our two paradigms has far-reaching implications for the exercise of Black Theology in this conflict-ridden country.

The Neglected Dialectic: A Personal Viewpoint
The reason why we started this paper with a kind of kaleidoscopic presentation of some important historical landmarks or phases of the black struggle in South Africa is because we believe that any analyti-

cal paradigm or theory worth its salt is, perforce, derivative. It is derived from contexts that are real, concrete and historical. In short, theory must have historical and empirical rootage. Reality fathers theory, and not the other way round. This is trite but true.

Therefore the two paradigms we have been discussing thus far will only be true and useful to the extent that they mirror the concrete, historical and contemporary situation in South Africa; and they will be false to the extent that they subject the South African situation to a kind of Procrustean solution: if the situation does not fit the theory, then alter the situation!

Which of the two paradigms is true to the South African situation? But before we can take the risk of answering this all-important question, let us first try to trace what we choose to call the historical roots of these two analytical approaches. This, of course, can only be done very sketchily here.

There is ample evidence that the two approaches share in the well-known mid-nineteenth-century conflict between *Hegelian idealism* and its Marxian rebuttal, which could be called *realism* or, to use the more common term, *materialism*. Idealism as the general mode of understanding and interpreting reality played and still plays the role of what may be called 'conventional wisdom', the commonsensical way people generally think about reality. Christian philosophy, history and practice, in particular, are marked by this mode of interpreting reality. Marx and Engels, in the mid-nineteenth-century European context, mounted a vicious and vitriolic attack against this well accepted, 'conventional wisdom'.[38]

What is idealism? At the risk of over-simplifying what German idealism stood for, and what idealist-philosophers like Hegel taught, let us say this: according to idealism, ultimate reality is 'spiritual' and not 'physical'. The spirit, the idea, the mind is supreme. All *that is* is simply an unfolding of the idea or thought. It is the idea which creates what we see in the external world. This is so important that we have to say it again: the idea is creative, thought is creative, and the world is merely a product of thought or *human consciousness*. This is, very briefly, the central point of idealism.

How would an idealist approach to reality affect one's strategies and tactics in the arena of social transformation? The answer is obvious. An idealist strategist would have his primary focus on the mind, attempting to change people's ideas with the hope that once the ideas have changed, the mind would *ipso facto* change. As we have just said, this would be strategically logical because in the idealist context it is ideas that are creative of reality. The tools that an idealist strategist would employ would be on the whole psychological: education, preaching, heuristically-oriented discussions, and so on and so forth.

As stated above, it was in the mid-nineteenth century that social analysts like Marx and Engels opposed this line of thinking very strongly. Ideas, Marx and Engels taught, are not the causes of things; on the contrary, ideas are the effects of things. This is materialism or realism. Realism, as a mode of understanding and interpreting reality, says that ultimate reality is material, not spiritual. Ideas are the product of the material conditions of life. All ideas, thoughts, are subject to extra-mental social conditions.

This is, very briefly, how these mid-nineteenth-century social gurus understood the relationship between human thought and *material conditions.*

How would this materialist approach to reality affect one's strategies and tactics? Obviously, a materialist strategist would not focus his transformative efforts on the mind or ideas, but on the material conditions of life, because for him these are the *fons et origo* of ideas.

So whilst an idealist strategist takes his point of departure in *human consciousness,* the materialist strategist takes off from the material or *economic relationships* among men. The latter believes, as Marx and Engels did, that:

> The mode of production of material life conditions the social, political, and intellectual life process in general. It is not the *consciousness of men* that determines their being, but, on the contrary, their social being that determines their consciousness.[39]

We, therefore, wish to suggest that there seems to be a very close relationship between the idealist approach and the race-analysis paradigm, on the one hand, and the materialist approach and the class-analysis paradigm, on the other hand.

Race-analysts are, strategically, mind-oriented; class-analysts focus almost exclusively on the material conditions of life.

How, then, does all this apply to our four phases of the struggle? What was the origin and nature of the conflict between the Khoisan and the white settler community at the Cape?

To us it does seem that to the Khoisan it would not really have mattered whether those seventeenth-century invaders at the Cape were white, yellow or black; what would have mattered was the fact that the invaders harboured interests, material interests, antithetical to the interests of the indigenous Khoisan. The settlers occupied and used the land, water and pasturage that the Khoisan had a stake in. Competition-for-scarce-resources, to use a hackneyed phrase, was at the heart of this Khoisan-settler conflict, it does seem. To describe this initial conflict in primarily racial terms would be to imply that the Khoisan would have easily acquiesced in the expropriation of their land, water and pasturage if only the expropriators had a different skin-colour or racial origin.

The dynamics at play in this struggle would indicate a definite de-emphasis of 'race' as the root-cause of the conflict, at least at this phase. The second phase of the struggle does not seem to be immune from this de-emphasis. In the tribalistic phase, the Xhosas clearly resented being continually pushed eastward across the Zuurveld, then the Fish River, then the Keiskama, then the Kei River, etc. The racial origin or pigmentation of the white settlers and the Xhosas was not one of the essential factors that motivated and sustained the settlers' persistent attacks against the indigenous people and their land, attacks that the Xhosas perceived as being part of a course of unjust usurpation of their land rights. In this conflictual situation, these settlers were, first and foremost, 'land-hungry grabbers' and only tangentially 'white'. The fact that they were 'white' and the natives were 'black', visible as it was, was coincidental and not essential to the reprehensible rapaciousness of the invading settlers. Again, competition-for-scarce-resources seems to have provided an explanatory key to the conflict. It was a clash of interests, not a clash of skin-colours; historico-empirical observation does point, unmistakably, to the fact that, at least in these first two phases of the struggle, the natives of this country fought valiantly and lost their lives in order to keep their LAND to themselves. And, as the historian C.W. de Kiewiet so rightly observes:

> ...the natives were in a process which gave the white com-
> munities more than possession of the bulk of the best land.
> It gave them a considerable measure of control over the
> services of the native. The *land wars* were also *labour
> wars*.[40]

Thus from being independent possessors of their land, the natives, through having lost the various battles over the land, were turned into servile, obsequious, dependent kitchen boys, garden boys, herders, tenants or renters on the newly acquired white man's land. The land wars, which the natives lost, were part of the classical process of proletarianization. The natives, thanks to this process, almost *en masse,* became dependent wage-earners. It is easy to see that almost all the crucial ingredients of the labour-capital model are already present in this scenario, at least embryonically.

So, a simple, straightforward response to the question of why there was conflict between the Khoisan/Xhosas and white settlers in the seventeenth and eighteenth centuries should be: the battle was over the possession of the land. All other considerations are historically subservient and secondary to this: the imbroglio centred around the land. And if the Khoisan and Xhosas gradually became, in the eyes of the white settlers, 'black vermin' or 'stinking black swine', it was because they had first become the white settlers' arch-rivals in the competition for land.

Therefore, it would seem that a class-analysis fits these two phases of the struggle almost like a glove. To understand fully these two phases one would have to start from a materialist point of departure. Something other than 'colour', which is some sort of prejudice lodging in the mind, became at this stage of our history the criterion of social segmentation.

But having said this, one would have to go on to say that because the protagonists on each side of the battle lines were of different races or colours (although the basic motivation for the battles was not at the level of race or colour, as we have tried to state above), as time went on, colour gradually became an operative symbol for distinguishing one's competitors from the members of one's in-group. It would seem that from the second half of the nineteenth century, when South Africa with its discovery of diamonds (1867) and gold (1886) began seriously to enter into the arena of world capitalism, the dividing line between the initial motivation of 'conflict of interests' and that of 'colour differences' had become dangerously blurred, especially in the minds of the white protagonists. 'Blackness' in the mining industry, manufacturing and agriculture somehow became an inseparable symbol of those who belonged to the other side of the great economic divide. Colour became increasingly significant in this way. From the initial stance of 'push them out because they disturb our peaceful possession of the land' to 'push them out because they are black' was a gradual but easy step of psychological association and internalization on the part of the white conquerors. Most of them would soon forget how this white-black polarity originated. But as it was stated above, this apparent 'naturalness' of racial antipathy is only skin-deep. Racism is acquired. It is not innate. Whether one explicitly recognizes its origin or not, racism is born out of man's rapaciousness, his competition-for-scarce-resources. And in South Africa this is not a theory, but it is an historico-empirical assertion.

Anyway, back to the point we wanted to make: with time the 'racial motivation' became inseparable from the motivation of the 'conflict of interests'. The third and fourth phases of the struggle coincided with the blurring of the line between these two motivational categories of conflict. South Africa soon became known as the colour-bar society — in which the indigenous people of colour were blatantly discriminated against solely on the basis of their colour.

This is also how the members of the African National Congress fundamentally perceived the conflict, especially judging from the strategies they employed. Their strategies were derived from and informed by what has been called in this paper 'conventional wisdom', namely, idealism. For congress the basic location of the South African problematic was in the minds of the discriminators. It was therefore not surprising that these early twentieth-century black leaders employed strategies that were characteristically psychological: tactics of moral persuasion, sonorous appeals for justice, endless attempts to enter into negotiatory talks with the dominant group. But what was even more fundamental in this approach was the fact that these early nationalists seemed to have had no basic quarrel with the economic system that was then operative in South Africa; their gripe was instead aimed at the state racism which prevented them from their full and rightful share in that economy. They were, as we know, ardent admirers of the Cape liberal tradition and the Westminster system. All they wanted was to prise open the doors of racial discrimination.[41] In short, their approach was idealistic — that is, their point of departure was the consciousness or ideas of those who discriminated against them; their approach was also moralistic — that is, they believed in the transformative powers of preaching and teaching. Change of heart and change of mind could be effected by the power of argument and logic. Yes, they believed strongly in the goodness, inherent goodness, of human nature and in the supremacy of reason and logic. So they kept on arguing, persuading...and hoping. The aim of their approach was also integrationist; that is, they wanted to be part of the current system. The only serious obstacle, they were convinced, was 'racism'.

Why, even an overtly trade union movement like the 1919 Industrial and Commercial Workers Union (ICU) failed to remain immunized against this idealistic, moralistic, and integrationist approach. For some time after its foundation in 1919, ICU, under the leadership of Clemens Kadalie and George Champion, to all intents and purposes, usurped the role of the ANC. It became the principal vehicle of African discontent. And in so doing it was derailed from clearly and directly addressing the South African problematic from a purely economic, industrial platform. It became, like the ANC, a populist movement with but a slight touch of trade unionism or worker concerns.

It is on record that when the ICU leadership was challenged on this 'confusion', their general retort and explanation were that in South Africa economic and political issues were inseparable; that these issues had to be fought concurrently, at one and the same time.[42] Their diagnosis might well have been correct, but their cure or prescription was of doubtful validity. Populism was substituted for trade unionism.

It is clear that both the ANC and ICU leaderships were held in thrall by the idealistic approach to problems. As Philip Bonner so rightly says in connection with the ICU:

> ...for the best part of the decade they mistook protest for pressure and numbers for strength, ignoring all the while there had to be some way for pressure to be brought to bear for it to have any effect.[43]

Whilst the reading of the conflict in South Africa from an idealistic point of view was not so explicitly articulated in the ANC and ICU, it did find an explicit and well articulated expression, we believe, in the fourth phase of our struggle, namely, the Black Consciousness phase. The Black Consciousness philosophy, particularly at the beginning, made it explicit that it would refuse to be derailed from viewing the South African problematic from the race-analysis point of departure. Without wishing to waste time in enunciating this well documented stance, it would suffice to cite the words of one of Black Consciousness' foremost ideologues and proponents of this point:

> [The liberals] tell us that the situation is a class struggle rather than a race one. Let them go to Van Tonder in the Free State and tell them this: We believe we know what the problem is and will stick by our findings...[44]

In a similar context, this ideologue, denouncing the motivations and repercussions of class analysis, said:

> A number of whites in this country adopt a class analysis primarily because they want to detach us from anything relating to race in case it has a rebound effect on them because they are white.[45]

It is assertions like these which led political scientists like Sam C. Noluntshungu to think that, despite some uneasiness with capitalism within the Black Consciousness philosophy:

> ...there was no systematic economic analysis of class, nor, even a political account of what the interests and roles of the various classes might be in the process of liberation.[46]

The black nationalists of the early twentieth century implicitly espoused the idealistic methodology of analysis and practice; the Black Consciousness leaders, while vehemently rejecting the integrationist tendencies of the earlier movement, explicitly adopted the latter's idealistic methodology: racial prejudice became the starting point of their struggle.

It was in the aftermath of the October 1977 bannings that objections against this idealistic approach were openly and persistently raised within black political circles, in favour of a materialist methodology. Matters have reached a stage where one is either an idealist in one's approach or a materialist.

But as we have suggested, this either/or dichotomy between idealism and materialism breaks down in front of what we have called the inseparability of the two motivational categories: 'conflict of interests' and 'colour differences'. We would like to suggest that the either/or manner of posing the problem introduces an air of artificiality into the race/class debate.

The materialist or class-analysis approach is certainly right in holding fast onto the idea that the material conditions of life are the root cause of the conflict between black and white in this country but they are less than right when they deny that 'beliefs' or 'ideas' pertaining to racism have also a role in shaping society. To subscribe to the fact that racial attitudes are the effect of infra-structural economic conditions does not carry the logical necessity of inextricably binding one to the acceptance of the relative unimportance or role-insignificance of racism and other non-economic ideas (e.g. those that generated and propelled the Christian Crusades in the eleventh century) in shaping and stratifying society and affecting the life-chances of a large section of members of this country. Heribert Adam, himself a strong believer in the determinative role of material conditions, is right in posing this question:

> Why should the independent role of beliefs [racism] not be granted, even in shaping an economic environment? Marxist [materialist] interpretations of South Africa rarely

go beyond the notion of base and superstructure. By mechanically relegating the realm of ideology to a mere reflection of underlying interests, Marxists usually ignore the
subjective reality. A peculiar sterility — therefore —
characterises much of the recent leftist writing on South
Africa.[47]

Those who grant an almost exclusive and absolute autonomy to
material, objective conditions, and deny even relative autonomy to a
system of beliefs, ideas, prejudices, etc., will be hard put to it to
explain some obvious South African examples which point to the
powerful influence and motivational dynamics of these beliefs, ideas,
prejudices, etc. Examples abound which show that a belief system
does play a role in shaping the course of history. For instance, as we
noted before, in 1963, Dr. H.F. Verwoerd, addressing a mammoth
Afrikaner crowd on the threat of economic sanctions against South
Africa, defiantly and feelingly declared:

I am absolutely opposed to concessions of any kind. I
personally would rather see South Africa poor but white
rather than rich and mixed.[48]

The 2,000 strong audience gave him a thunderous applause and
chorused, 'Amen'. It does seem that there are a hundred and one
factors, outside the purely economic sphere, which are as capable of
motivating individuals and groups of people as the so-called infra-
structural objective conditions of life advanced by the class-analysts.
Take another example, outside South Africa this time. The planned
return of Jews to Israel under the charismatic leadership of people
like Ben Gurion, Moshe Dayan, Golda Meir, etc., is one example
among numerous incidents in human history which simply refuse to
be unlocked by the explanatory key of economic determinism. Something much more than mere economics impelled this particular
people to some heroic feats. The Masada experience? The motivation
behind this wholesale self-emolation of men, women and children is
explainable only in other than mere economic terms. The tragedy
that occurred in Guyana among the followers of Reverend Jim
Jones? How can this be fully and adequately explained within the
parameters of the base-superstructural model alone? Reality seems
to be much more vast than this model allows. The South African
situation is such a complex reality which refuses to be subjected to the
over-simplification of the materialist, economic calculus. Says Heribert Adam, once more, in *Perspectives in Literature:*

> In the South African case, material rewards are at present only one part of the payoff that accounts for the maintenance of Afrikaner unity. Almost equally important would seem the cohesive power of a symbol system, rewards of esteem and status, the integrating role of ideology, which is frequently underestimated, if not altogether rejected in economic analysis. Only a genuine synthesis of the interplay between ideology (beliefs) and economy, not focus on either at the expense of the other, would seem to hold the key for deeper insights into the complex conflict.[49]

If the materialist or class-analysis approach errs, not by acknowledging the determinative role of material conditions, but by downplaying the determinative role of belief systems as mere reflections of the base, the idealist or race-analysis approach errs by down-playing and de-emphasizing the role of economic motivations in South Africa's social formation. It is not in what both camps uphold, but in what both camps tend to reject or de-emphasize that the fault lies. Heribert Adam's plea for '...a genuine synthesis of the interplay between ideology and economy' is crucial. The separation of these two possible motivational bases in the South African situation inevitably leads to 'a paucity of explanatory theory'. Yes, to gloss over the dialectical relationship between these two important variables — class and race — in the South African situation can only lead to a Procrustean explanation of the conflict.

As Deborah Posel says, in substance, it is disastrous to seek a uniform ranking of one variable over another. It is their concrete interrelationships, their dialectical relationships, that we should focus on.[50] We can neglect this dialectic at our own peril. Hermann Giliomee has written about this dialectical relationship between class analysis and race analysis. In an article in *Social Dynamics,* he suggests:

> The challenge in this case is to show how racial ideas and cleavages, on the one hand, and class relations, on the other hand, structured and reinforced each other.[51]

The phrase used by some people to describe the South African system—that is, 'racial capitalism'—may be more than just a fad, after all. This phrase tries to come to grips with the whole of South African reality. South Africa is both a racial oligarchy as well as a capitalist society. But the two do not run parallel; they are mixed and intertwined. Even the protagonists in the game do not know when they are being only racially motivated, or when capitalistically impelled.

The two variables reinforce each other all the time.

Analysis Informs Strategy

But it is important to realize that when one says that the two variables are mixed and intertwined, one speaks only of analysis — not of strategy or tactics. It is tragic to confuse analysis with strategy or diagnosis with the cure. It is this which probably led to the relative inefficiency of ICU. Although its leaders analyzed the situation in this country in political and economic terms, in the sense that in South Africa politics is inseparable from economics, they concentrated mainly on political manoeuvres to the virtual neglect of industrial, economic action, thus confusing analysis with the cure.

Now, how does this apply to our analysis of the situation in terms of racial capitalism? The determination of strategy to transform this kind of situation cannot be assumed automatically from hearing what the analysis is. For instance, there are those of us who believe that racial capitalism can be effectively combatted only on the basis of black solidarity, whereas others take the stand that it can be successfully fought only on the basis of forging trans-racial links and alliances with other people who are sympathetic to our cause. These are strategies which may or may not be the correct remedy for racial capitalism. But they are strategies — and it is important to remember that they are strategies and not principles (i.e. goals, the focal point of political actions). Strategies are by nature flexible: what may not be a good strategy today, may be okay tomorrow. Strategies have a flexibility which principles do not quite enjoy. That is why it is important to realize that disagreement, however deep, at the level of strategy is not disagreement about principles. Strategies and tactics are subservient to principles.

Ideological Differences

The term 'ideology' runs through our everyday political conversation like a greased pig. It is slippery; it lacks a precise content. But somehow we cannot allow this term to stride the world like a colossus. It must have some residual connotation that one can trap and look at.

In the contemporary scene, there seems to be some measure of agreement among social scientists that 'ideology' refers to a system of ideas or beliefs containing assertions about the nature of the desirable society and the actions required for the attainment or maintenance of that desirable society. It is, in short, a group's blueprint of, or visualization of the desirable society. But I think Albert Nolan is right when he clinches this notion of ideology by saying that this set of ideas about what society should be like '...is called an ideology only when the set of ideas is adhered to uncritically, dogmatically, and with a great deal of emotion rather than as a result of some kind of objective reasoning based upon facts'.[52]

In short, the term 'ideology' has come to have, in politics, almost the same meaning the terms 'creed' and 'faith' have in religion. It is for this reason that Daniel Bell regards ideology as '...a set of beliefs, infused with passion, [seeking] to transform the whole of a way of life'.[53] In essence, therefore, the residual meaning of 'ideology' is: a blueprint, adhered to with passion, of what society ought to be. If this notion of ideology is correct, it follows that only people who happen to possess such 'blueprints' may differ ideologically. 'Ideological differences' are differences at *blueprint level*. The challenge of the hour is to look at and examine our contemporary political groupings and clearly distinguish at least three distinct elements in their political doctrine and practice:

- Their blueprint
- Their strategy, and
- Their tactics.

Ideological differences are differences at the level of blueprints of society. And if this notion is strictly adhered to, then one may say there were no 'ideological differences', say, between the older ANC strategists and the white regime that the former so persistently fought against. This is so because the older ANC membership seemed to have had no serious quarrel with the basic blueprint of their society. Our plea here is simply this: let us distinguish our differences at the level of blueprints from our differences at the level of strategy or tactics. The two sets of differences are like day and night.

The first level is that of 'what-to-achieve' (the blueprint); the second level is that of 'how-to-achieve' (strategy, or general plan of action); the third level is that of 'what-specific-tools-to-use' (tactics, or immediate, specific plan of action). Differences at the second and third levels may be very important, but not half as serious as those at the first level. Untold confusion is often created when people pretend to have ideological differences whereas, in fact, their differences are merely strategic and tactical. Dr. Neville Alexander, in his 1983 Hammanskraal talk, seemed to sense this distinction. Inveighing against those who supported the thesis that our struggle is not for national, but class liberation, thereby de-emphasizing the race/colour category, Dr. Alexander said:

> To deny the reality of prejudice and perceived differences, whatever their origin, is to disarm oneself *strategically* and *tactically*.[54]

These words allow us to think that Dr. Alexander believes that at this juncture in our history the strategy and tactics of fighting the struggle at the level of national liberation and, by implication, on the basis of black exclusivity, carries decided advantages. To say this is not to say, automatically, that one's blueprint is Pan-Africanist, socialist or capitalistic. In fact to say what Dr. Alexander said above is not to speak about one's blueprint at all. This is a crucial distinction which must not be lost on us.

In our contemporary situation the million dollar questions are: Should we forge alliances trans-racially for the struggle, or operate solely on the basis of black solidarity, black unity? At what level do we locate this question? At the level of blueprints or at the level of strategy and tactics? The answer to these questions may yet bring about greater tolerance, effectiveness and sophistication in the formulations of our principles (blueprints), strategies and tactics, within the all-important struggle that all of us are engaged in.

When one looks at some of the National Forum Committee and United Democratic Front 1983 write-ups on their respective policy statements, one is stuck more by their similarities than dissimilarities. NFC explicitly visualizes what it terms 'anti-racist and socialist Azania'; but at the same time we know that the 1955 Freedom Charter, which most UDF affiliates accept and respect, has definite socialist elements in it. So it does seem that both the NFC and the UDF are attracted and fascinated by blueprints, albeit not completely spelled out, which are not that dissimilar. The challenge of the hour therefore is for this conference on Black Theology to ferret out the fundamental differences, dissimilarities between these two 'embryonic blueprints'. If there are dissimilarities, then we can truly say that the two seemingly irreconcilable camps differ ideologically, that is, they differ at the level of blueprints about the nature of the desirable society. In short, if they differ ideologically it means they have antagonistic visualizations of tomorrow's South Africa/Azania/Maluti, the name is immaterial.

But as we all know the most visible difference that one observes between the NFC and the UDF camps is that whilst the former operates on exclusive black solidarity, the latter operates on a non-racial basis. But even AZAPO, one of the moving spirits within NFC, has repeatedly declared that its racial exclusivity stance is only confined to what they term the 'pre-liberation phase of the struggle' — thus implying that in the 'post-liberation phase' the said exclusivity would be phased out. What this says to us then is that this exclusivity is not a principle or a goal or a blueprint; it is a strategy, as Dr. Neville

Alexander seemed to suggest; it is a broad plan of action to achieve a socio-political blueprint, namely, 'an anti-racist, socialist Azania'.

If this is the case, what we called the most visible difference between the UDF and NFC affiliates must be located at the level of strategy, not at the level of blueprints about how society should be organized. Differences at the blueprint level are more shattering than differences at any other level.

Black Theology: Bienvenu or Adieu?

As long as the black people in this country suffer a double bondage — racial oppression and economic exploitation — the task of Black Theology will always be double-pronged. Racial capitalism is the name of the game. This is the sin that Black Theology wants to uncover and eradicate in God's own name. The term 'black' must perforce remain prefixed to 'theology' because for the past 117 years 'blackness' in this country has been the symbol of economic, class exploitation. That prefix emphasizes this crucial point, which no black can forget in a hurry.

No, not yet adieu! But bienvenu, BLACK THEOLOGY!

NOTES

1. Gail M. Gerhart, *Black Power in South Africa: The Evolution of an Ideology* (Los Angeles: University of California Press, 1979), p. 238.

2. Edward Roux, *Time Longer Than Rope: A History of the Black Man's Struggle for Freedom in South Africa* (Madison, Wis., and London: University of Wisconsin Press, 1964), pp. 136–37.

3. T. R. H. Davenport, *South Africa: A Modern History* (Johannesburg: MacMillan, 1977), p. 3.

4. Richard Elphick and Hermann Giliomee, eds., *The Shaping of South African Society, 1652–1820* (Cape Town: Longman Penguin, 1979), pp. 11–12.

5. Ibid., p. 12.

6. Davenport, *South Africa*, p. 26.

7. W. M. MacMillan, *Bantu, Boer, and Briton: The Making of the South African Native Problem* (Westport, Conn.: Greenwood Press, 1963), p. 25.

8. Davenport, *South Africa*, p. 5.

9. Ibid.

10. MacMillan, *Bantu*, p. 25.

11. C. W. de Kiewiet, *A History of South Africa: Social and Economic* (London: Oxford University Press, 1957), p. 74.

12. Ibid., p. 75.

13. Ibid.

14. Ibid., p. 82.

15. Roux, *Time*, p. 95.

16. Peter Walshe, *Black Nationalism in South Africa: A Short History* (Johannesburg: Ravan Press, 1973), p. 5.

17. Ibid.

18. Ibid., p. 6.

19. Donald Denoon, *Southern Africa since 1800* (Essex: Longman Group, 1982), p. 110.

20. Davenport, *South Africa*, p. 144.

21. Peter Walshe, *The Rise of African Nationalism in South Africa: The African National Congress, 1912-1952* (Los Angeles: University of California Press, 1982), p. 38.

22. De Kiewiet, *History*, p. 144.

23. Ibid., p. 143.

24. Roux, *Time*, pp. 108-9.

25. Ibid., p. 110.

26. Walshe, *Rise*, p. 36.

27. Denoon, *Southern Africa*, p. 110.

28. Walshe, *Rise*, p. 34.

29. Ibid.

30. Ibid., p. 37.

31. Tom Lodge, *Black Politics in South Africa since 1945* (Johannesburg: Ravan Press, 1983), p. 322.

32. The citation from the document appears in van der Merwe.

33. Harrison M. Wright, *The Burden of the Present: Liberal-Radical Controversy over Southern African History* (Cape Town: David Philip, 1977), p. 18.

34. Jan Botha, *Verwoerd Is Dead* (Cape Town: Books of Africa, 1967), p. 111.

35. Gerhart, *Black Power*, p. 7.

36. James Cone, unpublished paper.

37. Cone, *God of the Oppressed* (New York: Seabury Press, 1975), p. 16.

38. Leszek Kolakowski, *Main Currents of Marxism: Its Rise, Growth, and Dissolution* (Oxford: Clarendon Press, 1978), 1:55-58.

39. Joseph M. Bochenski and Gerhart Niemeyer, eds., *Handbook on Communism* (New York: Frederick A. Praeger, 1962), p. 24.

40. De Kiewiet, *History*, p. 180.

41. Walshe, *Black Nationalism*, p. 33.

42. Philip Bonner, in *Essays on South African Labour History*, ed. Eddie Webster (Johannesburg: Ravan Press, 1978), p. 115.

43. Ibid.

44. Steve Biko, cited in No Sizwe, *One Azania, One Nation: The National Question in South Africa* (London: Zed Press, 1972), p. 125.

45. Steve Biko, cited in Sam C. Noluntshungu, *Changing South Africa: Political Considerations* (Cape Town: David Philip, 1983), p. 158.

46. Noluntshungu, *Changing South Africa*, p. 155.

47. Heribert Adam, *Perspectives in Literature*, p. 47.

48. Botha, *Verwoerd*, p. 111.

49. Adam, *Perspectives*, pp. 49-50.

50. Deborah Posel, in *Social Dynamics: A Journal of the Centre for African Studies* (Cape Town) 9, no. 1 (1983): 52.

51. Hermann Giliomee, in *Social Dynamics* 9, no. 1 (1983):18.

52. Nolan develops this theme in a number of his works.

53. Daniel Bell, in *The End of Ideology Debate*, ed. Chaim Waxman (New York: Simon and Schuster, 1968), p. 261.

54. Neville Alexander, in *National Forum Publication* (South Africa, 1983), p. 25.

Chapter 2

The Historical Origins of Black Theology
MOKGETHI MOTLHABI

Editors' Abstract

'To say, therefore, that Black Theology in South Africa stands with one leg in Africa and the other in Black America is to recognize our double advantage in the situation in which we find ourselves. As Africans, we share our background and experience of being what we are with other sons and daughters of Africa. As an oppressed people, we share the experience of disinheritance and oppression with our brothers and sisters in America'. Thus Motlhabi relates the dialectical relationship between American Black Theology and South African Black Theology. To the extent that it is an African Theology, Black Theology must seek to recover African forms of religious expression. This means paying special attention to the traditional cultural aspects that persist among mainline African Christians; but more importantly it means retapping the resources made available by the African Independent Churches. Motlhabi insists also on the relevance of African traditional religions for the liberation struggle today. In order to grasp the nature of this relevance black theologians will need to study and gain 'better insights into African traditional religions themselves'.

According to Motlhabi, paying attention to the crucial issues he raises will enable black theologians to 'embark on phase II of Black Theology', the phase beyond the prolegomena, the phase of actually doing Black Theology.

Introduction
There is something pretentious about the present topic, viewed from
the South African perspective. Unless it is taken broadly to include
the origins of Black Theology in America, it falsely gives the impression that South African black theologians have achieved something in
the study and development of Black Theology and can, therefore,
leisurely look back at its origins and put it in perspective. Nothing
can, of course, be further from the truth. Black Theology in South
Africa, as a discipline, has been a 'non-starter'. Perhaps it is because
blacks here in general are so impatient to move ahead that, as in
writing an examination, they had rather deal with what seems 'man-
ageable' first and return to unfinished business later. This, unfortunately, makes us perpetual late-comers who have to depend on other
people to do or begin things for us, which we then adopt and adapt to
our own taste — if we succeed in doing this at all.

American black theologians have advanced far ahead of us in
Black Theology and could justly produce a documentary history of it
a few years back. This paper cannot but depend to a large extent on
their contributions. It is not, however, a study of Black Theology as
such but of its origins and sources.

Two approaches have often been cited in the quest for the roots of
Black Theology. The first one grounds it in the historical past of black
people in the United States and South Africa, taking into account and
interpreting their cultural heritage; its religion and philosophy; the
impact made by western culture, particularly through its Christian
religion, on it; and the general historical and contemporary experience of black people in a white, colonized world. The second approach considers what may be called the 'literary origins' of Black
Theology, that is, it treats it as an intellectual discipline. The first
involves sometimes different, though frequently identical, emphases
on the historical past and experiences of black people in these countries. In the second, there is general agreement that Black Theology
originated in the United States when, in 1969, James Cone produced
his pioneering work on the topic, titled *Black Theology and Black
Power*.[1] Cone acknowledged that in that 'latter' period Black Theology owed its new inspiration and rebirth to the new black mood in
America and its movement of the time, black power. These approaches have not, generally, been treated in an exclusivistic manner
but rather as continuous.

The present paper will be based on both approaches under four
broad sub-topics, which will be seen as inspirational sources for Black
Theology. The second approach mentioned will be used to treat two

topics, 'The Roots of Black Theology in America' and 'Black Theology in South Africa'. A few authors representing each will be selected for cursory examination. In general, though not exclusively, Cone will be taken as the representative of American Black Theology. Under the first approach the influences of the African Independent Churches and of African traditional religions will be examined. Not much work, if any, has been done in determining the basis of Black Theology in these two sources. Those black theologians in South Africa who have dealt with the question at all have tended to stop at pointing out the need for performing this task rather than actually engaging in the necessary research and construction. The nature of this paper, from the topic given, is such that nothing more can be done here than examining how these ideas were put forth by some theologians and perhaps offering a few more suggestions.

Prelude
Cone's work, as a useful source in determining the roots of Black Theology, has itself depended on three main sources. These are western theology, scripture, and both past and contemporary Afro-American writings and sermons on religion and the black experience. In his writings, in addition to what he learned from his predecessors' writings regarding the black experience, he cites his own upbringing and the social influence he received as a member of the black community. He writes, 'More often than not, it is a theologian's personal history, in a particular socio-political setting, that serves as the most important factor in shaping the methodology and content of his or her theological perspective...'[2] The third of the above sources, in particular, shows that while Cone set himself the task of articulating Black Theology in a systematic manner, using his training in Western theology and the Bible as a tool, he nevertheless depended mostly on his black predecessors and contemporaries in and outside the church for the raw material of Black Theology. These people should be given credit for both their religious practice and its interpretation, and for their analysis of the black religious experience in general, which could later serve as the basis for the understanding and development of Black Theology (as a theory).

A second source of interest to us in discovering the roots of Black Theology is what our own black theologians in South Africa have said or do say regarding its basis and role. Except for the writings of one or two outstanding theologians, South Africa's writing on Black Theology has been less vigorous than black American writing. It has mainly bordered on definitions and has not successfully outgrown this stage. While some of our key theologians have continued their pastoral practices and preaching in accordance with their understanding of the Black Theology approach, no clear analysis has been made, on the theoretical level, of how to go about the task of actually doing Black Theology.[3] In other words, Black Theology might have been given content in the actual practice of theologians in preaching and in executing their pastoral duties, but this content has not yet been analyzed systematically for the benefit of learning and scholarship.

The disadvantage here is that we are able to study and learn from other theologies, like Latin American Liberation Theology, American Black Theology, even Feminist Theology, etc., but the people from these schools of thought cannot learn from us because our theology is still basically in its 'oral form' (if at all), as if waiting for some western anthropologist to research and analyze it for us. What seems to be required to move out of this impasse is an intermediate stage between defining Black Theology and actually doing it. This intermediate stage involves not only showing how Black Theology is to be done but also giving it theoretical content before it can be applied to a practical setting. Once this approach has been started there will, of course, be mutual interplay between theory and practice, to their mutual enrichment.

Thirdly, a case can be made for finding the roots of Black Theology in the African Independent Churches, just as in America it also depends partly on the black church for its understanding and nourishment. Both the African Independent Churches and the American black church have often been accused of being fundamentalistic and other-worldly, characteristics not conducive to involvement in a this-worldly struggle for change and justice. It is our duty as theologians, however, to find out what it is about them that makes them so attractive and appealing particularly to people at the grassroots. It is often argued, of course, that the reason for this is their closeness to tradition and African culture (in the case of African Independent Churches). Black Theology must analyze and confirm or disprove the basis of this claim.

Finally, traditional African religion, philosophy and culture must have a bearing on Black Theology not only in South Africa but also in the United States, as American black theologians already acknowledge. Some black theologians in South Africa used to make a distinction between Black Theology, interpreted as a contextual theology, and African Theology, seen as an indigenous theology.[4] Is contextualization incompatible with indigenization, and is African Theology, because it is indigenous, forward or backward looking? These questions have to be answered carefully and any superficial problems about them exposed.

The Roots of Black Theology in America

At least four main sources of Black Theology have been identified by some American black theologians. These are the Bible, the black experience, the black church, and the influence of African culture on American black religion and religious experience. Not all of these sources are always stated or made explicit in the writings of individual theologians, and their emphases often differ. For instance, Cone has accused Gayraud Wilmore, his friend and colleague in the exposition of Black Theology, of omitting reference to scripture in naming the sources of Black Theology in his major work on black religion.[5] In his book Gayraud Wilmore names the three sources as black folk religion, the writings and addresses of the black preachers and public men of the past, and the traditional religions of Africa.[6] Cone argues that such an approach to Black Theology 'will be more acceptable among non-Christian Blacks (especially nationalists) than among Black Christians in the institutional Church, for whom Jesus Christ is the most important religious symbol'.[7]

One does not quite understand Cone's concern on this question. Apart from the fact that Wilmore writes as a Christian theologian and gives no grounds for the impression that he is denying the scriptural basis of Christian theology, his reference to and acceptance of black religion and black preaching would seem to be an implicit recognition of the biblical basis of Black Theology, which is also implicit in his acknowledgement of the role of the black church.

In his second book on Black Theology, Cone mentions six sources of Black Theology without any reference to either African traditional religion or even black religion itself. These sources are the black experience, black history, black culture, revelation, scripture, and tradition.[8] This failure to mention black religion, especially, as a source of Black Theology reflects the earlier influence of Cone's theological training and that he, in fact, perceived himself as fashioning a Black Theology for the black church completely *de novo*. Perhaps he acknowledges this judgement on him indirectly when he later states in the preface of his *God of the Oppressed*, 'Because of the encouragement and critique of my black colleagues, I have been motivated to probe more deeply the resources of the black experience as primary datum for the development of a Black Theology'.[9] Indeed, one of the chapters in that book is devoted to the black experience itself as a source of Black Theology, with special reference to black religion. As already seen, Cone had not completely neglected the black experience, as he had taken up the challenge of black power and attempted a theological response. His theology, following closely on the heels of the black power movement, was partly a response to the concerns raised and addressed by this movement. He had, however, perhaps overemphasized this aspect to the neglect of the black experience in general, including the black religious experience. Later Cone, together with Wilmore, also acknowledged the role of African and black religions, as well as the black experience, in the search for Black Theology as follows, 'The search for a Black Theology takes us not only into the survivals of African religions and the syncretistic religion of the slaves yearning for freedom, but also into the Black experience in the Black ghetto today'.[10]

As Cone rightly states, Black Theology derives its inspiration from scripture, and Luke 4:18 may be said to be its liberatory creed.[11] It also derives inspiration from the Old Testament story of the Exodus, which is often cited as proof that God, as the liberator of the oppressed who freed the children of Israel from their bondage in Egypt, would surely hear the cry of black people in America (and South Africa) and deliver them from their anguish. The fact that Jesus' gospel was addressed to the poor of this world, with whom he identified, was also a source of inspiration for Black Theology.

One of the great proponents of this Exodus/Christ-identity tenet was a radical, American, black preacher, Jaramogi Abebe Agieman, formerly Albert Cleage. His two books, the *Black Messiah* and *Black Christian Nationalism,* portray Christ as a black Jew whose main mission was to form a Black Christian Nation for the purpose of uniting black people against white oppression, thus enabling them to struggle together for their liberation. For him the early Jews, including Jesus' ancestors, were black and gained their light complexion only as a result of migrations and intermingling with lighter races, which almost amounted to selling their birth-right. Moses, to wit, was the black liberator of the black Jewish nation. Both he and Jesus were great nation-builders who showed the importance of nationalism in fighting against the enemies of the nation. An important aspect of Cleage's church is its baptism, which is an initiation into the black nation. His morality tended to be in-group morality, interested in the well-being of the black oppressed and almost hostile towards the oppressor, who must be shaken off the black man's (and woman's) back.[12]

Cleage's claims have been rejected by other black theologians, particularly J. Deotis Roberts, as wild, with nothing concrete to offer in their support. Roberts has also been critical of Cone's work, especially because of the latter's apparent alienation of white Christians and white theology. For Roberts the counterpart of liberation, which he accepts as the basis and goal of Black Theology, is reconciliation, and the two go together. While the former is a precondition for the latter, Black Theology must always keep reconciliation in view in the struggle against oppression. However, Cone has rightly criticized Roberts of inconsistency when the latter writes that

> a black theology that takes reconciliation seriously must work at the task of inter-communication between blacks and whites under the assumption that for those who are open to the truth, there may be communication from the inside out, but at the same time there may be communication from the outside in. In the latter sense, white Christians may be led to understand and work with blacks for liberation and reconciliation on an interracial basis.[13]

Roberts seems to want to have his cake and eat it too. If liberation is a precondition for reconciliation, there is no way whites and blacks can begin to act as if already reconciled and work for 'liberation and reconciliation' together.

All these theologians and their other colleagues have come under severe criticism from William Jones, a Unitarian minister, especially in his prolegomenon to Black Theology. Jones conducts his arguments from the perspective of theodicy and black humanism, asking, 'If there is a just God, why do people suffer (undeservedly)?' Black theologians base their claims that God is the liberator of all the oppressed in the Exodus story, but what proof, what historical example, is there in the black experience to warrant these claims? For such a claim to be justified, blacks should be able to point at events in black history which reflect the liberatory acts of God, just as the Israelites could point at the Exodus event to show that God was their liberator and father. Black people have no right to make claims on other people's histories and base their hopes on them as if they were their own history. Since there is no historical event to which they can point that shows that the biblical God is on their side as their liberator, their claims have no basis. Indeed, their continuing oppression in America points to the contrary. Because God would seem to favour whites in all respects, it would appear more that he is on their side than on that of blacks.[14]

Many criticisms from black theologians against Jones's argument have tended to be *ad hominem*, shrugging it off as non-theological because of his humanistic approach. Dismissing him as a philosopher of religion rather than a theologian, Roberts goes on to remark that black theologians must make a decision whether they are 'church' theologians or not, and act accordingly.[15] Cone, on the other hand, sees Jones's argument as an 'external critique from the vantage point of black humanism'. Nevertheless, he grants, it remains a serious challenge of Black Theology and must be taken seriously by black theologians. He proceeds to offer two points in solution to the problem. 'First', he writes, 'suffering is the source of faith. That is, without human suffering there would be no need for the Christian gospel in particular or religion in general'. The gospel, with its message of salvation, is the Christian answer to human misery. 'Second, while the Christian faith arises out of suffering, suffering is the most serious contradiction of faith. This is the paradox'.[16] These considerations give some strong flavour to American reflection on Black Theology and the issues that should be faced. These issues form the basis of this reflection, thus resulting in the development of Black Theology as a theoretical discipline like western theology and other disciplines.

Black Theology in South Africa
The pioneering effort in the bringing of Black Theology to South Africa, as an intellectual discipline, was made by the University Christian Movement in 1971. Through its director of theological concerns, Basil Moore, 'Black Theology' was imported from the United States and placed under a separate project bearing that name, with its own director. Through this project Black Theology was propagated throughout South Africa by means of seminars and ministers' caucuses which discussed the relevance of the church and its teaching in a situation of oppression such as South Africa. Some of the papers read at these seminars were later made available in book form. This book was, however, banned in South Africa within a month of its publication but appeared later overseas under different titles.[17] Among its essay contributions there were three on Black Consciousness, which, as black power in United States, was the inspiration behind Black Theology in South Africa. Black Theology in this country was thus a logical result and religious counterpart of Black Consciousness. It was, therefore, natural that it follow shortly after the latter had made its impact in South Africa.

The first director of the Black Theology Project, Sabelo Ntwasa, was banned while the book was with the publishers and this resulted in the removal of his essays from the book and the deletion of his name as editor. A significant prelude to his banning was a comment on Black Theology in the South African Radio propaganda programme, 'Current Affairs'. The comment related the historical links between 'Black Theology'[18] and black power in America. Associating the latter with violence and hostility to whites, it saw black power's link with Black Theology as the politicizing of theology, hence the revolutionizing and consequently the distortion of the church's teaching, which was likely to have harmful effects for South African society. In view of this reaction, the government's subsequent actions against Black Theology and its director did not come as a surprise.

From the very beginning Black Theology in South Africa was seen to stand with one leg in Africa and the other in black America. In Africa, there was a recognition that the missionary drive, in spite of its enlightening effort through education and other 'civilizing' activities, resulted partly in the betrayal of the African people. Although it had not quite succeeded in stripping the Africans of their culture and traditions, it had managed to distort them and to make the Africans ashamed of themselves and their heritage by regarding everything African as 'uncivilized' and 'savage', among other disparaging remarks, and African beliefs as 'superstition'. One writer, whose comments on colonialism in general are equally true of some missionary approaches, aptly put it as follows:

> Colonialism is never satisfied with having the native in its grip but, by some strange logic, it turns to his past and disfigures and distorts it. Hence the history of the black man in this country is the most disappointing history to read about. It is merely presented as a long lamentation of repeated defeats. The Xhosas were thieves who went to war for stolen property. The Boers never provoked the Xhosas but merely went on 'punitive expeditions' to teach the thieves a lesson. Heroes like Makana who were essentially revolutionaries are painted as superstitious troublemakers...Great nation-builders like Shaka are cruel tyrants who frequently attacked smaller tribes for...some sadistic purposes. Not only is there no objectivity in the history taught but frequently there is an appalling misrepresentation of facts that is sickening even to the uninformed students.[19]

Part of the task of Black Theology was to discover what basis African forms of religious expression, which still have 'remnants' in black 'mainline' Protestant churches but are prevalent most in the African Independent Churches, had in African traditional culture and beliefs. It was hoped that through this exercise what was good in traditional beliefs and, therefore, compatible with Christian theology could still be retrieved and used to inspire and give meaningful form to our Christian convictions. The discovery and exposition of such traditional practices and their successful relation to Christian teaching would show that traditional beliefs are not necessarily incompatible with Christianity but are, in fact, 'latent' Christianity, so to say — if only because they are not mutually contradictory with it.

The same source quoted above goes on to state that Christianity 'has proved to be a very adaptable religion which does not seek to supplement [sic] existing orders but — like an universal truth — to find application within a particular situation'. While the statement is only partly true, for Christianity does seek to *supplant* injustice and unjust orders, if it is to be faithful to its founder,[20] no one can dispute the basic argument contained in it. Indeed, Desmond Tutu repeats more forcefully the platitude that theology, as the interpretation of the word of God contained in the Christian teaching, possesses the 'limitations and the particularities of those who are theologising. [Thus] it can speak relevantly only when it speaks to a particular· historically and spatio-temporally conditioned Christian community'. Consequently, this human activity — which theology is — 'must have the humility to accept the scandal of its particularity as well as its transcience [sic]'.[21] From this perspective, according to Tutu, Black Theology is for black South Africans an African theology, concerned with indigenization and the gospel in its relation to the peculiarities of the South African situation.

At the same time, black South Africans recognized that the situation addressed through Black Theology in America was very similar to their own and hence, if Black Theology proved meaningful there, it could equally be adapted to produce similar fruits in South Africa. Black Americans were an oppressed minority. While not a minority in their own land, black South Africans were oppressed by a militarily strong minority. The message of Black Theology, as already seen, is liberation: 'to set the downtrodden free'. Thus it fell within the umbrella of Liberation Theology. It recognized that blacks needed to be liberated not only from socio-political bondage, which the church tended to ignore for a pie-in-the-sky, literal interpretation of passages such as, 'My Kingdom is not of this world' and 'Render unto Caesar the things that are Caesar's', but that they needed to be liberated also from religious enslavement to 'heretical' churches which fashioned the Christian teaching according to their human inclinations and socio-political interests. In South Africa, for instance, the white Dutch Reformed churches preach apartheid in the name of scripture,[22] and many other churches have not vigorously spoken out against it and have actually collaborated with it.[23] *Anathema sint.* In these circumstances Black Theology wanted to serve as a challenge to the conscience of the church for the benefit of genuine Christian love and its implication in the struggle for justice.

Black Theology, therefore, rejected most of 'white theology's' interpretation of the gospel and saw it as mostly self-serving. Through its unfaithfulness to the gospel it had implicitly declared the death of God just as, in the Exodus story, the children of Israel had apostasized during Moses' absence and created themselves a golden calf. Black Theologians saw as part of their agenda the discovery of the original Christian teaching — the message behind the distorting tendencies of 'white theology' — and its recasting in accordance with black people's understanding and the demands of their experience. In short, they sought 'to interpret the Gospel of Christ in the light of the black condition'.[24]

The leading black theologian in this country at the time of its first championing was Manas Buthelezi. In one of his earliest articles to be published in South Africa he was concerned to draw proper distinctions between African Theology and Black Theology. Seeing the former's concern as being chiefly with indigenization in the ethnographical sense and thus preoccupied with a 'reconstruction of the African past', he opted for the latter, which he saw also as concerned with indigenization but in the contextual, anthropological sense which took present-day realities in South Africa into account and desired to address them. Buthelezi was suspicious of the 'tendency to romanticize the ethnographically reconstructed past at the expense of the anthropological dynamics of the present situation'. He believed that concentrating on the exigencies of present-day life would 'instinctively', as it were, lead to the activation of spiritual insights contained in the old African world-view, to the enrichment of African Theology and without the pretenses inherent in the claim that we can know how much of the past can influence the present.[25]

One can understand Buthelezi's apprehension with African Theology as it has often been narrowly interpreted by some theologians. However, he might have moved from one extreme view to another. A present without a past is barren. From the study of sociology we know that human beings only become part of a society by being socialized into it. Without tracing our socialization into the African past in some way, it is wishful thinking to imagine that we can reflect the traces of that past in our life and actions, even instinctively. Nor do we need to recall the past merely for the sake of being romantic about it. 'The child is the father of the man'; but once a man is of age, he abandons all childlike acts, though his childhood remains part of what he is as an adult. A man without childhood experiences, like one without a past, is like an uprooted tree which has lost all contact with the earth responsible for its nurture.

To say, therefore, that Black Theology in South Africa stands with one leg in Africa and the other in Black America is to recognize our double advantage in the situation in which we find ourselves. As Africans, we share our background and experience of being what we are with the other sons and daughters of Africa. As an oppressed people, we share the experience of disinheritance and oppression with our brothers and sisters in America. We can learn from both as well as benefit both. To be truly African, Christianity 'must speak in tones that strike a responsive chord in the African breast and must convict the African of his peculiar African sinfulness'. On the other hand, Black Theology, with its political emphasis, has 'an existential urgency which African theology has so far appeared to lack'. 'It cannot be lulled into complacency by a doctrine of pie in the sky which is a reprehensible travesty of the gospel of the Incarnation'.[26] On this basis, therefore, a theologian like Tutu sees himself not only as an exponent of Black Theology but, *eo facto,* of African Theology without the narrow connotations placed on it by theologians such as John Mbiti.[27]

It is tempting to interpret the South African views of Black Theology described here, as well as others, as almost contradictory and perhaps representing irreconcilable schools of thought. However, one should understand them more as formative stages in determining the method of Black Theology, which may ultimately be reconciled as issues and interconnections become clearer and Black Theology itself matures.

David Bosch has, for instance, discovered five trends of Black Theology in South Africa, each with its own representatives.[28] The first trend he sees is that which follows the American model. Its emphasis is on contextualization, seeking to address current bread and butter issues of the liberation struggle, rather than on indigenization as negatively defined by Buthelezi. The second trend would, according to Bosch, equate Black Theology with African Theology, almost as the view represented by Tutu above. It sees Black Theology as African Theology in the Southern African context, which is perceived as possessing an aspect absent from independent Africa. The third trend views Black Theology as related to African traditional religions in a harmonius way, since the Christian teaching does not, according to it, seem to have anything new to offer that is not already present in traditional religions. According to the fourth trend, Black Theology may be said to have found its earliest expressions in the African Independent Churches and the theological causes leading to their secessions from the missionary churches. Finally, Bosch sees as a separate trend the view presented earlier that Black Theology in South Africa stands mid-way between African Theology and American Theology, thus forming a bridge between them.

While one may not question the presence of some of these trends, one does wish to question the validity or timing of such an analysis, made at the very beginning of the quest and without acknowledging that they represent the initial groping of individual minds in search of meaning and relevance, which may end up in the melting pot of common discovery and theological refinement.[29] Indeed, this kind of melting pot has already been reached in America in the discussion of the sources of Black Theology, as already seen in the previous section. Even the communique of the Pan African Conference of Third World Theologians in its statement on African Theology recognized the need for this integration when it stated that the methodology of studying Christianity in Africa must move towards a 'more critical approach that starts from African worldviews, examines the impact of Christianity, and *evaluates the varieties of African responses'.*[30] The communique also lists Black Theology in South Africa among the approaches in African Theology, one which 'takes into consideration the experiences of oppression and the struggle for liberation and gets its inspiration from the biblical faith as expressed in African language and categories as well as from the experience and reflections of black North Americans'.[31]

In fairness to Bosch, he does make some concession that 'it seems as though in South Africa the two theological trends of Black Theology and African Theology can indeed merge into a meaningful symbiosis'. However, he sees this as a possibility only of the first two trends, culminating in the fifth, but leaving out (it seems) the contributions that might be derived from the African Independent Churches and African traditional religions in the understanding of Black Theology. This brings into question the earlier argument in his paper that early manifestations of Black Theology are found in the secessions of African Independent Churches from the white mainline churches. It is the contention of this paper that African traditional religions and the African Independent Churches are some of the sources of African religious expression which need to be taken seriously in any positive search for the roots of Black Theology in South Africa even as they are taken seriously in African Theology itself.

African Independent Churches

More research still needs to be done into the theological roots of the African Independent Churches as a protest movement against the mainline white churches and how these roots can be seen as rudimentary or inspirational to Black Theology. Much has been written about the political causes for their break-away, such as leadership disputes, lack of participation by blacks in decision-making processes, the unwillingness of missionaries to prepare local leadership for eventual take-over by blacks, money disputes, etc. Theological reasons for disaffections, however, if there are any, are merely glossed over and often stated in very vague terms.

Appiah-Kubi has argued that 'spiritual hunger', rather than most of the causes often stated, was the main cause of the emergence of the African Independent Churches. This hunger he describes as the 'religious need of healing, divinity, prophesying, and visioning'. These needs, he says, 'are fulfilled by Christian means in these churches'.[32] Two white South African theologians, in an attempt to interpret Black Theology, have also made similar claims. Bosch relates the story of a Congolese girl, Kimpa Vita, who, as a result of her vision, led a protest movement against the Catholic Church in about 1700. She taught that Christ 'appeared as a black man in Sao Salvador and that all his apostles were black'. He identified himself with the Africans and took their side in their suffering and oppression as against their white oppressors. She prophesied, therefore, that Christ would eventually 'restore the old Congolese Kingdom and establish a paradise on earth'. Bosch sees Vita's teachings as possibly the first manifestation of Black Theology in Africa, since the latter is, according to him, pre-eminently a 'protest against an interpretation of the gospel which has been channelled according to white intentions'.[33]

This narrative provides a good example of how Black Theology can be grounded in the African Independent Churches and their theological protest against missionary churches. Very often, however, there is no sufficient documentary evidence for claims made and this warrants further research by black theologians to authenticate the claims and to establish firm bases for Black Theology. In his book *Bantu Pro-*

phets in South Africa, Sundkler makes a few allusions to some of these theological roots which do not, however, seem to be primary among the causes of secessions from white churches for those who espoused them. After stating, for instance, that Mokone's break-away from the Methodist Church was the result of racial segregation in the church, he goes on to point out that Mokone 'had heard missionaries who referred in their sermons to Psalms 68:31, *"Ethiopia shall soon stretch out her hands unto God",* and to other references such as Acts 8:27'.[34] According to Sundkler, Mokone took this statement to mean the self-government of the African church under African leaders. The superficiality with which this cause is linked to the secession is witnessed by the fact that Sundkler does not even mention it in his typology of African Independent Churches. Speaking of the Ethiopian type, he writes, 'As Ethiopians I classify such independent Bantu Churches as have (a) seceded from White Mission Churches chiefly on racial grounds, or (b) other Bantu Churches seceding from the Bantu leaders classified under (a)'.[35] A second type, which he classifies as Zionist, is described as 'deliberately nativistic', likely to serve as a bridge from Christianity back to heathenism.[36] With such a conclusion, it is difficult to see how he can even imagine a theological basis for the African Independent Churches.

It may be that some of the religious practices incorporated into the African Independent Churches after the secessions from missionary churches reflect the implicit yearnings of those people who finally broke away and implicity remain, therefore, causes for the breakaways. Sundkler describes these practices in his book and they can, hopefully, provide useful material for an investigation of the roots of Black Theology in the African Independent Churches. We need to examine not only how these churches came about and what theological push-factors prompted their departure from white churches. Their teachings, sermons and the content of their hymns must be analyzed theologically, their practices examined for theological significance, and their attitudes to white churches scrutinized to establish their points of difference from white Christianity. This kind of study would certainly reveal certain parallels with the origins and theology of the black churches in the United States, but our goal will not be to imitate them but to find out what is unique about the emergence of the African Independent Churches and their ways.

Sundkler shows that some of the hymns of the African Independent Chuches, like the freedom-loving black American Spirituals, contain strong nationalistic tones. Consider, for instance, the following hymn from Rev. Shembe's hymnbook:

> Africa, rise!
> And seek thy Saviour
> Today our sons and daughters are slaves.

The Saviour is, of course, the Christian Messiah whose second coming is often emphasized with fundamentalistic zeal. But salvation is not always seen as an other-worldly affair, as the following verse shows:

> Jesus, come
> With your father
> People are dying
> here on earth...[37]

The yearning for a God who truly appealed to the African imagination and aspirations, in protest against the God of white theology, was expressed in the following sermon by Shembe:

> You, my people, were once told of a God who has neither arms nor legs, who cannot see, who has neither love nor pity. But Isaiah Shembe showed you a God who walks on feet and who heals with his hands, and who can be known by men, a God who loves and who has compassion.[38]

While it may be true that the African Independent Churches are generally inclined towards a fundamentalistic approach to theology, they are not necessarily blind to their surroundings or to the facts of their socio-political conditions. They may not always be explicitly 'political' in their sermons, so to say, but even in their prayers ministers and individual congregants reveal that they are not only interested in the life to come but they do not accept their present condition as intended by God. Black Theology must, therefore, take these churches seriously and try to understand not only their beginnings but also what message these beginnings have for black Christians in general and how their Christian understanding and theology can profit from them.

This aspect of Black Theology, together with the following one, did not receive as much prominence in the early days of Black Theology in South Africa as that concerned with the immediate needs of liberation and protest against the church's complacency with the status quo. For this reason this section has been included mainly as a recommendation for the future development of Black Theology, but also as an example of the second approach—mentioned at the beginning of this paper—to discovering the roots of Black Theology.

African Traditional Religions

As already seen, not every black theologian originally agreed on the use of the traditional worldview and its religion in the quest and development of Black Theology. Surprisingly, this seemed to be more a South African problem than a black American problem. Perhaps African Theology, it was felt, as the theology of independent Africa, might justly spare the time and luxury of seeking Africa's heritage and relating it to the Christian teaching. However, as a contextual theology, Black Theology must concern itself with the present-day struggle not only against socio-political oppression but also against enslavement to the nonliberatory aspects of the cultural past and outmoded traditions.

The emphasis of African Theology itself has shifted since it was accused of what may be called 'negative indigenization'. It has already been seen that it also makes room for Black Theology as one form of its application in a situation like South Africa. The African Theology communique cited earlier has also made it clear that African Theology must be responsive to the demands of all the situations it seeks to address. It must be contextual — dealing with the liberation of people from cultural captivity; it must be a liberation theology — concerned with liberation from socio-economic exploitation; and it must also struggle against sexism. Its nurture is seen as coming not only from the Bible and the Christian heritage, but also from African anthropology, African traditional religion, the African Independent Churches, and other African realities.[39]

These ideas would have found implicit support from some of the early proponents of Black Theology in South Africa. Although Rev. Simon Lediga is cited as supporting the alignment of Black Theology with African traditional religion, it can safely be assumed that this alignment was not viewed to the exclusion of the other sources mentioned.[40]

Such an alignment, with its presuppositions of the role of traditional religions, receives more emphasis from Tutu, who sees African Theology and Black Theology as soul mates rather than antagonists. Affirming the role of traditional religions in the development of African Theology, he writes, 'African theology has done a wonderful service in rehabilitating the African religious consciousness'. This he sees as repudiating the idea that 'worthwhile religion in Africa had to await the advent of the white man'.[41]

Just as black American theologians have referred to their religious heritage for the early manifestations of Black Theology in their country and for present inspiration, so, therefore, it seems, must black

South African theologians also examine their traditional religions for the unique religious and cultural contributions that can be made by them to the Christian teaching and Black Theology. Cone and Wilmore have supported this idea, seeing as one of the first tasks of African (or Black) Theology the 'reconstruction of the Christian faith in Africa which takes seriously the fact that God had revealed himself in the traditional religions and that by a selective process African theologians can use this revelatory content to throw light on the message and meaning of Jesus Christ'.[42] Theologians may have already been overtaken by their congregations on this if it is true, as it is often claimed, that for many Africans conversion to Christianity has 'not meant the exchange of the indigenous religion for the new one but rather an amalgamation of the two, made the more possible by their common belief in spirits'.[43] If this claim is true, we must find out exactly what aspects of the Christian teaching were assimilable into traditional religious beliefs and how this was done to suit the African's understanding and his/her religious expression. This, however, cannot be successfully attempted until we have gained better insights into African traditional religions themselves, and on this South Africans still have a long way to go compared to their fellowmen on the continent.

Conclusion

In many ways black South Africa can be said to be the 'last ox' (*agter os*), to use an Afrikaner expression, in the kraal of development and progress in the African continent. This is so not only in the political sphere but also in its relative lack of disciplined, intellectual growth or expression. We have to do away with our tradition of being perpetual beginners who never approach the middle course or reach the end of our initiatives. In discussing this paper's topic with a friend, he argued that we should stop writing prolegomena to Black Theology and 'get down to real business', that is, begin giving content to this type of theology. I share his observation. One of the reasons for our lack of success is the little attention we pay to research and our overdependence on intellectual imaginativeness, which we mistake for originality. Until we take research seriously, both to obtain facts and to stimulate our thinking, we will continue in this stalemate of 'genesisism' and can make no noteworthy contribution to Black Theology in particular, let alone to scholarship in general. We may be at the tale end of events, but it is better to be late than never to be there at all. It is time to embark on phase II of Black Theology.

NOTES

1. James Cone, *Black Theology and Black Power* (New York: Seabury Press, 1969).

2. Cone, *God of the Oppressed* (New York: Seabury Press, 1975), p. vi.

3. Both Manas Buthelezi and Desmond Tutu have objected to this statement by suggesting that Black Theology is reflected in their pastoral work and preaching. That is granted. The main argument here is that no systematic rationale has been given for these activities. Boganjalo Goba has written about how to do theology in South Africa in this article 'Doing Theology in South Africa: A Black Christian Perspective', *Journal of Theology for Southern Africa* 31 (June 1980): 23-35. This still leaves out, however, the actual content of Black Theology.

4. For an examination of Black Theology in South Africa, see David J. Bosch, 'Currents and Crosscurrents in South African Black Theology', in *Black Theology: A Documentary History, 1966-1979*, ed. Gayraud S. Wilmore and James H. Cone (Maryknoll, N.Y.: Orbis Books, 1979), pp. 220-37.

5. Cone, 'Epilogue: An Interpretation of the Debate among Black Theologians', in *Black Theology: A Documentary History*, p. 618.

6. Wilmore, *Black Religion and Black Radicalism* (Garden City, N.Y.: Anchor Press/Doubleday, 1973), pp. 298-302.

7. Cone, 'Epilogue,' p. 618.

8. Cone, *A Black Theology of Liberation* (Philadelphia: Lippincott Co., 1970), pp. 54-69.

9. Cone, *God of the Oppressed*, p. vii.

10. Cone and Wilmore, 'Black Theology and African Theology: Considerations for Dialogue, Critique, and Integration', in *Black Theology: A Documentary History*, p. 469.

11. In the Jerusalem Bible the passage reads: 'The spirit of the Lord has been given to me,/for he has anointed me./ He has sent me to bring the good news to the poor,/ to proclaim liberty to captives/ and to the blind new sight,/ to set the downtrodden free,/ to proclaim the lord's year of favour'. Unlike Cone, I do not see the need for insisting on the mention of scripture among the sources of Black Theology because scripture is, understandably, the primary source of all theology. What I am concerned about is what distinguishes Black Theology from white theology. This, I think, is the reason why Wilmore also seems to take scripture for granted in naming his sources.

12. For a summary of his views see Albert B. Cleage, Jr., 'The Black Messiah and the Black Revolution', in *Quest for a Black Theology*, ed. James J. Gardiner and J. Deotis Roberts (Philadelphia: Pilgrim Press, 1971), pp. 1-27. Cleage's two books referred to are: *The Black Messiah* (New York: Sheed and Ward, 1969); and *Black Christian Nationalism* (New York: William Morrow and Co., 1972).

13. J. Deotis Roberts, *Liberation and Reconciliation: A Black Theology* (Philadelphia: Westminster Press, 1971), p. 23. For his criticism of Robert's position, see Cone, 'Epilogue'.

14. See William R. Jones, *Is God a White Racist?* (Garden City, N.Y.: Anchor Press/Doubleday, 1973).

15. Roberts, 'Liberation Theism', in *Black Theology II*, ed. Calvin E. Bruce and William R. Jones (Lewisburg, Pa.: Bucknell University Press, 1978), p. 236.

16. Cone, 'Epilogue', p. 622.

17. The South African title was *Essays on Black Theology*. See n. 1 of the Introduction, above, for information about the British and U.S. editions.

18. See chap. 3, below.

19. Steve Biko, 'Black Consciousness and the Quest for a True Humanity' (mimeograph).

20. See Desmond Tutu, *Hope and Suffering: Sermons and Speeches* (Johannesburg: Skotaville Publishers, 1983), p. 125.

21. Tutu, 'Black Theology/African Theology—Soul Mates or Antagonists?', in *Black Theology: A Documentary History*, p. 488.

22. See Tutu's repudiation of their claim in *Hope and Suffering*, p. 130.

23. For a discussion of the churches and their racial practices and reactions to apartheid, see M. B. G. Motlhabi, *The Theory and Practice of Black Resistance to Apartheid* (Johannesburg: Skotaville Publishers, 1984).

24. Cone, *Black Theology of Liberation*, p. 23.

25. Buthelezi, 'An African Theology or a Black Theology' (mimeograph).

26. Tutu, 'Black Theology/African Theology,' pp. 487, 489.

27. John Mbiti, 'An African Views American Black Theology', in *Black Theology: A Documentary History*, pp. 477–82.

28. Bosch, 'Currents and Crosscurrents', p. 224–37.

29. See, however, the last paragraph of this section.

30. See 'Communique, Pan-African Conference of Third World Theologians, Accra, Ghana, December 17–23, 1977', in *Black Theology: A Documentary History*, p. 505 (emphasis added).

31. Ibid., p. 506.

32. Kofi Appiah-Kubi, 'Indigenous African Christian Churches: Signs of Authenticity', in *African Theology en Route*, ed. Kofi Appiah-Kubi and Sergio Torres (Maryknoll, N.Y.: Orbis Books, 1979), pp. 117–18.

33. Bosch, 'Currents and Crosscurrents', pp. 220–21.

34. B. G. M. Sundkler, *Bantu Prophets in South Africa* (Oxford: Oxford University Press, 1961), p. 39.

35. Ibid., pp. 53–54.

36. Ibid., p. 55.

37. Ibid., pp. 196, 279.

38. Ibid., p. 27.

39. 'Communique', pp. 506–7, 509.

40. See Bosch, 'Currents and Crosscurrents', p. 227.

41. Tutu, 'Black Theology/African Theology', pp. 488–89.

42. Cone and Wilmore, 'Black Theology and African Theology', p. 471.

43. Kwasi Wiredu, *Philosophy and an African Culture* (Cambridge: Cambridge University Press, 1980), p. 45.

Chapter 3

The Black Consciousness Movement: Its Impact on Black Theology
BONGANJALO GOBA

Editors' Abstract

Black Theology is the child of Black Consciousness. The latter, as the ideology of the black struggle for liberation, has provided a fundamental matrix for developing a black theological hermeneutic. The black experience as a hermeneutical point of departure for Black Theology spawns a qualitatively different approach to the scriptures and traditions of Christians. The marriage of Black Theology and Black Consciousness has also led to a questioning of the role of the church in the process of radical social change. Goba is not, however, uncritical of Black Consciousness as the ideology of the black struggle for liberation. He invokes three aspects of Frantz Fanon's philosophy as a basis for critiquing Black Consciousness. These are: the rural base of the revolution; the nationalistic character of the revolution; and the fundamental problem of violence in the revolutionary process.

Goba notes that the first (the rural base of the revolution) and the third (the problem of violence) aspects of the revolution have not been adequately addressed by the Black Consciousness philosophy, which focuses on the urban context of the black struggle and ignores the rural hinterland where the majority of black people are being confined by apartheid policies. Goba calls for a critical development of both Black Theology and Black Consciousness. The present phase of the black struggle is a critical one which demands an inbuilt element of self-criticism.

Note that the following paper opens with the formalities of a speech in order to emphasize the historic occasion of the seminar.

'Our blackness is a given thing: We are born black and in view of this,
no choice is open to us'
(J. Deotis Roberts)

Introduction

The Chairperson and Friends:

Thank you very much for this invitation to participate in this very important seminar on Black Theology. This brings back sad and pleasant memories because the first Black Theology seminar in South Africa was held in this place during the early seventies. Therefore for some of us this is an important occasion to reflect again on the development of a very important movement within the black Christian community. As we participate in this workshop we are actually reaffirming a vision that was born long ago, when some of the early black Christian leaders such as Rev. Dwane and Rev. Mokone decided to break away from the imperial theology that dominated the lives of the black Christians in this country. There is therefore a sense in which we are involved in a theological pilgrimage that has continued and will continue to give an expression to our faith within the ongoing struggle for liberation. So the significance of this seminar is not that we are here to resuscitate Black Theology from its slumber, but we are here to sharpen and deepen our respective *methodologies* vis-à-vis the current ongoing struggle. In Zulu I would say *'Sizolola Izik-hali':* we are here to sharpen our tools or 'swords' in order to challenge again the black Christian community to participate meaningfully in the struggle for *authentic* liberation.

This is important because there are those who have the false impression that Black Theology is something of the past or it is dead. Black Theology is alive because it has become the way of doing theology — a vehicle through which we articulate and express our faith. It is dead only to those who continue to be enslaved to a colonial type of theology, or a reactionary theology that has failed miserably to address itself to our situation of dehumanization and oppression. What must be emphasized is that Black Theology expresses itself within the context of our experience of oppression. It portrays the Christian story within the experience of pain and suffering. Further, it brings a message of God's promise for the liberation of the poor and oppressed — a message which affirms that God is on the side of the oppressed as one who challenges them through the coming of our Lord Jesus Christ to engage in his mission of liberation of the world. This for me is the essence of the gospel.

With these few remarks, let me attempt to spell out briefly some of the issues involved in our topic. The topic as it stands presupposes a profound relationship between Black Consciousness and Black Theology. There is a sense in which this is true. However, we must be careful not to overlook certain problems, especially when we try and define both these concepts. I believe we must take into consideration the following points:

(a) We must examine the various definitions of both Black Consciousness and Black Theology.

(b) We must also examine various political dynamics that have influenced both these movements — here, I have in mind the sociopolitical context.

(c) There is also a need for us to examine the shifting ideological alliances within the current black struggle in South Africa today. This, I am aware, may be a very sensitive area, but it must be approached because it reflects certain political perceptions about our present political situation.

(d) Finally, we have to address ourselves to the problem of ideological consciousness as a theological issue vis-à-vis the praxis of liberation.

These are some of the areas I hope to examine briefly in this paper and I am tempted to think that the other speakers may say something about some of these issues.

The Problem of Definitions

Having made these few remarks let us attempt to examine some of the common definitions of these concepts. To define both these ideas is not easy. Nevertheless, when we examine ideas associated with Black Consciousness we find the following notions: Black Consciousness is defined as a programme of black political self-awareness, a quest for black pride — hence the slogan 'black is beautiful'. Black Consciousness is an attitude of mind or a way of life. In this context, Black Consciousness is referred to as an ontological concept, one which pertains to the meaning of being black in the world. Hence Allan Boesak defines it as follows: 'Blackness is a reality that embraces the totality of black existence'.[1] Black Consciousness is an existential category which depicts a mode of existence that has an aesthetical orientation (e.g. concern about culture and art as well as a commitment to the past) as well as a political one that becomes a political philosophy that justifies a strategy in engaging in the process of liberation. This is why we get an emphasis on ideas such as dignity and solidarity in a given context of a political struggle.

We can tentatively define Black Consciousness as a kind of a political philosophy whose goal is to forge and promote the struggle for black liberation in a world of white domination. I have used the word 'tentatively' because we are dealing with a phenomenon that is in the making: that is, an idea that still needs to be fully defined, a kind of a prolegomenon that must be fully developed within a concrete struggle. One of the problems which we have to remember when attempting to define this concept is that in our situation, Black Consciousness is vaguely defined and there is a state of confusion about it. Black Consciousness is an ideology which is claimed by both radicals and reactionaries in our context. For example even a movement such as Black Alliance regards itself as a Black Consciousness movement. It is my hope that during this seminar we will attempt to deepen our understanding of this very important idea in our struggle.

Having given this rather general description of what Black Consciousness entails let me also give a definition of Black Theology. It is also very difficult to give a satisfactory definition of Black Theology. To my mind one of the most comprehensive definitions of Black Theology is the one which is contained in a statement by the National Committee of Black Churchmen made in June 1969:

> Black Theology is a theology of black liberation. It seeks to plumb the black condition in the light of God's revelation in Jesus Christ, so that the black community can see that the gospel is commensurate with the achievement of black humanity. Black Theology is a theology of "blackness". It is the affirmation of black humanity that emancipates black people from white racism, thus providing authentic freedom for both white and black people.[2]

This definition has been the basis of many approaches in Black Theology. Even in our own situation we have retained some of the basic elements of this definition. I have defined Black Theology elsewhere as follows:

> Black Theological reflection is a critical reflection on the praxis of Christian Faith, one which participates in the ongoing process of liberation with the black Christian community.[3]

This definition, like many others, attempts to explicate the relevance of the gospel within the context of the black struggle. Black Theology is a way of reflecting about our faith as we engage meaningfully in the struggle of our people. Black Theology is a way of thinking and acting by black Christians as they attempt to discover the political implications of their faith in a given situation. Therefore, having said this, we also have to be careful because Black Theology today is claimed by both radicals and reactionaries. For example even those black ministers who collaborate with the existing political system of apartheid and so-called independent states will tell you that they are doing Black Theology. This is one of the dilemmas we must examine in this seminar. Apart from this, there are those who have confused Black Theology with African Theology, those who think when we focus our attention on the challenge of Africanization we are actually doing Black Theology. The problem here has to do with the kind of hermeneutic that one uses in his or her theological programme. Black Theology in its method of interpretation is intentionally political; on the other hand, African Theology tends to be more ethnographical, particularly in its emphasis on African cultural values. Therefore we must make a clear distinction when we talk about the two. But at the same time we must also realize that it is possible to embody both interests in the kind of theological hermeneutic that we choose. Both these rather general definitions of Black Consciousness and Black Theology will become useful as we explore further the nature of the relationship between these two movements.

A Brief Examination of the Political Dynamics that Influenced Both These Movements

I want to suggest that one way of understanding the relationship between Black Consciousness and Black Theology is to examine the socio-political context out of which both these movements emerged especially in the late sixties. Many theories can be presented in trying to assess the origins of both Black Consciousness and Black Theology. My own view on this is that every context of a political struggle has tremendous influence on the political perceptions of those who engage in it. This is true of our own situation. There is a sense in which one can describe Black Consciousness and Black Theology as parallel movements both arising from black experience. They both attempt to articulate a way of engaging in a struggle for liberation which takes seriously the existential experience of being oppressed in the South African context.

Black Consciousness represents a culmination of an ideological struggle that began in the late forties and found a new impetus in the late sixties. It represents a creative response to the collapse of the so-called non-racial politics of the sixties which whites, particularly in NUSAS and UCM, dominated. I need not give all the details about this because these have been covered by Dr. Motlhabi's paper. When Steve Biko sounded the call for a black student organization in 1968 there was tremendous response from various campuses in the country. I can still remember serving on the SRC of the Federal Theological Seminary and how important the challenge was for us. It was important because it challenged us to focus on our black identity and its relationship to the struggle. One can safely say that the emergence of Black Consciousness in the late sixties represented a kind of a political reawakening at a time when there was an absence of black political leadership in the country. You will remember that at this time most of the significant political organizations had been banned. It was a period of political confusion in the black community.

So when Black Consciousness emerged under the dynamic leadership of Biko it brought a new ray of hope, a new commitment to the struggle for liberation. Its impact was not just felt in the various black university campuses, but also in the various black seminaries. When the decision came to resign from white dominated student organizations such as NUSAS and UCM a new organization had to be found, one that would embody this new political vision throughout the country and that body became SASO. At the same time a number of us were members of the University Christian Movement, a liberal Christian movement that had broken away from the SCA. Because of this dynamic movement of Black Consciousness, we decided to dissociate ourselves from UCM and to establish the Black Theology movement which represented a theological response to the challenge of Black Consciousness.

It is important to remember that this black political reawakening in South Africa coincided with the black civil rights movement in the United States. It is difficult to determine how much this influenced Black Consciousness in South Africa because of the different political situations. But when we examine the political thrust of black power in South Africa, we see a symbolic relationship in terms of ideas and strategy. As we wrestled with the challenge of Black Consciousness we were really influenced by the writing of James Cone. We discovered in his theological hermeneutic a fresh approach in engaging in the liberation struggle in our situation within an ecclesiastical context. I can remember how Cone's ideas dominated our Black Theology seminar at Wilgespruit in 1970 and became a useful basis for developing a Black Theology arising out of the South African context. It is also important to note the presence of a number of leading exponents of Black Consciousness at this seminar. People like Biko, Harry Nengwenkulu and Barney Pityana had a tremendous influence on our approach.

Black Theology emerged also at a critical period within the church in South Africa, a period which was characterized by a failure of the white dominated Christian church to respond to the political crisis that was in the country. This is why there was a negative response to Black Theology coming from white theologians as well as some of our reactionary black Christian leaders. The significance of Black Theology at that time was that it forced the black Christian community to take seriously the challenge of Black Consciousness within the black struggle itself. Apart from that it brought about a need within the black Christian community to reinterpret the nature of the Christian faith within the context of the black struggle in South Africa.

Let me conclude this section by suggesting that the relationship between Black Consciousness and Black Theology can be described as that of soul mates walking together in the ongoing struggle of black liberation. Both these movements are an expression of a vision of liberation whose goal is to conscientize and involve members of the black community in the struggle for a just social order. Black Consciousness and Black Theology are like the hands of a potter who is trying to mould something symbolic and yet concrete in terms of the vision for the future. But this is not enough: we still have to explore their relationship in the light of the present struggle, particularly in terms of our praxis of liberation. In the late sixties both these movements were a response to a crisis situation of intense repression, an attempt to provide a vision for liberation in the black community. But we must also assess in what way they continue to offer that vision of liberation to the black community today.

The Problem of Shifting Ideological Alliances in the Black Struggle Today

This brings me to the present situation. In what way do these movements have any relevance for our struggle today? This I believe is a question which could help us determine their relationship in terms of our present situation. In what way has the situation changed from that of the late sixties? Another question to ask is: In what way is Black Theology involved in this context of conflict?

Today as before there is an ongoing conflict within the black community at two levels. There is conflict among those who, whilst sharing a deep concern about the programme of black liberation, differ ideologically as well as in terms of strategy. There is a division between those who work within and outside the existing pseudo-political structures — that is those who collaborate with the status quo and those who work outside the existing political system. These divisions are so deep that any person committed to the black struggle must think about this state of affairs. With the recent euphoria about the so-called constitutional reform in South Africa these ideological conflicts have rekindled. However, it must be stated that the source seems to be centred on the theory-praxis debate in any revolutionary struggle. The so-called constitutional reforms should merely be seen as a political context in which present political divisions express themselves — at a much broader level these conflicts are centred on ideology and strategy. Whilst both the United Democratic Front and the National Forum are committed to the liberation struggle, they differ both in terms of ideology and strategy. The UDF is more inclined to a broad political vision of a democratic society reflecting certain basic tenets of the Freedom Charter. As far as its strategy is concerned it is an open one in which all progressive democrats participate irrespective of race, religion or class. On the other hand the National Forum is inclined to a Pan-Africanist ideology reflecting an exclusive kind of black nationalism and a strategy that excludes whites as participants in the revolutionary process.

As I have already indicated, this situation is not new. Conflict has always been part of our struggle. However, one of the ironies of our struggle is that the conflicting parties share something in common and that is a search for political solidarity with the goal of engaging in the ongoing process of authentic liberation. My real concern about this conflict has to do with the future of the black struggle in this country. And this future can only be clear when we understand the political goals which are projected by both these movements. Unfortunately when we examine various documents reflecting various positions of these movements, we get a rather vague picture. For example the UDF is committed to a democratic, non-racial, unitary state in which democrats participate irrespective of race, religion and colour. The declaration makes no critical statement about, for example, capitalism. In other words the declaration does not spell out what is understood by a democratic state in terms of the projected socio-political structures which are envisaged. On the other hand the statement of the National Forum reflects a commitment to some kind of socialism which rejects a system of racial capitalism. But this is also not spelled out, even if the statement in a very general way mentions a commitment to establish a democratic, socialist state with a clear rejection of whites participating. As they put it, they are opposed 'to all alliances with the ruling class parties'.

There is no doubt in my mind that both these movements are committed to liberation. Unfortunately, their ideological commitments and strategies differ profoundly and this brings me to the question of what is really at stake in the conflict. One of the basic problems which generates this conflict has to do with a clash of ideologies (and at a deeper level with personalities). For example the National Forum embraces a democratic political vision that is committed to an exclusive black nationalism and its social praxis automatically excludes whites. I am aware this may be an oversimplification of the problem at stake. However, it is important to mention this because one has to assess in which way is the broad vision of Black Consciousness related to the issue. Further how does this ideological conflict influence one's black theological hermeneutic in terms of our present situation? Is it possible for black theologians to escape this ideological conflict in terms of their respective methodologies? I am mentioning these shifting ideological alliances in passing because they pose a serious problem to the way one examines the impact of Black Consciousness on Black Theology. One could even go further and say they demand a new reinterpretation of the relationship between the two. And here again there is bound to be a serious division between us as black theologians. The problem has to do with how one defines Black Consciousness as a necessary political philosophy for developing a relevant black theological hermeneutic. For example is it possible that one can define a black theological hermeneutic in terms of the political vision projected by the United Democratic Front? And on the other hand could one develop a theological hermeneutic that reflects the political vision of the National Forum? There is still a third possibility which projects a critical perspective in terms of these two ideological camps. The third option must examine critically the role of an ideology within a given struggle particularly as it projects a comprehensive theological praxis. I do not have all the answers to this problem and perhaps this could be an issue to be debated by the conference.

The Problem of Ideological Consciousness in Black Theology
I want to emphasize that all theology is ideological in the sense that it projects a political vision of those who participate in it. This is why I disagree with Allan Boesak when he makes the following statement:

> Christian faith transcends all ideologies and all nationalistic ideals. It transcends specific groups and nations within specific ideals and interests.[4]

This to my mind reflects a profound misunderstanding of the nature of a theological hermeneutic, a dangerous ahistorical perspective which contradicts Allan Boesak's view of the black experience. I make this observation because the starting point of a relevant theology is actual involvement in the struggle and as such involvement reflects or embodies the emancipatory interests of those who are in it. So Black Theology occurs within the context of the black struggle and inescapably will reflect the ideological interests of the black community. If it doesn't it ceases to be Black Theology.

This brings me to the problem of ideological consciousness and theology, especially as it relates to the impact of Black Consciousness on Black Theology. Let me attempt to give you my own assessment of Black Consciousness. I want to suggest that Black Consciousness as an ideology of the black struggle is not to be confined to the realm of aesthetics but constitutes the programme of political action. Black Consciousness is an ideology which seeks to conscientize blacks about the nature and praxis of their struggle. Its goal is to bring about total authentic liberation. Its concern is not simply to promote psychological black self-affirmation. In other words Black Consciousness is not just a therapy to make us feel good about our blackness. But it constitutes a serious political programme of action. It is political in the sense that it identifies, clearly for us, white oppressive socio-political structures. In other words, Black Consciousness is the critical starting point of engaging in the black struggle because it takes seriously the particularity of black experience.

As an ideology Black Consciousness represents a social totality of the goals of our liberation. I am using ideology here in the Althusserian sense in which an ideology is a system of representations which embodies the totality of all our experience. In other words for me Black Consciousness does not represent a kind of social aberration or what is sometimes referred to as false consciousness. But it is basic to the way we perceive the political reality of our situation. So Black Consciousness as a central ideology in the black struggle is unique in that it arises out of a socio-political context in which we have been oppressed and dehumanized as black people in this country. This to me is the essence of the political vision that continues to inform my view of the black struggle in South Africa. I am aware that such a statement is bound to raise the old complex debate of class and race. In response to this I have always maintained that what distinguishes the political reality of our situation from others in the world is that we are oppressed first and foremost because we are black. This is a fundamental truth that even my own mother understands. To speak about a pocket of the emerging black bourgeois class is to create confusion in the minds of our people. Because as far as the average black person is concerned the black middle class is part and parcel of the oppressive socio-political status quo in this country. Anyone who underestimates this fact will present a truncated view of the black struggle. Those who emphasize class as an important political variable in our struggle must provide a clear understanding of what they mean by class, particularly as a collective heuristic concept that defines the nature of our present struggle. Apart from that, this debate belongs to the intellectual elite in our society who continue to benefit from the present status quo.

I believe in defining Black Consciousness we must begin to project the values of our people whose perceptions of blackness are reflected in their daily experience of suffering and oppression. To many of our people the existential issue or question is: Why is this happening to us as black people? As Vilakazi puts it in one of his poems, 'my beingness oppresses me'. In other words my oppression is ontological; it pertains to who I am. Having said this I am not suggesting that a class analysis is not important, only that such an analysis must take into consideration the historical-political dynamics that have shaped and continue to shape our struggle. I think the fundamental question we have to ask is: How do we define the necessary connection between ideology and social analysis for the black liberation struggle? This is important to ask because our social analysis must be informed by a comprehensive ideology and that ideology for me continues to be Black Consciousness, because it projects for us a reality which says racism is a concept that speaks to the total system, the essential nature of the South African social order as perceived by black people. This is why those who view the black problem as part of the general problem of class oppression make a big mistake — they tragically underestimate the uniqueness of the black situation and experience as a whole. Black Consciousness poses a challenge to Black Theology because of its commitment to the uniqueness of black experience.

Having made these rather general statements about very serious issues which require a deeper analysis, I want to suggest that Black Consciousness as an ideology provides an important context for developing a theological hermeneutic of the oppressed. However, for theologians to develop their hermeneutic, there is a need to define how this ideology should function in terms of deepening the social analysis of our present socio-political situation. We need to spell out what kind of society we envisage and how we will work for it, given our present political situation. For example, if we are committed to a socialist state, what do we mean by that? Let me conclude this section by stating, once more, that our theological hermeneutic is not something purely abstract, but emerges within the prophetic vision of those who engage in a concrete struggle. Therefore there is a sense in which Black Consciousness is part of this prophetic vision in which we as theologians respond to the challenge of the liberating gospel of Christ.

The Impact of Black Consciousness on Black Theology

Let me conclude this presentation by making a few remarks about what I consider to be the real contribution of Black Consciousness to Black Theology and then move on to make some projection of what should happen in the future, particularly in terms of our theological praxis. Black Consciousness has provided a very important context for developing a black theological hermeneutic. It has challenged black theologians to take seriously the particularity of black experience. This has been extremely meaningful, particularly in approaching scripture and Christian tradition. But its most significant contribution has been in the area of praxis. Black theologians, because of Black Consciousness, have had to wrestle with the challenge of how they can meaningfully participate in the ongoing struggles for liberation. This has challenged them to examine the role of the church in the process of radical social change. So we can say Black Consciousness has been the nerve centre of Black Theology which has given it a unique character in the entire black theological enterprise. Black Consciousness has played and continues to play an important role because it compels black theologians to reflect the emancipatory interests of the black community as the agenda for the task of doing theology in the South African context. Because of the Black Consciousness Movement we have been compelled to look at ourselves within the context of oppression, to discover within ourselves the power to assert our theological insights without making any apology. In other words Black Consciousness has enabled us to see Jesus Christ as he is, particularly in our situation. But having said this, we also state there is still a challenge before us to explore the real meaning of Black Consciousness as an ideology of the black struggle.

For there are those who regard it as a bourgeois ideology of the black elite. In redefining consciousness for ourselves there is a need for us to go back to Frantz Fanon and examine three important aspects in his philosophy. These are: (1) the rural base of the revolution; (2) the nationalistic character of our revolution; (3) the fundamental problem of violence in the revolutionary process.

I mention Fanon because I believe he may provide us with very interesting ideological insights for our particular context. Black

Consciousness has tended to be an urban phenomenon and this points to one of its central weaknesses. As an ideology it is inadequate because masses of black people are in the so-called independent states. Finally we must be realistic in our political goals: we are confronted with a violent social order and therefore the problem of violence will also pose a serious enigma to our black theological enterprise as a whole. What all this suggests to me is a need for us to redefine our theological hermeneutic as well as praxis within the context of our struggle. This requires what I may call a hodogenic methodology. We need a method that weaves its way out of the concrete struggle, one that in essence represents the theological efforts of the oppressed themselves as they forge a new Christian praxis. For this to take place we need a much more comprehensive analysis of our own situation, one which avoids ideological reductionism current in some of the vulgar materialistically orientated approaches in our situation. This means that we need a critical perspective that will force us as black theologians to question our existing categories of thought which may be foreign to the existential understanding of our situation. To achieve this, there is a need for popular theology which reflects the total experience of our people reflected in song, poetry and their stories forged within the actual struggle itself.

Black Consciousness has played a very significant role in the development of Black Theology. But the question we have to ask is: Is it still adequate for our present situation? In what way is the present situation challenging us to reexamine our theological hermeneutic and praxis as black theologians? Which is important, race or class, in terms of our theological project? Or are both needed for a comprehensive analysis? These are some of the questions we have to answer as we enter this critical phase of the black struggle. And it is in responding to these questions that we will be able to assess the ongoing impact of Black Consciousness on Black Theology.

NOTES

1. Allan Boesak, *Farewell to Innocence* (Maryknoll, N.Y.: Orbis Books, 1977), p. 26.

2. 'Black Theology: Statement by the National Committee of Black Churchmen, June 13, 1969', in *Black Theology: A Documentary History, 1966-1979*, ed. Gayraud S. Wilmore and James H. Cone (Maryknoll, N.Y.: Orbis Books, 1979), p. 101.

3. Bonganjalo Goba, 'Doing Theology in South Africa: A Black Christian Perspective', *Journal of Theology for Southern Africa* 31 (June 1980): 25.

4. Boesak, *Farewell*, p. 121.

Chapter 4

Theological Roots of the African Independent Churches and Their Challenge to Black Theology

J.B. NGUBANE

Editors' Abstract

'For the African Christians, this break meant, more than anything else, their spiritual freedom from mission control and support'. Ngubane presses the point that it is the desire for this freedom which underlies the theological roots of African Independent Churches. The missionary, with the support of the armed colonial forces and the commercial agents of merchant capital, had attempted to undermine African society by withdrawing from it the theological freedom that was a part of its cultural fabric. According to Ngubane the missionary was dismally unsuccessful. Africans accepted Christianity not as a replacement of African religion but as a new perspective to be added to a stock of historically accumulated perspectives. The Zion churches in particular never allowed African religion to be Christianized, rather they Africanized Christianity.

Ngubane argues that Black Theology represents a horizontal dimension of black life while the faith of African Independent Churches expresses a vertical dimension. Thus for him Black Theology needs the faith of the AICs as much as the AICs need Black Theology. In addition, the spirit of love which permeates the African Churches constitutes a challenge for Black Theology. 'Black Theology and all of us have a "black" mission to preach love to the white man so that he may have the courage to see...that his security is not necessarily tied to his rejection of the black man'.

The biggest challenge of the Independent Churches is their down-to-earth form of contextualization. They deal not only with the theological issues raised by white oppressive structures but also and perhaps more importantly with the issues of 'Africanness', past, present, and future.

In treating a topic of this nature one ought to keep in mind what Christian theology is all about. To date, there is no definition of Christian theology universally accepted by theologians. Various theologians have offered various definitions, highlighting and underscoring perspectives of their interests, as there are different branches and different aspects of this discipline. For the purpose of this paper, I have chosen Langdon Gilkey's definition, which, I hope, will illumine our course in this paper. Gilkey defines Christian theology as follows:

> A *reflection on our human existence,* on its character and its destiny, and on the 'world' (in the widest sense of the term) in which we live from the perspective of the Christian faith.
>
> or,
>
> A *coherent reflective explication of the contents of the Christian faith,* a delineation in contemporary terms of the 'revelation' on which the Christian community and thus the faith of those who are in it are founded.[1]

These definitions, namely, an examination of general experience (the basic nature of our human existence and our life in history: their goals, possibilities, hopes, obligations, problems, and destiny) and an explication of Christian symbols (the contents of the Christian faith), are ultimately interrelated and form a unity based on the contents of the Christian faith. This faith deploys symbols, e.g. sacred words, sacred actions (ritual, liturgy), sacred images, sacred objects, etc., in order to interpret, illumine and clarify the character of our existence and history.

The importance of looking at the contents of our faith as well as at our actual life in history in our theologizing is essential if our faith is effectively to influence our life. Gilkey underscores this point when he says:

> This 'correlation' between our human existence and history and Christian revelation, between our ordinary experience of self and community and the symbols characteristic of the Christian tradition, is fundamental for all theology.[2]

Many theories have been advanced by research workers and missionaries regarding reasons for the emergence and growth of African Church Independentism, e.g. socio-political factors, the Land Act of 1913, leadership struggles in the mission churches, etc. G.C. Oosthuizen in 'Fort Hare Papers' has enumerated twelve major 'Causes of Religious Independentism in Africa', the twelfth being 'Theological Causes'. He also says elsewhere that search for a ritual or liturgy was one of the main causes. He says:

> The liturgy of the Bantu churches in South Africa is still alien...Independent Churches, in South Africa especially, are being established due to frustration in the field of independence and indigenous development especially in the liturgical field.[3]

Some of the many reasons given so far may be misleading, though they might have occasioned or conditioned the emergence and growth of African Church Independentism. They are helpful, though, in providing insights into contributory factors and conditions of the time. It seems to me that in talking about 'churches' in any connexion, theological reasoning must be the basis of it all. Obviously, before breaking away from the existing church establishments or founding new churches, the leaders of such moves must have done a lot of theologizing. As men and women of Christian faith, I presume these leaders reflected on and examined their ordinary human experiences as Christians in their respective Christian communities and in their 'world' in the light of the contents of their Christian faith. Evidently, the result of this reflection and examination led them to act as they did.

African Independent Churches are usually classified into two main categories, namely, 'Ethiopian' or 'Separatist', on the one hand, and 'Zionist' or 'Spirit' or 'Charismatic' or 'Prophetic' etc., on the other. But some researchers have proposed a third group, the 'Messianic' group, which appears distinct from the other two, though closer to the 'Zionist' type. M.L. Martin lists traits of the Messianic churches:
(1) they are led by a prophet who becomes the new Moses, a saviour, a black Christ, so that Jesus Christ is pushed into the background;
(2) the charismatic leader promises total liberation from suffering, political domination, etc., and gives assurance of material prosperity and good health. Salvation is expected from the leaders' activity;
(3) eschatological ideas are secularized, and the complete transformation of all things is said to be imminent.[4]

This kind of assessment is tantamount to saying that these churches hardly deserve to be called 'Christian'. Such analysis appears to me open to a number of serious queries from several angles. There is ample evidence that these churches claim to be fully Christian, and do not see themselves as relegating Jesus Christ to the background. And it appears that there is no evidence that the leaders of these churches ever claimed or pretended to usurp the place of Christ in the church. However, a detailed discussion of this issue will serve no useful purpose for this paper. For our purpose, we shall consider this group of churches as part of the Zionist et al. churches.

The Ethiopian-Zionist dichotomy was, it seems, arrived at for the convenience of dealing with the complex phenomenon of African Church Independentism. Although we cannot avoid using group names to some extent, we better not insist on classification. But the best thing, I assume, is to see African Church Independentism as a movement taking different forms that can be placed at the different points of a spectrum, ranging from a separatist 'imitation' of a mission church to an original, creative attempt at synthesis of traditional and Christian beliefs, an attempt to establish a new African Christian identity, a creative effort to formulate an African Christian religion. In all of these churches, it appears, 'religious ideas and religious language are used to interpret changed intellectual, social, economic and political conditions and to give expression to the perceived change in such a way that action can be organized and directed'.[5] In dealing with these churches, one should avoid making negative impressionistic conclusions resulting from a lack of years of sustained contact with them and preparedness to learn from them with an open mind and heart. Some researchers have fallen into this pit; for instance, Sundkler[6] sees Shembe and Lekganyane as usurping the position of Christ; Martin, as pointed out above, considers 'Messianic' churches as relegating Christ to a decidedly secondary position;[7] Beyerhaus sees all Zionists as working with a closed Bible, where Christian terminology is stripped of all true biblical meanings.[8]

We cannot ignore the immense problems faced by almost all Independent Churches because of the lack of trained theologians and exegetes in their ranks. This offers a challenge to black theologians and exegetes of the mainline churches. But in taking up this challenge, they must address themselves to theological questions that are uppermost in the African's mind, related to his worldview and culture; black theologians will contribute a great deal if they consider theological insights of these churches, especially those relating to synthesizing African traditional beliefs and the Christian tradition; black exegetes should be willing to apply African insights and perspective to the interpretation of the sacred scriptures and theologically generalized Christian truth based on the scriptures. One must admit, however, that western-trained black theologians do face a problem in this task because they are generally equipped with western tools only. To be effectively involved in this task, they would have to see how to modify and adapt their tools. Efforts of black theologians and exegetes in this direction are feasible. John S. Mbiti, for instance, has set up an example. He, with seven other Africans, has attempted to deal with theological issues relevant to Africa in the volume: *Biblical Revelation and African Beliefs* (1969), and in his praiseworthy volume: *New Testament Eschatology in an African Background* (1971); in this latter volume he looks at Christian eschatology from the two-dimensional background of the culture and concept of time of his people, the Akamba.

In the face of the rapid proliferation and staggering size of membership of the Independent Churches — 1970 South African official statistics put their membership at 49,2% of all African Christians (South Africa, 1982, *Official Yearbook of the Republic of South Africa:* 739-58) — one cannot but ask oneself what theological factors attract people so much to these churches. What makes them tick? What are the basic theological grounds motivating their thoughts and activity? Oosthuizen sees these churches as representing 'Christianity on the march', guided by unwritten yet alive theology expressed in dances and song and liturgy and ritual.[9] The following three factors seem to be the theological roots for this phenomenon.

1. Theological Search for Human-Cultural-Spiritual Freedom as Children of God

When missionaries came to preach the gospel in Africa, they brought along a whole range of western values. They appeared determined to instill in their converts these western values and a distaste especially for traditional religious values and African culture, which were considered inferior and primitive. African converts were expected to adopt a new identity based on the western-Christian order. It was expedient to belong to a church; Africans appreciated the discipline of church membership and accruing benefits, such as acceptance by missionaries and colonial powers, access to schooling, acquisition of jobs, etc.; so, a growing number of Africans embraced Christianity. But this did not mean full loyalties and fellowship with the church, for Africans as a whole were not convinced about the inferiority of their religious and cultural values. Therefore the majority of African Christians remained only partially converted according to the expectations of the missionaries. They were attached to their traditional and cultural values, and therefore did not always pursue their new faith within the bounds of missionary orthodoxy. They thus lived, as it appears to be still the case today among many so-called 'orthodox' African Christians, on two unreconciled levels. They subscribed to a statement of faith, but 'below the system of conscious beliefs are deeply embedded traditions and customs implying quite a different interpretation of the universe and the world of Spirit from the Christian interpretation'.[10]

In the major crises of life, e.g. birth, illness, death, etc., and in performing the 'rites of passage' the traditional rituals have often 'far much more influence than the Christian belief. In these great moments the Church is an alien thing'.[11] Thus, traditional religion remains vital or may be only superficially affected.[12]

Here we have an example of a clash of cultures over religion. Religion has always been the medium in which different cultures encounter and perceive one another most acutely and in which they interact most intimately because it provides the symbol language in which they communicate. But it is also in religion where African and western cultures clashed, and still clash, most violently and with far-reaching consequences. Early missionaries theologized according to their own cultural frames of reference, for any theologizing is culture-bound, though Spirit-led. Unfortunately early missionaries failed to reproduce in contemporary African cultural contexts the theologizing process which was exemplified by St. Paul and others. Paul and the early church leaders did not simply condemn and jettison the Greek mystery religions and Greek philosophy. But these provided the matrix for the theologizing of the early church. This theologizing was translated and communicated in Greek religious and philosophical frames of reference. Further evolution of Christianity was based both on the scriptures and on these frames of reference.[13]

As it appears from the above, African Christians found themselves in a serious dilemma. Some leaders among them did some theologizing and positively searched for traditional values or treatment of needs not catered for in the mission churches or rejected outright, as pointed out above. Strange enough, most of these values and needs were recognized and sanctioned by either the Old or New Testament: e.g., in the Old Testament: revelation through dreams and visions, complex rituals, purification, polygamy, the descent of God's Spirit on the prophets, etc.; in the New Testament: healing, expulsion of evil spirits, apocalyptic and eschatological doctrines, denunciation of the Pharisees, etc. What exacerbated the issue was the discriminatory attitude of some missionaries and white Christians towards their black counterparts. This attitude, though less pronounced in the church, was similar to that of the colonial powers. Besides, some missionaries were characterized by authoritarianism of which Africans found themselves at the receiving end, relegated to inferior positions, and offered no scope for leadership or initiative. All this was against the gospel and Christian doctrine about the equality of all people before God. So, some leading African Christians, both ministers and laity, sought to reconcile the two levels on which they lived: they sought to rehabilitate African culture and the African way of life in the context of their new faith, and expressed an active reaction against the domination which was also reflected in the mission churches. Thus the break with these churches was inevitable, and followed, for different reasons, the pattern of Protestant tradition of which these African leaders were part. For the African Christians, this break meant, more than anything else, their spiritual freedom from mission control and support.

The first recorded secession in Southern Africa was that of 1872; it was made by 150 Africans of the Hermon mission station of the Paris Evangelical Mission in Lesotho.[14] This secession was, however, short-lived. Then in South Africa, Rev. Nehemiah Tile (Methodist) in 1882 formed the 'Thembu National Church' in which the Thembu 'king' (Ukumkani) would hold a position similar to that held by the British monarch in the Church of England.[15] In 1885 some leading Maidi church members formed the 'Native Independent Congregation for the Maidi' from the London Missionary Society. In 1889 the 'Lutheran Bapedi Church' was formed from the Berlin Mission. In 1892 Rev. Mangena Mokone (Methodist) formed in Pretoria the 'Ethiopian Church'. From then on all separatist churches were called 'Ethiopian' or 'African'. In 1896 the 'Zulu Congregational Church' seceded from the American Board Mission. In 1898 Rev. P.J. Mzimba of the Free Church of Scotland in South Africa formed the 'Presbyterian Church of Africa'.

I have given the above examples to show the rate of early proliferation of church Ethiopianism in Southern Africa. This process continued although it slowed down from the 1960s when attention was focused on solidification. It is significant that most of the churches enumerated above bear the name of a particular linguistic group. I think this underlies the feeling of joy for freedom from foreign domination in the church, and also is an expression of the importance of traditional values.

The Ethiopian type of churches, in the main, retained the basic organization, liturgy, hymnbook and catechism of the church they had left behind, although major adaptations, additions and transformations to suit the African ethos have been made. For example, Musana Disco Christ Church (Army of the Cross of Christ Church), formed in Ghana in 1919 from the Methodist Church by the prophet Jehu-Appiah, introduced the rosary in its liturgy and introduced elements of the traditional Akan structure in its organization, based on war organization, and the head of the church (prophet) bearing the title of Akan kings, *Nana*. Some of these churches did not, however, accept the basic structural forms of the churches they left behind. For instance, in Nigeria the Ethiopian Church was born in 1921 out of discontent regarding a rigid adherence to foreign forms. The name 'Ethiopian' or 'African' is evocatory, highlighting the desire to have a truly African church, an indigenous church. Besides, these words stress the scriptural origin (e.g., Psalms 68:31; 87:4) of the names of the churches and evoke an ancient African heritage because they are 'a symbol of African pride in indigenous culture and achievement'.[16] Moreover, Africans took justifiable pride in the fact of history that Christianity penetrated northern Africa long before it reached most of Europe.

The second member of the dichotomy, the Zionist et al. group of churches, the gloriously black movement of the Spirit, was, paradoxically, initiated by a few white people early this century. These whites were devotees of 'Zion City', in Illinois, USA. This 'Zion City' was an apocalyptic, healing movement founded by John Alexander Dowie in 1896, and called 'The Christian Catholic Apostolic Church in Zion'. Daniel Bryant, an 'overseer' of this church, baptized the first group of African Zionists, twenty-seven people, on May 8, 1904, in Johannesburg by 'triune immersion'.[17] Edgar Mahon, a member of the Salvation Army, and Petrus Louis Le Roux, a Dutch Reformed Church minister at Wakkerstroom, were instrumental in the founding of the Zionist liturgies. Le Roux and Mahon were only catalysts: The whole movement soon passed into the hands of the Africans themselves and with rapid proliferation. Some important African leaders of the Zionist movement were: Daniel Nkonyana, Paul Mabiletsa, Elias Mahlangu, Titus Msibi, Ignatius Lekganyane, etc. Beside the other reasons mentioned above, the later Zionist groups emerged perhaps because, for one reason, there was no mission church in their area. One may argue, however, that the activity of the missionary or some other Christian and the Bible they introduced must have been sufficiently close for the seed of the faith to be sown and new ideas stimulated. But, on the other hand, some who might have joined a local mission church could not do so for various reasons, perhaps chief among these being the strict disciplinary requirements of mission churches, e.g., long periods of preparation and probation before receiving baptism and other sacraments, social prohibitions, for example, polygamy, initiation, etc. It is true, however, that some of the leaders belonged to some other church before they founded their 'Spirit' groups of churches. These churches were not, of course, offshoots of any other church. The leaders' contact and experience in their former churches stood them a good stead in their new undertaking. For example, Isaiah Shembe was originally a member of an African Baptist Church; Simon Kimbangu was formerly a catechist in the Baptist Missionary Society at N'Kamba, Zaire; Josiah Oshitelu, founder of the 'Church of the Lord' *(Aladura),* was educated in Anglican mission schools, and became a teacher-catechist in the Church Missionary Society at Ogere, north of Lagos; Timothy Cekwane was a local preacher in Mzimba's 'Presbyterian Church of Africa' at Heimville, Natal.

Although the beginnings of African Zionist movement have some links with Dowie's movement and white 'catalysts', the actual African Zionist groups of churches were and are founded by Africans themselves. They are founded and led by charismatic prophet-healers who receive a call through revelation in 'voices', visions and dreams to proclaim messages of prayer and miraculous healing. Both Old and New Testaments are called upon to confirm the validity and acceptability of such revelations. From the founders' revelations grow religious movements which reflect the immediate precedent of African religion far more than the mission churches, and even more than the Ethiopian type, for that matter.[18] Prophetic leaders are often sources of creative religious and social change,[19] and attempt to contextualize Christianity, making it relevant to everyday life, especially through the use of practical ritual techniques which are not found in mission churches.

The freedom of the Independents as the children of God has allowed them to indigenize and Africanize the church. I make a distinction between the concepts indigenization and Africanization. I see the church as indigenized when it has at its helm sons and daughters of the soil, in full control, irrespective of colour or race. In this sense the Dutch Reformed Church in South Africa can be said to be indigenized. For the same reasons, the Ethiopian churches are indigenized because they are fully controlled by Africans themselves. But they may not be considered fully Africanized, for Africanization implies taking into consideration the culture of the people of Africa, their thought-patterns, their beliefs and their entire world view when creating structures and forms of the church. One, of course, may not say that the Ethiopian-type churches have not made efforts towards Africanization, but as long as they are still caught up in the general structures and forms (which are foreign) of the churches they left behind, they cannot be expected to Africanize fully. Africanization involves dynamic originality and tireless creativity on the part of the leaders, especially the founders. Zionist churches had, and have, as a whole, leaders of this calibre, e.g., Isaiah Shembe, Ignatius Lekganyane, George Khambule, etc.

All in all, although at present with some syncretic weaknesses, Independent Churches have, through their leaders, attempted to make a creative synthesis of traditional and Christian beliefs, creatively formulating a truly African Christianity which gives Africans an African identity: they represent radical indigenization and Africanization of Christianity.

At this juncture, I believe, parallels should be drawn between the rise of African Independent Churches and that of Black Theology in the United States of America and South Africa. As shown above, African Church Independentism emerged towards the end of the last century, in the 1870s and 1880s, whereas Black Theology appeared as such in the 1960s. By the way, G.C. Oosthuizen[20] argues that true 'Black Theology' did not start only in the 1960s but, albeit unwritten, started in South Africa with the rise of African Church Independentism. By this he means, I think, unwritten *African* theology. In one sense he is right, for African Christians became independent because they sought liberation as children of God from an oppressive church situation and from 'deculturizing', de-Africanizing, detribalizing treatment, and reacted, as some still do, against 'a foreign, unadapted, western oriented Church which does not take note of the African approach and world view'.[21] In another sense he is not right, for Black Theology, which came into being in the 1960s, though similar to African Theology in some respects, differs from it in others. Some points of similarity are that black Americans who initiated Black Theology trace their roots like Africans to Africa. Black Americans and the blacks in Africa, especially in South Africa and Zimbabwe (Rhodesia), were subjected to discrimination on the basis of the colour of their skin and raped by colonialism: both were the underprivileged and the disinherited of the earth. Moreover, for both, religion was an integral part of their experience, though the emphasis was not on the same kind of religion. For the Africans, it was the traditional religion plus Christianity, and Islam in some parts of Africa; whereas for the black Americans it was Christianity, as shown by their 'spirituals', and Islam was peripheral. Therefore African Theology deals with more religions than Black Theology. Besides, and more importantly, Black Theology and African Theology differ in that, through generations of absence from Africa, the black Americans' social and cultural landscape has become radically different.

The protagonists of Church Independentism and those of Black Theology theologized about their respective oppressive situations in the light of their faith and the gospel. We have already seen the causes of African Church Independentism, and we have mentioned that Black Theology as such came into existence as a theology of protest against discrimination based on skin pigmentation; it came as an antithesis to conceived white supremacy and arrogance. Its beginnings are associated with the rise of the black self-concept movement (Black Consciousness Movement) in the United States of America and later in South Africa. It was associated with the antithetical black power slogan: 'Black is beautiful'. In America as in South Africa, to be black had become associated with poverty, ignorance, illiteracy, terror, humiliation, insult, and exploitation by white people. It was a symbol of sin, evil, wretchedness, damnation, etc. In short, it meant loss of God-given human dignity and exposure to dehumanizing treatment. Unfortunately for Christianity, the above conception of white supremacy and arrogance were reflected in the white-dominated churches. The term 'Black Theology' was probably used for the first time by James H. Cone in his volume *Black Theology and Black Power* (1969). It was first taken up by some mainline black churchmen in America and used as an attack on 'white' religion and 'white' churches. The concept of a Black Theology was an attempt by the black people to understand 'the relevance of the Gospel for Black liberation conceived mainly by Black pastors and church executives who were struggling to define their faith *vis-a-vis* a White religious establishment which had betrayed them'.[22] Some outstanding black churchmen like Albert B. Cleage, Jr., Lawrence Lucas (R.C.C. priest) and Calvin Marshall (A.M.E. Zion minister) hammered out every Sunday the first tenets of Black Theology on the anvil of their experience in the ghettos of the poor.

I think Oosthuizen[23] has made a good going in his observation that the theology of the Independents, which is African Theology of Liberation, concentrates more on the vertical dimension, while Black Theology concentrates more on the horizontal dimension. These two dimensions need each other, and a balance should be struck between them. The challenge here offered to Black Theology is that it should be instrumental in further developing the horizontal dimension in the theology of the Independents. At the same time it should itself link up with the vertical dimension of the Independents. The importance of this dimension is underscored by Manas Buthelezi in his article 'Daring to Live for Christ'.[24] He says daring to live for Christ means having impact on the structures of all sorts which have manacled and spiritually debilitated the black man. To dare to live for Christ requires a strong vertical dimension of an oppressed Christian. In all his struggles the Christian needs God's grace, divine guidance and strength from above, while he works for both his human and spiritual liberation. In this way, the suffering of a Christian with a strong vertical dimension ceases to be 'oppressive suffering' and becomes 'redemptive suffering' based on the mode of Christ, and it generates true freedom of the children of God. Likewise, Bonganjalo Goba reminds us that in our search for true liberation we should keep in mind that 'Christ opens the path of liberation as he shares our common humanity, and God in His forsakenness suffers with us as the one who is crucified'.[25] With a strong vertical dimension firmly embedded in Christ and a Christ-guided horizontal dimension, Black Theology will become less propositional, speculative and principally for the educated and the sophisticated; but will become, like that of the Independents, existential at the grass roots level of the ordinary people, and will embrace the totality of human experience (religious, cultural, social, political and economic).

The balancing of the two above-mentioned dimensions will of necessity lead from antithesis to synthesis where there will be total reconciliation in Christ, for 'when anyone is joined to Christ, he is a new being; the old is gone, the new has come. All this is done by God, who through Christ changed us from enemies into his friends and gave us the task of making his friends also. Our message is that God was making all mankind his friends through Christ. God did not keep an account of their sins, and he has given us the message which tells how he makes his friends' (2 Corinthians 5:17-19).

2.   Christian Love, a Binding Force under the Guidance of the Holy Spirit

This, though applicable to all indigenous churches, is specially true of the Zionist-type churches which are, by the way, the largest in numbers and membership of the Independent Churches. The 1970 statistics in the *Official Yearbook of the Republic of South Africa* (South Africa 1982:739-58) are: 'Separatist': 2 761 120 (18,4%) and 'the Other and Unspecified', i.e., Zionist et al.: 4 626 260 (30,8%) of all

South African black Christians. It is known, however, that these figures have increased a great deal since that time. In connection with Christian communal solidarity of believers which the Independent Churches attempt to achieve, one is reminded of the solidarity of love which obtained among early Christians:

> All the believers continued together in close fellowship and shared their belongings with one another...Day after day they met as a group in the Temple, and they had their meals together in their homes, eating with glad and humble hearts, praising God, and enjoying the good will of all people. And every day the Lord added to their group those who were saved (Acts 2: 44–47).

During the first two centuries of Christianity there were no church buildings. Christians formed small communities and worshipped in different houses. The Independent Churches, especially the Zionist-type, have taken up this model as well as that of the Old Testament. They have their own 'Holy Cities', 'Jerusalems', 'Mount Zions', 'Bethesdas', and so forth: for example, Kimbangu's 'New Jerusalem' at N'Kamba, Zaire; Shembe's 'Jerusalem' at Ekuphakameni, near Durban, and his 'Zion' on Mt. Nhlangakazi, further north; Ma Nku's 'Temple of Jerusalem on Mount Zion' at Evaton; Lekganyane's 'Zion City Morija' (Mount Moriah), near Pietersburg, etc. At these holy places, salvation is experienced here-and-now in the context of a salvational dimension of traditional African ritual systems. Even the smaller Zionist groups have their 'Holy Places' where healing and salvation are brought about; they also see mountain experience as essential for spiritual growth: The leaders frequently take their flock for a time of seclusion to a mountaintop for prayer, meditation, fasting and purification. Sundkler[26] gives probable reasons for the importance of mountain experience: firstly, there is the sense of nearness to God on a high mountain; secondly, the ascetic aspect is enhanced, for both the mountain and 'much water', i.e., fountain, pool, river and sea, have purifying power.

The Independent Churches have realized a community based at some centre, and at the same time broken up into closely-knit smaller communities resembling traditional closely-knit extended families in which every member has the sense of belonging. Oosthuizen rightly says that these churches 'have adapted themselves to the existing structure of the traditional society with the family as the nucleus giving them not only a psychological but also an organisational advantage to the historical churches. They often form small "house congregations", the most familiar concept of the Church among the independent movements; they are not over-institutionalised bodies'.[27] At the same time, as pointed out above, this community resembles the early church which consisted of small closely-knit communities. In the church community of the Independents and through it 'immediate human needs, social, psychological and physical are appropriately met. Too many such needs had not been met at all in a meaningful way by the mission churches'.[28] Here 'the existential needs of the people are considered in their own idiom and not in terms of some alien Westernised formula or creed [and] the kingship of Christ and the liberating power of the Holy Spirit acquires meaning. Here too, the church emerges as a community of believers with an emphasis on loving care for each other — a "place to feel at home"'.[29]

The church community of the Independents is not exclusive in its concern, care and love. In cases of misfortune, illness, death or funeral, the Independents will always be there, to pray and console; their leaders or elders read from the holy scriptures, and give words of encouragement and consolation. In this community the commandment of love seems to be observed. In my long ministry, I do not remember going on an *umlindelo* (vigil for the deceased before funeral) without finding that some member of the Zionist group of churches was already there praying for my deceased parishioner and the bereaved. Besides, traditional mutual respect, *inhlonipho,* now reinforced by Christian tenets, is accorded each person. The members of the community call one another 'brother' or 'sister', and greet each other by the Christian, biblical greeting of 'peace be with you!'

Besides the power of the Holy Spirit and the love flowing thereof, a stable centre is essential for keeping the larger and smaller communities together. Oosthuizen[30] rightly points out that 'Africa's religious and tribal life was always dependent on a metaphysical being as its centre, and in these movements one finds the prophet or leader and his genealogical relationship with "their" supernatural world as such a centre. They satisfy the deep longing for a magical personality who controls the supernatural world'. But now the prophet or leader works under the influence of the Holy Spirit. Especially in the Zionist groups, the Holy Spirit holds a very prominent place. It is for this reason that these churches are also called 'Spirit' churches. The Holy Spirit reveals various things to them in dreams and visions, and they emphasize its healing effects through charismatic prophet-healers and bishops. Because of the dynamic activity of the Spirit and its purifying effects, the Zionists et al. stress a practical this-worldly notion of salvation which is accompanied by healing. In many cases, the Holy Spirit has replaced the traditional ancestral spirit, and in some instances takes on some of the function of the latter, e.g., revelation through dreams and visions. One must admit that there may be some confusion between the two types of 'spirit', and sometimes some speak indiscriminately of Spirit and Angel. As a whole, African Christians (orthodox or not) do distinguish between the Holy Spirit and the ancestors; most Zionists differentiate between Holy Spirit and Angel. Sundkler[31] gives an interesting discussion on this score.

In spite of some confusion and misunderstanding, it is significant that these churches assign a prominent position to the Holy Spirit in

The Independents also see, in their own way, the importance of the Holy Spirit as portrayed by the above passage and try to show example, in *Lumen Gentium* (1964: 4) we read the following:

> When the work which the Father gave the Son to do on earth (cf. Jn. 17:4) was accomplished, the Holy Spirit was sent on the day of Pentecost in order that he might continually sanctify the Church, and that, consequently, those who believe might have access through Christ in one Spirit to the Father (cf. Eph. 2:18). He is the Spirit of life, the fountain of water springing up to eternal life (cf. Jn. 4:14; 7:38-39). To men, dead in sin, the Father gives life through him, until the day when, in Christ, he raises to life their mortal bodies (cf. Rom. 8:10-11). The Spirit dwells in the Church and in the hearts of the faithful, as in a temple (cf. 1 Cor. 3:16; 6:19). In them he prays and bears witness to their adopted sonship (cf. Gal. 4:6; Rom. 8:15-16 and 26).

The Independents also see, in their own way, the importance osp the Holy Spirit as portrayed by the above passage and try to show this appreciation in their own lives as individuals and communities, as pointed out above. Here is another challenge for the protagonists of Black Theology: They better listen attentively to what the Spirit of God is saying to them through these churches. In seeking liberation, they must seek it in the spirit of love in Christ who gives true and complete liberation. As persons liberated through the death and resurrection of Christ, the promoters of Black Theology and all of us have a 'black' mission to preach love and reconciliation to the very people we feel treated us unjustly: 'to preach love to the white man so that he may have the courage to see...that his security is not necessarily tied to his rejection of the black man'.[32] Democratization of oppressive systems should be sought in the spirit of love, and there should be no reversal of positions, 'this time with the oppressed in the saddle and seat of power treating their former oppressors to a dose of their own medicine'.[33]

3.   The Ritual: Dialogue and Confrontation

In discussing Gilkey's definition of theology we saw that our Christian faith deploys symbols, including sacred words, actions (ritual, liturgy), sacred images, sacred objects, etc., in order to interpret, illumine and clarify the character of our existence and history. Among the Africans, the importance of archetypal symbols in religion, especially the ritual, was highlighted long before Christianity came to Africa. In the traditional universe archetypal symbols (gods, ancestors, sacred actions or objects) are enshrined and communicated in myth and ritual. These provide 'a network of symbolic forms, uniting social, ecological and conceptual elements into locally bounded cultural systems. They give order to experience by framing the world in terms of sacred figures and patterns. Thus encapsulated within local universes of archetypal forms, traditional African thought tends to abolish both time and chance by shaping experience to interrelated moral and ritual patterns'.[34]

We may say, therefore, that, among other things, one of the main reasons for the emergence of the Independent Churches, especially those of the Zionist type, was a quest for meaningful and suitable ritual, especially that of healing, and a realized community, as discussed above. They looked for a ritual to compensate for what was lost or was being lost or threatened to be lost in the new westernized society. Contextualized Christianity would give vitality to some traditional aspects that were in danger of being lost. Rituals of healing and purification were among the most important in traditional society, and the Independent Churches sought to establish 'accessible rites of healing with a Christian reference and within a caring community led by gifted and spiritual individuals claiming an initiative effectively denied them in the older Churches'.[35] Healing has attracted many people from mainline churches to Zionist-type churches and, to a lesser degree, to the Ethiopian-type as well since the ministry of healing is exercised there also. When I ask former Catholics why they joined Zionist churches, I invariably get the answer that they were sick and recovered after the Zionists prayed for them.

Martin West[36] gives three categories of the ritual of healing in the African Independent Churches: healing during church services, healing by immersion, healing through consultation with a prophet. The Ethiopian churches usually have the healing ritual during church services; this consists of prayer and the laying-on of hands. The Zion-ist-type of churches use the three methods. In all cases of healing the Holy Spirit is invoked to heal the patient. The smaller Zionist churches also have their 'Holy Places', circles on the floor of a build-ing or out in the open where they perform the rites of healing. Heal-ing is not only for physical diseases, but also a way of purification and it also cures psychological ailments and protects one from the unseen evil forces. Holy water is often used in healing, also as a means of protection.

One of the greatest contributions of the Independent Churches to theology and Christianity is found in the process of original and genu-ine contextualization of their faith and theology. This comes out more strongly in the context of dialogue and confrontation which they create between the Christian message and traditional religions.[37] This happens repeatedly, especially in sermons and ritual context. In traditional African religion archetypal symbols, which are models of behaviour as well as modes of thought, and ritual acts are used to structure collective communal rites which recreate the members' experi-ence of the world.[38]

Sundkler[39] gives an interesting example of adaptation and confron-tation (which he regards as a Bantu syncretism) under the chapter 'New Wine in Old Wineskins'. Two groups come together at dawn to a stream; one is of novices for divination led by the diviner Dlakude, the other is of the Sabbath Zionist Church led by the prophet Elliot Buthelezi. The two groups are each on the opposite sides of the stream. Their behaviour appears very much alike, yet they represent two different things. They both dance around the leader as they come half-running down the slope of the stream. They sing similar melodies but the words are not quite the same. One addresses itself to the Christian God and the Holy Spirit. The traditional group gets first to the stream and performs its rites of purification and strengthening, using the stream water mixed with some traditional medicine *(ubu-lawu);* they drink this frothy mixture and begin to vomit. In the meantime the other group is waiting. A short but sarcastic verbal confrontation occurs when the prophet asks the novices' leader: 'When are you going to finish, preacher?' After the first group has finished, the second group begins its rites, using the same stream water, but blessed this time. The prophet administers it 'In the name of the Father and of the Son and of the Holy Spirit', and the group is told that this blessed water will take away illness from the sick per-son. Then follows the laying-on of hands on the patient and the calling upon the Holy Spirit and speaking in tongues by the prophet and patient. Thereafter the whole group drinks of the blessed water and all vomit on the rocks.

There are many more examples of similar radical efforts at contextualization and adaptive remoulding of Christianity by the Zionists and other Christian indigenous churches. For instance, in African cosmology, pollution (Z. *Umnyamumswazi;* S.Ts. *bolwetse, seila)* is seen as a 'mystical force' which covers a very large spectrum in life, and one must constantly keep away from it or be purified from it. This kind of pollution is more than biblical defilement; it may be caused by physical and temporal environment, contact with some kinds of disease, bereavement, death, giving birth, bodily emission, crossing paths or highways where dangerous substances have been discarded, also by impersonal, unseen forces of evil and machination of evil people. In the African worldview pollution or misfortune can be treated medicinally or by appealing to the ancestors.[40]

The Zionists deal with all these types of pollution, and their concept of purification covers also the Old Testament model plus a whole complex of avoidances and taboos against things which cause pollution or defilement. They achieve purification by prayer, invocation of the Holy Spirit, use of holy water, holy staffs and immersion in 'much water', viz., fountain, pool, river and sea. Mountain experience has also a purifying effect. Similar examples of adaptation and replacement of traditional rituals by the Christian ones among the Shona Zionists in Zimbabwe are given by Daneel.[41] For example, the traditional rituals whereby tribal spirits are addressed at the graves of the ancestors on the mountains have been replaced by prophetic ceremonies of 'fasting on the mountains'. He discusses, among other things, how dialogue and confrontation are carried on in words and action by the Independents in relation to traditional beliefs, ritual and structures, and how this is achieved in the context of ritual symbolism, e.g. 'Jordan baptism'. He also shows how the Shona Zionists have introduced both facets of continuity and discontinuity of the God of Africa: they have accepted the remoteness of the traditional God, but at the same time have drawn him to be 'inside the orbit of their daily living'. Another interesting case, though obviously controversial, is that given by Nussbaum of the animal sacrifice introduced into the ritual of some Independent Churches in Lesotho. He suggests that this could be seen as an 'evangelical sacrifice' for Jesus and his needy family. He ends on this note: 'If we take the independent church challenge seriously and reflect on it carefully, both we and they may come to a more well-rounded understanding of the Gospel and some more effective ways of communicating it'.

From all that has been said above there is no doubt that the Independent Churches have on various theological issues flung down the gauntlet for Black Theology or any other theology, for that matter, to pick up. Their theological contextualization is 'down to earth', and they grapple with different facets of existential issues in a theological context. The greatest challenge offered Black Theology by these churches, I think, is the need for Black Theology to undertake self-examination and self-definition. Is it concerned principally with the social aspect relating to oppressive situations created by discrimination on the basis of one's skin colour? If so, it is situational and it has no lasting home among us, for if the situation changes, what then? Or is it more comprehensive, concerned not only with oppressive societal issues, but also with cultural and philosophical issues?[42]

If so, it has a better chance of permanence even after the disappearance of the oppressive societal structures. If the Independent Churches supply 'raw material' for Black Theology, how does this theology use this material?[43]

Finally, any theology becomes relevant only if it appeals 'to a religious instinct and susceptibility that already exists in its audience, and it cannot reach these without taking account of the traditional forms in which religious feeling is embodied, and without speaking a language which men accustomed to these forms can understand'.[44]

NOTES

1. Langdon Gilkey, *Message and Existence: An Introduction to Christian Theology* (New York: Seabury Press, 1977), p. 7.

2. Ibid., p. 8.

3. G. C. Oosthuizen, *Theological Battleground in Asia and Africa* (London: Billing and Sons, 1971), p. 320.

4. M. L. Martin, *The Biblical Concept of Messianism and Messianism in South Africa* (Morija: Morija Sesuto Book Depot, 1964).

5. J. Fabian, 'Religion and Change,' in *The African Experience*, vol. 1, ed. J. N. Paden and E. W. Soja (Evanston, Ill.: Northwestern University Press, 1970), p. 395.

6. B. G. M. Sundkler, *Bantu Prophets in South Africa* (London: Oxford University Press, 1961), p. 323.

7. Martin, *Biblical Concept*, pp. 165f.

8. P. Beyerhaus, 'An Approach to the African Independent Church Movement', *Ministry* 9 (1969): 131.

9. Oosthuizen, 'Black Theology in Historical Perspective', *The South African Journal of African Affairs* 3 (1973): 77.

10. Oosthuizen, *Battleground*, p. 311.

11. Ibid.

12. P. L. van den Berghe, 'Major Themes in Social Change', in *The African Experience*, vol. 1, p. 261.

13. See C. H. Kraft, *Christianity in Culture* (Maryknoll, N.Y.: Orbis Books, 1970), pp. 291ff.

14. B. A. Pauw, in *Bantu Speaking Peoples of Southern Africa*, ed. W. D. Hammond-Tooke (London: Routledge and Kegan Paul, 1974), p. 418.

15. Pauw, *Christianity and Xhosa Tradition* (London: Oxford University Press, 1975), p. 25.

16. G. Shepperson, 'Ethiopianism, Past and Present', in *Christianity in Tropical Africa*, ed. C. G. Baeta (London: Oxford University Press, 1968), p. 258.

17. Sundkler, *Bantu Prophets*, p. 48.

18. A. Hastings, *A History of African Christianity, 1950–1975* (Cambridge: Cambridge University Press, 1979), p. 71.

19. B. C. Ray, *African Religions* (Englewood Cliffs, N.J.: Prentice-Hall, 1976), p. 111.

20. Oosthuizen, 'Black Theology', p. 77.

21. Ibid.

22. Gayraud S. Wilmore, in *Black Theology: A Documentary History, 1966–1979*, ed. Wilmore and James H. Cone (Maryknoll, N.Y.: Orbis Books, 1979), p. 67.

23. Oosthuizen, 'Black Theology', p. 77.

24. Manas Buthelezi, 'Daring to Live for Christ', in *Mission Trends, No. 3: Third World Theologies*, ed. G. H. Anderson and T. F. Stransky (Grand Rapids, Mich.: Eerdmans, 1976), p. 178.

25. Bonganjalo Goba, 'Doing Theology in South Africa: A Black Christian Perspective', *Journal of Theology for Southern Africa* 31 (1980): 27.

26. B. G. M. Sundkler, *Zulu Zion* (London: Oxford University Press, 1976), p. 315.

27. Oosthuizen, 'Fort Hare Papers', p. 11.

28. Hastings, *African Christianity*, p. 72.

29. M. L. Daneel, 'Towards a Theologia Africana? The Contribution of Independent Churches to African Theology', *Missionalia* 12, no. 2 (1984): 70.

30. Oosthuizen, 'Black Theology', p. 77.

31. Sundkler, *Bantu Prophets*, pp. 242ff.

32. Manas Buthelezi, cited in David J. Bosch, 'Currents and Crosscurrents in South African Black Theology', in *Black Theology: A Documentary History*, p. 232.

33. J. S. Pobee, *Toward an African Theology* (Nashville: Abingdon, 1979), p. 141.

34. Ray, *African Religions*, p. 17.

35. Hastings, *African Christianity*, p. 72.

36. M. West, *Bishops and Prophets in a Black City* (Cape Town: David Philip, 1975), pp. 91ff.

37. Daneel, 'Theologia Africana?', p. 68.

38. C. Ernst, 'Theological Methodology', in *Encyclopedia of Theology: The Concise Sacramentum Mundi*, ed. K. Rahner (London: Burns and Oates, 1975), p. 1672.

39. Sundkler, *Bantu Prophets*, pp. 237ff.

40. H. Ngubane, *Body and Mind in Zulu Medicine* (London: Academic Press, 1977), pp. 77ff.; G. M. Setiloane, *The Image of God among the Sotho-Tswana* (Rotterdam: Balkema, 1976), pp. 44ff.

41. See Daneel, 'Theologia Africana?'.

42. D. Makhatini, 'Black Theology', in *Relevant Theology for Africa*, ed. H. J. Becken (Durban: Lutheran, 1973), pp. 8ff.

43. E. W. Fashole-Luke, 'The Quest for African Christian Theologies', in *Mission Trends, No. 3*, pp. 144ff.

44. Robertson Smith, cited by Desmond Tutu, 'Black Theology/African Theology—Soul Mates or Antagonists?', in *Black Theology: A Documentary History*, p. 487.

Chapter 5

The Relevance of African Traditional Religions and Their Challenge to Black Theology

ITUMELENG MOSALA

Editors' Abstract

African traditional religions reflect the historical and social struggles which the African people have engaged in with nature and with one another at various stages in the evolution of their societies. African religions belong to the ideological sphere of the total life of African societies. At the level of the ideological the contradictions encountered in material life — in the process of production and reproduction of life — were resolved. The forms that African religions assumed developed in accordance with the changes in the processes of production and reproduction. African religions were, however, not merely mirror images of the material life of African societies, they were rather cultural weapons of struggle that were capable of transforming material life.

According to Mosala, African traditional religions reflect the point at which the historical development of the African was halted and arrested by colonialism.

The relevance of African religions for the contemporary black struggle can be appreciated when it is realized that the notion of culture as an act of liberation is at the heart of a progressive understanding of these religions. Black Christians by seeking a hermeneutical connexion with historical African culture discover a standpoint from which to oppose the oppressive culture of the dominant classes of our present society. This is above all fundamental to a rediscovery of the liberative aspects of black working-class culture under conditions of monopoly capitalism.

Introduction
I wish to approach the question of the relevance of African traditional religion for contemporary society by examining at least four
factors briefly. These are: (1) religion and society (2) African traditional religion and pre-capitalist African societies (3) The articulation
of modes of production (4) African traditional religion as a progressive protest movement within contemporary society.

Religion and Society
It is necessary to establish the relationship of religion and society
generally in order to search for the relevance of a particular religion
to a particular society. What such a relationship is deemed to be is a
consequence of ideological and theoretical commitment. Accordingly, therefore, let me clarify my own theoretical position.

First about society. The latter is not simply the total number of
individuals living together in the same area, as is sometimes naively
implied. On the contrary, as Peter Berger expresses it, 'Society is a
dialectic phenomenon in that it is a human product, and nothing but a
human product, that yet continuously acts back on its producer'.[1] Or
even more accurately, as Hindess and Hirst argue:

> It designates a complex structure of social relations, a
> unity of economic, ideological and, in certain cases, politi-
> cal structural levels in which the role of economy is deter-
> minant.[2]

The complex social relations which make up society are themselves
a product of human history which is based on two basic relations —
the relations between man and nature, and relations between man
and man.

At the risk of distortion let me attempt to simplify this complexity
of relations, the outcome of which is society. Man is an integral part
of nature. Nature relates to him as a source of his means of life. Using
his labour power he acts on nature to produce food, clothing, and
shelter, and he uses other means to meet other needs. Through this
process he produces wealth. The use of tools which serve as the
instruments of labour make his labour power more powerful. With
time his skills and ability to utilize the tools improve and with his
cooperation with other men the struggle to wrestle a living from
nature becomes relatively easier.

Man's relationship with nature is characterized by both harmony
and conflict:

> harmony because being part of nature, whatever man does
> is a manifestation of nature; and conflict because he must
> detach himself from nature, act on it, change it, turn it into
> a slave, compel it to meet his needs. Nature itself is not
> passive and often acts hostile to man. Struggle is the es-
> sence of man's relations with nature.[3]

On the other hand, in the process of struggling to tame nature to
meet human needs, man enters into relations with other men. So the
struggle against nature is a cooperative act. This relation with other
people to struggle against nature gives birth to another form of social
relations; i.e.,

> man must share out the fruits, the products, the wealth
> resulting from that cooperative struggle with nature.[4]

These relations between man and man and between man and nature constitute the relations of production and form the economic
structure of society.

In the process of carrying out their economic life men and women
work out norms and rules that regulate their life, and they evolve
institutions through which these norms and regulations are enforced.
Thus society is also a political community with some form of state.
And, as Ngugi wa Thiong'o aptly summarizes the evolution of society:

> In the process of their economic and political life, the
> community develops a way of life seemingly unique to that
> society. They evolve language, song, dance, literature,
> religion, theatre, art, architecture and an education sys-
> tem...Thus our economic and political community evolves
> a cultural life...It is a community of culture, linked to-
> gether by a shared way of life.[5]

That, therefore, is the concept of society which is assumed in this
paper. Secondly, and as a consequence, religion is seen here to form
part of the cultural sphere of society. It is thoroughly pertinent to,
and issues from as well as relates back to the two basic relations on
which society hinges, namely the relationship between man and nature and the relationship between man and man. Thus the definition
of religion which approximates the theoretical position elaborated
above is the one given by Peter Berger. He writes:

> Religion is the human enterprise by which sacred cosmos

> is established. Put differently, religion is cosmization in a
> sacred mode...This quality may be attributed to natural or
> artificial objects, to animals or to men, or to the objectiva-
> tions of human culture...The sacred is apprehended as
> 'sticking out' from the normal routines of everyday life, as
> something extraordinary and potentially dangerous,
> though its dangers can be domesticated and its potency
> harnessed to the needs of everyday life...The cosmos pos-
> ited by religion thus both transcends and includes man.[6]

Religion may, therefore, be pushed back to its material, social-
historical base. Man's understanding and positing of divine reality
must of necessity correspond in some important ways with the level of
development of historical society.

African Traditional Religions and Precapitalist African Societies
This, it seems to me, is the perspective from which African traditional
religions must be seen. To study them in isolation from the societies
and historial milieu in which they were rooted is to court the danger
of ahistoricism and therefore to risk making idealist conclusions. This
point is noted with enviable clarity by Kwesi Prah in his discussion of
feudalism in Africa. He writes:

> The discussion on feudalism in Africa has suffered very
> much from ahistoricism. This latter is a total lack of either
> a systematic periodisation perspective within which feu-
> dalism is placed, or of the internal historical structure of
> feudalism in the analysis of African society. It is a reified
> conception of the nature of African society, a reconstruc-
> tion which fits no historical period. Often it uses the dicho-
> tomy 'traditional and modern society'...'Traditional'
> society, defined in a historically unstructured form, is vir-
> tually surrealistic. It is incoherent both spatially and tem-
> porally. In other words it is a complete distortion of
> reality. Reality is spatio-temporal in its materiality, and as
> such is ceaselessly changing...To take history out of social
> analysis is to make society lifeless; a structure without a
> dynamic, like a heart which does not beat.[7]

What Prah says about discussions of feudalism applies without
exception to discussions on African traditional religions. The latter
suffer from the same kind of ahistoricism, particularly in their total
lack of 'periodisation perspective', when making reference to traditional societies and their religions. African traditional society is rei-

fied and it is not clear what period in history is thought of and what are regarded as its salient features. The view is gaining ground, however, that immediately precolonial societies in Africa were going through a feudal period after the disintegration of tribal democracies during the communal stage. It would therefore be conceptually and methodologically useful if an attempt was made, in talking of African traditional religions, to situate them within definite, concrete, historical-social relations.

In most African societies in precolonial times the slave mode of production, in which the contradiction between man and nature was overcome through the exploitative use of slave labour without reward, was not widespread. This leaves us with only two historically known precapitalist modes of production within which we must try to situate African traditional religions, i.e., primitive communal society and feudal society. Although the forms which these two societies assumed in various parts of the world are different, evidence does point to their incidence in many parts of Africa.[8]

Primitive communal society is characterized by communal ownership of the means of production — cattle, land, etc. Thus the social products of labour are socially appropriated. There exists no fundamental social contradictions between members of this society since all partake in production activities and have equal access to the products of social labour. There are, however, certain impending contradictions in this society. The level of development of the forces of production, i.e. technology and the ability to use it, remained very low, thus hindering a progressive harnessing of the forces of nature and their submission to human need. Very often in this society nature acted hostilely to man and, in the absence of technological ability to tame it, necessitated ideological and cultural mechanisms of dealing with it. African traditional religions formed an indispensable part of these cultural-ideological means for handling hostile natural forces. This is clearly illustrated by precolonial Africans' attitudes towards animals, plants and other natural objects and phenomena. In fact, one can hazard the suggestion that in the primitive communal stage with its low level of technological and scientific development, nature occupied a dominant role in the religious consciousness of Africans. John Mbiti writes in this regard that:

> Cattle, sheep and goats are used for sacrificial and other religious purposes...Creeping animals feature in religious concepts more than do other wild animals...Mythical trees feature in a number of stories...The sun, moon and stars feature in myths and beliefs of many peoples...Rain is

> regarded by African peoples to be one of the greatest
> blessings of God. For that reason, He is commonly re-
> ferred to as 'the Rain Giver'...Thunder is taken by many,
> such as the Bambuti, Barenda, Ewe and Ila, to be God's
> voice.[9]

It is possible, therefore, that those aspects of African traditional
religions which lay emphasis on the religious significance of natural
phenomena and animals belong more properly to the lower stage of
the evolution of African societies.

However, with the disintegration of communal society and the
emergence of feudal relations in precapitalist Africa some changes
begin to occur in the religious concepts of Africans. The emphasis on
the religious significance of natural phenomena gives way to beliefs in
supreme beings and the importance of the ancestors as a link between
the divine and the people. Setiloane's argument that 'Badimo' (the
living dead) are agents of 'Modimo' (God) through their participation
in 'Bomodimo' (the numinous sphere) and that they are connected to
the biologically living who have seniority and authority is an example.
Members of the community share derivatively from 'Badimo' in this
'Bomodimo' and this points to the coincidence of this religious out-
look with the emergence of feudal forms of social organization. Although technological development began to advance with the advent
of feudalism, the emergence of this society was so gradual that for a
long time communal values persisted. Thus Markovitz argues well
that although religious beliefs began to alter with altered social relations many other concepts persisted. He writes:

> Who was the chief in Asante society? What role of a chief
> was of primary significance? According to K.A. Busia,
> above all the chief was 'he who sits upon the stool of the
> ancestors'. The major political significance of the chief
> stemmed from a cosmological belief. The Asante believed
> that they composed an ongoing community of the 'dead',
> the living, and those yet to be born. The 'dead', though
> unseen, nevertheless influenced the course of the living:
> they could cause crops to fail and prevent women from
> conceiving...The chief, as successor of the royal ancestors,
> acted as a bridge for the tribe between the living and the
> dead.[10]

It needs to be stated, however, that feudal societies in Africa did
not assume the same characteristics that they displayed in other parts
of the world. This is particularly important to note in a study of
African traditional religions because of the way in which concepts

and ideas emanating from different historical cultures in Africa are blended and left to coexist. It is appropriate to embrace the caution shown by Rodney when he writes:

> Feudalism involved great inequality in distribution of land and social products. The landlord class and its bureaucracy controlled the state and used it as an instrument for oppressing peasants, serfs, slaves, and even craftsmen and merchants. The movement from communalism to feudalism in every continent took several centuries and in some instances the interruption of internal evolution never allowed the process to mature. In Africa there is no doubt that the societies which eventually reached feudalism were extremely few. So long as the feudal state was still in the making, elements that were communal coexisted with elements that were feudal and with some peculiarities due to African conditions.[11]

African traditional religions, therefore, are a product of two precapitalist, African, historical-social bases, namely primitive African communal societies and African feudal socio-economic set-ups. In order to comprehend the role of African religions in society it is vital to understand the role of culture within these two precapitalist social formations. *But* what is more, in order to appreciate the relevance or otherwise of these religions today, it is crucial to have a perception of the social, material conditions in which they took root and flourished.

Articulation of Modes of Production
There is truth in the view that while it is easy to impose domination on a people, such domination can be continued only through a permanent, organized siege on the cultural life of the people in question. Unless one liquidates, physically, the people to be dominated, thus emptying domination of its content and object, their suppression is incomplete. The only other option is to harmonize economic and political domination with the cultural identity of the people. The total success of the latter is not historically attested, however. This is the problem which various forms of colonialism in Africa were burdened with. The indigenous populations of Africa could not be totally liquidated without defeating the object of colonialism: the colonized people. On the other hand, they could not all be drawn immediately out of their social relations into the relations of the new profit-making system without creating contradictions for the new system. One such contradiction was that the labour of the colonized people must be

bought as cheaply as possible. Therefore it was necessary to leave them rooted with one foot in the traditional society where their families would foot the bill for requisite social services. The other contradiction was that while the native's assimilation of the new culture would enable him to fit into the work routine of the new system, in the long run his tastes and demands might as a result become too expensive.

This, therefore, meant that two modes of production were left to articulate with one another even though the one was gradually being left to degenerate. It was the continued existence of traditional ways of life alongside the new so-called modern society that became the ground for the maintenance and reproduction of traditional culture. But because the traditional society has been caused to be systematically underdeveloped, men and women are drawn unavoidably into the other system where an alien culture confronts them now as a friend and now as an enemy.

African Traditional Religion as a Religious Protest against Alienating Forces

The most significant fact about African traditional religions is their subject matter, their content. This is what gives them their relevance. The subject matter of these religions is the historical and social struggles of the Africans in the process of their evolution. It originates from the history of the Africans and is the vehicle through which the achievements and failures, joys and pains of Africans are expressed.

African traditional religion has 'its social base in a people's production of their material life — in the practical activity of human beings co-operating and communicating in labour to wrestle with nature to procure their material means of life — food, clothing and shelter'.[12]

In fact, to understand the relevance of African traditional religion one must comprehend the significance of culture. To speak of a people's religion is to speak of their history, and to speak of their history is to speak of their culture. African traditional religions reflect the point at which the historical development of the Africans was arrested and halted. And since the subjugation of a people requires the suppression of their culture to be successful, an attempt to liberate a people requires the negation of the oppressor culture as an important starting point. Culture is not only the outcome of a people's history. It is a determinant of that history. To want to liberate people is to desire to restore them to the centre of the historical process. Commitment to a people's liberation is reflected by commitment to their culture. It is here where African traditional religion can make a lasting contribution. For as Michael McKale observes:

> Historically, culture has been fused with religion, for being an American Indian is not something you do on Sunday for one hour. It is a way of life which includes every aspect of one's existence. Religion was life and the sum total of one's way of life for all these indigenous cultures.

But:

> As imperial culture dominates the world it tends to force people to conform to its world view. The result is the destruction of human perception as mediated by traditional cultures.

And it is important to note that:

> People do not...become radical just because they lack food and basic necessities. Millions of people starve every year and they don't become anything except dead. It is when people perceive the moral contradictions between their own culture and history and the culture and history of capitalism which is imposed on them that they are radicalized.[13]

The point must be made unequivocally, therefore, without creating the impression that all elements of African traditional culture and religion are progressive and relevant for contemporary society, that without a creative reappropriation of traditional African religions and societies both African and Black Theologies will build their houses on sand. A Black Theology of Liberation must draw its cultural hermeneutics of struggle from a critical reappropriation of black culture just as an African Theology must arm itself with the political hermeneutics that arise from the contemporary social struggles of black people under apartheid capitalism.

NOTES

1. P. Berger, *The Social Reality of Religion* (Middlesex: Penguin, 1967), p. 13.

2. B. Hindess and P. Q. Hirst, *Pre-Capitalist Modes of Production* (London: Routledge and Kegan Paul, 1975), p. 13.

3. Ngugi wa Thiong'o, *Education for a National Culture* (Harare: Zimbabwe Publishing House, 1981), p. 2.

4. Ibid., p. 3.

5. Ibid.

6. Berger, *Social Reality*, pp. 34f.

7. K. K. Prah, *Notes and Comments on Aspects of Tswana Feudalism in the Precolonial Period* (Gaborone: National Institute for Research in Development and African Studies Documentation Unit, 1977), p. 2.

8. See I. L. Markovitz, *Power and Class in Africa* (Englewood Cliffs, N.J.: Prentice-Hall, 1977), pp. 99ff.; see also Prah, *Notes and Comments.*

9. J. Mbiti, *African Religions and Philosophy* (London: Heinemann, 1969), pp. 50ff.

10. Markovitz, *Power*, p. 104.

11. W. Rodney, *How Europe Underdeveloped Africa* (Washington, D.C.: Howard University Press, 1974), p. 39.

12. Ngugi wa Thiong'o, *Writers in Politics* (London: Heinemann, 1981), p. 59.

13. M. McKale, 'Culture and Human Liberation', *Radical Religion* 5, no. 2 (1980): 11f.

Chapter 6

Current Themes and Emphases in Black Theology
SIMON MAIMELA

Editors' Abstract

*Black Theology is a product of an awareness that black op-
pression and black exploitation are man-made. There is a
class of oppressors, white oppressors, who wield political and
economic power over black people. God has nothing to do
with it. When, however, black people decide to liberate themselves from this oppression they also commit themselves to
reflecting theologically on their suffering. According to Maimela, therefore, 'Black theologians are thrown into a situation
in which they cannot avoid seeing the world as a battleground
for the white oppressors and oppressed blacks'. Conversion
issues out of the conflict created by the existence of oppressors
and oppressed. True conversion cannot bypass this situation.
Qualitatively new human relationships are also a product of
an honest handling of this conflict. These themes compose the
first emphasis of Black Theology.*

*Secondly, since the struggle between classes, races, and
sexes is one of life and death, black theologians have an obli-
gation to see reality from the point of view of the poor, of the
little ones, of the marginalized and of the oppressed black
people. In short, Black Theology must take a preferential option for the oppressed. The third emphasis of Black Theology
is the conception of salvation as historical-social fact. This
means that the old division of the human being into body and
soul is no longer tenable. The salvation of the soul is no longer
a separate future fact. The fourth important factor of Black
Theology is the realization that 'the world is History-in-the-
Making'. According to this perspective the world and humanity are not given, finished, and static realities. On the contrary
humanity and the world are in the continual process of being
made. This understanding of the world and humanity calls for
transformative human action in which black theologians are to
participate.*

The theme which has been assigned to me is rather broad and open-ended. It does not seem possible to cover all its aspects, and I will therefore confine myself to a few themes or emphases which I hear proponents of Black Theology making. May I also state at the outset that I discuss Black Theology within the broader context of Liberation Theology, of which Black Theology is just but a part. Consequently, it should not surprise the readers if they find commonalities between Black Theology and other types of Liberation Theology in their treatment of these themes.

The World Is in Conflict between the Oppressor and the Oppressed

Black Theology as a conscious and systematic reflection on the black situation of racial oppression in South Africa is born out of a historical experience of suffering, of domination and humiliation of the powerless by the powerful racial group, which denies their fellow South Africans the right to become creators of their own history. It is born out of the awareness by blacks that they are not poor and oppressed by accident or by divine design. Rather *they are made* poor and powerless, and they are oppressed by another racial group, the rich and socio-politically powerful whites. Black Theology is born of this and the decision made by powerless and oppressed blacks that they will not accept the world the way it is, ordered by the ruling elites, and that they must opt for a radical change which may involve them in a confrontation with those who want to maintain the present unequal material relationships. In short, Black Theology, like every theology of liberation, arises when, in protest against the inhumanity to which they have been subjected by the dominant whites, the oppressed blacks not only decide to liberate themselves historically by taking away the power to shape history from their oppressors, but also commit themselves to reflecting theologically on their historical suffering, a suffering which they regard as a theological problem so as to find new ways out of that suffering.

From these few remarks it is obvious that, by beginning their theological reflection where pain and suffering are, black theologians are thrown into a situation in which they cannot avoid seeing the world as a battleground for the white oppressors and the oppressed blacks. Indeed, the fact that the ruling elite would like to encourage their victims, namely the oppressed black majority, to accept the already established social order despite the fact that it is unjust, oppressive and dehumanizing to blacks is, to liberation theologians, conclusive evidence that far from being serene and normal the world is already in a state of conflict. It is a world polarized between two groups because the institutionalized violence that characterizes our world is designed to benefit the powerful racial class at the expense of the poor and the dominated black persons.

By looking at the world from the point of view of the oppressed and the downtrodden, where the world is experienced as a conflict because the major constituents are polarized and are unable to work together toward the liberation and realization of dignity for all human beings, and by insisting that the reality of our conflictual world should become a subject for theological reflection, Liberation Theology raises embarrassing and uncomfortable questions for traditional theology. For the conflictual character of human history and the reality of confrontations among human beings, be they of class, race, or sex, are issues that traditional theology has tried its best to avoid reflecting on. It has done this by trying to understand human nature and society individually and spiritually. It has presented the gospel as something addressed exclusively to individuals, and dealing with their personal salvation, thereby reducing the Christian message to the private property of the few converted individuals.

Of course this attempt by traditional theology to close the eyes of many Christians to the reality of conflict is understandable, when it is remembered that theology was done from the point of view of the privileged, the powerful, the well-fed, and the rich. This was done to serve the interests of those who were comfortably situated and protected by the prevailing social arrangements against the rough edges of the oppressive structures. Being prevented from experiencing and discussing the oppressive social structures that keep the black majority in misery, traditional theologians are unable to see that the oppressed are made poor, dependent and powerless socially, economically and politically not by reason of laziness but by man-made social structures. Consequently, they focus on the love for the enemy and the oppressor, believing that it is un-Christian to talk about the polarity of human history between the oppressor and the oppressed, between blacks and whites, and that it is possible for the polarized blacks and whites to work together and to share the Lord's supper without also demanding that the oppressor should stop acting unjustly and oppressively towards the oppressed and poorer members of society.

Yet it is only when the reality of the conflictual nature of our world is acknowledged that any realistic hope of working towards overcoming this conflict can be entertained. Then Christians, confronted by the reality of the sinful alienation from one another on account of class, race and sex, will struggle to find one another and join hands in order to liberate their fellow human beings from all the forms of oppression which give birth to various structural conflicts among people. Indeed, Liberation Theology ought to be commended for pointing out that the reality of the conflictual nature of our world is symptomatic of human fallenness into that fundamental sin, namely, one of breach of fellowship between God and human beings and among human beings themselves. It is a refusal to love and to be available for the well being of one's neighbour. This fundamental sin, this alienated human existence, according to black liberation theologians, is the cause of injustice, oppression, and the will to dominate — all of which individually and collectively breed conflict and polarization among people. Put differently, Liberation Theology wants to drive home to theology that behind every form of injustice and oppression and, therefore, behind every polarization among people, there is a personal or collective will responsible for rejecting God's will that we should love our neighbours as ourselves. Consequently, the overcoming of this alienation, which breeds oppression and domination and ultimately conflicts, with a view to effecting reconciliation, requires that Christians should do more than convert or change a few people within the dehumanizing social system. Rather the radical transformation of the system itself must be aimed at. In this way all human beings can become the subjects of history and the creators of human destiny. As Christians, they can work together with God in building up a more just and humanizing social order in which class, race and sex are transcended as determinants of personal value.

Finally, Black Theology (and the same goes for all Liberation Theology) does not just wish to focus on the conflictual nature of the human situation out of its weddedness to Marxist class analysis, as its critics often charge. For as Gutierrez points out, the reality of confrontation among human beings is something that St. Paul also acknowledges, and had to deal with, when he reminds us that the Christian life involves a painful conflict between the old and the new Adam, and a transition from bondage to freedom. These tensions are experienced when, in obedience to the call of the gospel, the oppressor is converted to the position of the oppressed classes, the despised races, and the dominated sex. Conversion which alone overcomes human conflicts thus involves a total break with past oppressive and exploitative tendencies, behaviour and ways of relating to the neighbour. This would bring about a profound solidarity between the oppressor and the oppressed, as well as a commitment by the oppressor to the process of liberation on behalf of and together with the poor and the downtrodden. Also, this transformation (conversion) will lead to qualitatively new ways to becoming human in our relationship with others. To summarize: until that fundamental fellowship of brotherhood and sisterhood to which the gospel calls all people is experienced and actualized as a gift from Christ, a fellowship beyond the present divisions in society on account of race, sex and class, the need to acknowledge and try to overcome the conflictual nature of the human situation is something which any Christian theology worth the name will have to put high on its agenda.

Theology Must Take a Preferential Option for the Oppressed

Given the fact that the world is in conflict and the majority of the human family suffers from injustice and exploitation on account of colour while the whites, the powerful few, benefit from the status quo, it follows that any theology which acknowledges this conflict can no longer afford to remain socially and politically neutral. For the struggle between classes, races and sexes is one of life and death; it is the struggle before and in the midst of which the church and Black Theology must take sides out of a conviction that the demands of the gospel are incompatible with unjust, alienating, and polarizing social arrangements. Because it is impossible to be Christian without also committing oneself to the process of liberation, black theologians are persuaded that a point is reached when all theologians must ask themselves: What is my social location in this conflictual society as a theologian? Whose interests and concerns am I serving or promoting? How is my faith related to the struggle of liberation of the oppressed and the people of colour?

It is as one confronts these and similar questions frankly and honestly that it becomes obvious that no neutrality is possible for a theologian, because in a conflict for life and against death, one cannot equally embrace the oppressor and the oppressed: one is forced to be for one and against the other. Since the situation in which the oppressed majority find themselves is closer to reality, the reality of the conflictory and unacceptable nature of our world, black theologians argue that, in order to see reality as it is, it is imperative that Christian theologians should try to see and understand society from the point of view of the poor, of the little ones, of the marginalized, and of the oppressed black. This preferential option for the poor is one which theologians should make so as to be able to see society in a new light, as a society which has sentenced the oppressed black majority to a life of misery and suffering.

It should be noted that this insistence on the preferential option for the oppressed and marginalized by Black Theology is not based on the compassionate feeling for the underdogs, but on what black theologians believe is biblical revelation. According to Black Theology, God has already taken sides with the oppressed, the outcasts and the despised when God elected to liberate Israel from Egyptian bondage. It is a preferential option for the poor which was brought to a new height in the coming of Jesus, who was himself a poor and oppressed man of sorrows, who suffered and was crucified as the criminal and the rejected outcast. In the light of this revealed preferential thrust, black theologians, struggling for justice, believe that Christians and churches must also take the side of the poor, to claim solidarity with them in their struggle, thereby liberating the oppressed from misery and marginality, and bringing down the powerful from their thrones. Put differently, the preferential option for the poor is grounded on the fact that God has taken sides. In consequence, this call for a theological commitment and re-orientation is based on the belief that it is among the struggling poor that God is to be found at work. Also this requires of theologians that they re-read the Bible in the light of those struggles of the poor for freedom, if God's promise of liberation of the captive is to be correctly understood in the oppressive society in which we live today. This re-reading of the Bible from the point of view of the poor and oppressed, based on what is called the 'hermeneutical privilege' of the poor, has led black theologians to a better understanding of God's suffering not as an abstract theological idea but as relating to the concrete historical suffering of the dominated people for whom God suffers in order to break all the chains which have subjected them to spiritual and physical bondage.

In Black Theology, the fact that God has taken sides with the poor is very important, for it implies that God is not prepared to put up with social situations in which the black majority are oppressed and humiliated. Consequently, black theologians argue, just as God liberated Israel not only from spiritual sin and guilt but also from oppressive political and economic deprivation, God will again liberate all oppressed people not only from personal sins and guilt but also from the historical structures that are evil, exploitative and alienating. This, according to Black Theology, is the message of the Exodus story and the Lucan story where Jesus declares that his ministry is to free those who are in bondage.

In the light of this preferential option for the poor, the church is called upon to abandon its false neutrality (which is nothing but an implicit support for the ruling and economic elite), to move out of its position of ghetto power, and to shake off the protection given it by the beneficiaries of the unjust status quo. In doing this the church would be taking its position for and with the poor who struggle to control their destiny, thus committing itself unequivocally to human liberation. In other words, God's prophets will be reading the signs of the times, openly denouncing ameliorative measures which prolong and give injustice and oppression respectability, calling for and advocating a radical transformation of the existing structures. In doing so, the church becomes that institution which joins forces with God to work for the liberation, dignity, and justice for all people, thereby rejecting the misuse of the gospel to legitimize class and racial oppression as well as sexual domination. Should the church take an option for the poor and the oppressed, something it has never done when it served the interest of the dominant whites, it would, according to Black Theology, become the vehicle of reconciliation and peace among the alienated, polarized, and conflictual humankind in our part of the world.

Salvation as Historical-Social Fact

Behind the claims made in the preceding subsections, that the death and resurrection of Jesus Christ offer effective remedy for polarization between the oppressor and the oppressed, between the black and white, lies the conviction that the gospel has a social meaning and that human restoration through the Christ-event is not separable from the renewal of political, economic and social institutions. It is out of this conviction that black theologians have had to reject traditional theology's emphasis on spiritualization of the gospel — as if the gift of salvation which Christ offers has no relation to the material conditions of the poor and the oppressed, and as if salvation is not concerned with the whole person in his/her physical and spiritual dimensions. Accordingly liberation theologians accuse traditional theology of a false, deliberate reductionism used to limit the understanding of the gospel to the 'spiritual sphere', to the personal life, implying thereby that Christ's work only touches social structures tangentially and not at their root where social and racial classes struggle to free themselves from political bondage to which they have been subjected by the dominant groups. In succumbing to this reductionist temptation, traditional theology is accused not only of refusing to acknowledge that Christ's salvation involves the all-comprehensive work of liberating human beings from all social misery but also of portraying salvation as if it were 'a pie in the sky', an eschatological reality and a flight from this world of tears. In doing this, it offers salvation as if it were a tranquilizing instrument, an instrument which oppressors are all too ready to use to cover up social injustices so that the poor will not rise up to challenge the prevailing oppressive material relationships.

Obviously, it would be incorrect to exaggerate the claim that traditional theology was not altogether aware of the social implications of the gospel, because the church as an institution located in society did exert cultural and political influence. But this awareness was overshadowed by the overriding concern to save individuals from the pangs of hell, thereby preparing them in this life for salvation in the life hereafter. This spiritualistic trend became even more pronounced in the pietism of both Protestant and Catholic churches, the pietism that had a marked influence on traditional theology's tendency to focus more on the individual than on the social reality of salvation on this side of the grave. Therefore, without minimizing the personal or spiritual reality of salvation — thereby reducing the gospel message to one formula, namely, the social and economic formula — the recovery of and emphasis on the social reality of salvation in Black Theology of Liberation should be understood as a necessary corrective to an undue overemphasis on the spiritual nature of human life at the expense of its physical dimension.

The claim that salvation should be understood also as a social fact has to be understood against a modern background in theology where there has been an increasing appreciation that human beings exist in the totality of their body and spirit in their social relationship with others. This modern awareness has broadened our understanding that individual salvation in the afterlife must also include salvation in this life in society. Salvation thus has to do also with liberation from those things that keep human beings in slavery and oppression, thereby denying them joy and wholeness as individuals and community. Put differently, salvation is no longer understood as an escape from this miserable world but as a divine power and possibility of transforming the social structures, of restoring creation and of seeking to overcome suffering. It is only as salvation is understood to be bound up with the institutions and structures that bind men and women of flesh and blood that it could become good news for the oppressed, the hungry, the alienated, the sorrowful and the outcasts.

This broad conceptualization of salvation has been made possible by a redefinition of sin by liberation theologians. For them sin, as something which is opposite to liberation, is not merely a private matter but rather is eminently a political, social term; it describes an oppressive situation, one in which there is no fellowship, no mutual caring among people, and there is no room to live as a whole human being in freedom and joy. That is, the term 'sin' depicts a structural existence which characterizes the fallen human existence; it describes the reality which includes both the personal sins and the collective sins of my people, my class and my race. Besides, sin refers to a structural reality; it is never something we encounter in-itself but it is met only in concrete, particular instances of alienations between God and humanity, of exploitative relationships between one class or racial group and another.

In the perspective of Black Liberation Theology, sin is therefore a deeply rooted reality in human existence. In consequence, the removal and elimination of sin requires much more than the conversion of a few men and women; its elimination demands a radical liberation and transformation of society and humanity itself — as men and women together with and under God struggle to build up a just society, thus jointly contributing to the building up and growth of the Kingdom of God in history. Black liberation theologians ground this defiant hope of a radical liberation in the gift which Christ offers to our world. For by his death and resurrection, according to Liberation Theology, Jesus procured for humanity an effective remedy for sin and all its personal and social consequences such as greed, hatred, prejudice, misery and inhumane as well as exploitative tendencies and behaviour. Indeed, the Christian message to sinful humanity is that the work of Jesus Christ is intended to deal with what is deepest and fundamental in human life: the healing of the most stubborn and virulent disease of the human heart, namely, lovelessness and hopelessness.

Expressed somewhat differently, black theologians argue that God's redeeming work in Christ should be understood as holding out the divine promise and possibility of a social and personal renewal in the sense that God in Christ intends redirecting, reinvigorating and regenerating the perverted and alienated human existence by lifting it up to himself in order to liberate humanity from sin, thereby actualizing a complete fellowship of God and humanity, and of people among themselves. In view of this all-embracing, cosmic salvation involving the transformation not only of pious individuals but also of the entire human existence, Black Theology of Liberation is justified in arguing that salvation is real only when it includes the social relationships in which men and women of flesh and blood live. For until the totality of that situation — characterized by human brokenness, alienation and, therefore, lack of social justice, freedom, and personal wholeness — is saved, transformed, and liberated there can be no genuine and tangible salvation for humanity. To be sure, by itself the process of liberation, which Christians are called to participate in, cannot, however radical it may be, conquer the very roots of oppression and exploitation, namely, sin. Nor can it automatically create heaven on earth. For the conquering of the cause of suffering and domination remains a divine gift from above. But this does not mean that salvation and historical liberation are not closely related. Indeed they are, and without collapsing them into one another, Liberation Theology is correct when it argues that salvation already achieved and promised in Christ is the precondition for historical liberation, and for human attempts to transform the fallen, alienating social conditions into a more just and humane society. For this very reason, historical liberation remains the joint effort of both God and Christians while ultimate salvation is a divine gift, and historical liberation draws its lifeblood from ultimate salvation.

The World Is History-in-the Making
The strong emphasis placed on the transformative nature of salvation for the human condition, and the claim that salvation to be genuine must effect historical liberation from suffering, distress, and oppression, are understandable when it is remembered that Liberation Theology is written from the point of view that the world and humanity are to be understood as historical, and as both changing and changeable. Black Theology of Liberation thus shares the fundamental biblical conviction which holds that the world and humanity are not given, finished, and static realities but they are dynamic realities that are undergoing continuous change and development in response to God, who leads them towards their completion in the eschaton. Put differently, liberation theologians cannot, even for a moment, believe that the world in which we now live is a given world, one which comes directly from the hands of the Creator, and is a world which humanity must accommodate itself to and accept in gratitude. For they know from experience that the world is too awful, too distorted, too unjust, and too oppressive to be the kind of world which derives directly from God's hand. On the contrary, they look upon the world as something that is made by people and is therefore amendable to human transformative action. Accordingly, as the world is the product of humans' structuring of their environment, it is a world which is engaged in the history of its making and therefore is open to all sorts of possibilities, possibilities that lend themselves to the restructuring of society in such a way as to demonstrate a respect for the human dignity and worth of every single one of its members.

This perspective, one from which liberation theologians view the world, is grounded in the fundamental biblical faith which holds that the world and humankind are in the hands of the victorious God who makes promises of and is capable of making all things new (2 Cor. 5:17; Rev. 21:5). In other words, biblical faith thinks of the world and humanity as in a process of change from past and present to the future. It understands life in terms of the human response to the hope of divine promises which liberate mankind from the limits imposed by existing structures of this world and enable humanity to think and behave according to the possibilities which God's future holds out to them. In consequence, believers impelled by the possibilities that the divine future creates, rather than fix their gaze on the world beyond as the 'true life', now feel themselves called upon to turn to their present world in order to transform it socially, economically, and politically so as to actualize the vision of the future which God has placed at their disposal and to find fulfilment in their present life.

In view of the fact that the world in its process of making is open to human intervention, planning and transformation, Black Theology of Liberation finds it necessary to call and inspire men and women to engage themselves in a struggle to change the social realities of this oppressive and life-denying world so that they, together with God, can shape the world into what was intended by their Creator. Furthermore, in order to underline the meaningfulness of human involvement in the ongoing dynamics of creatively shaping and transforming the world towards its intended goal and completion, Liberation Theology often reminds its readers that it is for the realization of the city, New Jerusalem, and not the jungle in some distant past known as paradise in Eden, that God is actively engaged in the work of continuing creation. In this process of transforming the world in anticipation of the coming Kingdom in which God will realize the divine objectives of bringing about the absolute state of peace, liberation and justice for God's new humanity, ordered and guided by love, Black Theology of Liberation calls men and women to play their part and to be on the cutting edge of human liberation from all forms of social and spiritual oppression, thus becoming partners with their Creator in the refashioning of this unjust world into one in which they will at last find fulfilment. In doing this, Liberation Theology teaches people that social structures and interpersonal relationships are not fated to be eternally oppressive and destructive. Rather they are alterable for the better because all historical structures are neither perfect nor can they fully encapsulate the life-giving and life prompting will of God. Accordingly, it remains human responsibility to join hands with God in order to build up, nurture and transform all social structures and institutions so that they may serve human needs better and better.

Finally, Black Theology of Liberation is fully aware that, in order for people to become responsible creators of their individual and collective history, they should become conscious of their own God-given potential for creative action in shaping the world. Therefore, to instill and affirm this human ability to intervene and re-create the world within the all-embracing context of God's ongoing and forward thrusting creative activity of transforming the world, Liberation Theology believes that one of its tasks is that of teaching people to believe in themselves and in their creative ability to shape and complete the world. In this respect, Black Theology of Liberation tries to overcome the tendency of traditional theology to belittle human creativity and its contribution on the grounds that human beings cannot bring about God's Kingdom on earth. Without denying this important insight, Black Theology reminds people that their creative involvement with and under the guidance of God in overcoming sin and its destructive consequences is not futile, and not totally unnecessary and irrelevant to the final victory that will arrive with God's coming Kingdom. Rather this victory emerges out of the partial historical victories which God and committed Christians now win against evil, oppression and lovelessness. To be sure, God's coming Kingdom will include far more than these limited historical victories which God's saints and their Creator gradually win, but God's coming Kingdom is not entirely divorced from the present struggles in which the Saviour and his disciples are engaged, as they try together to humanize social conditions. And because of the continuity between the human political work of liberation and God's gift of final liberation at the end of all historical struggles, Black Theology of Liberation argues that earthly and historical progress in the social sphere, to the extent that it contributes towards the moulding and ordering of the world into one of justice and peace, is necessarily of vital importance to the growth of the Kingdom whose final realization will be brought about by God in the eschaton. Indeed, it could not be otherwise for the world which is involved in the history of its making into the kind of world that God had intended it to be.

Chapter 7

The Evolution of the Black Struggle and the Role of Black Theology

TAKATSO MOFOKENG

Editors' Abstract

As long as the black struggle expressed itself in terms of accommodation to the status quo, black religious protest remained at the level of a struggle of black people for integration into the religious status quo. According to Mofokeng the courageous struggles of black people against colonialism, settler colonialism, and apartheid capitalism prior to the advent of the Black Consciousness Movement heralded neither a theoretical nor a political-praxiological break with white capitalist ideology and social practice. It is for this reason that only with the rise of the Black Consciousness Movement was it possible to evolve a Black Theology of Liberation. The Black Consciousness Movement questioned the fundamental production system of apartheid South Africa by contrasting it initially with precapitalist African social formations and then by envisioning a modern open society premised on the communal values of traditional African societies. The Black Consciousness Movement identified a cultural contradiction between the oppressing white minority regime and the black oppressed masses. Thus both the material basis and the ideological superstructure of white capitalism were rejected as antithetical to the interests of the oppressed and exploited black masses. As a corollary of this, Black Theology, as a tool of struggle for the materially and culturally oppressed black people, emerged as an expression of a complete ideological break with white capitalist society.

Introduction
The arrival of armed colonial Europeans in our country determined the response of our forefathers to this incursion. Their act of forcing a foreign, capitalist economic system upon our forefathers as well as that of relegating them to a position of cheap labourers determined the nature of the social, political and economic history of South Africa.[1] These unprovoked violent acts disturbed the natural development of African socio-economic history. It was totally derailed and put on a radically new rail. From then onwards the socio-economic history of black South Africans became an essentially changed one. It became a protracted struggle against institutionalized, violent exploitation and oppression as well as a struggle to regain their land on which they could be free to establish a new social, political and economic system, a system in which they would be the owners of the means of production and of the produce of their labour as well as being those who would determine the system of distribution.

The introduction of Christian religion at gunpoint, as it were, by these European colonizers and settlers determined the history of the Christian church in South Africa.[2] If Christian religion had been introduced in a different manner and for a totally different purpose the history of the church in South Africa would have developed differently and made the church a blessing. Instead it became a history of an organized religion that harboured tensions, contradictions and conflicts within itself. For our forefathers the history of black organized Christian religion became a history of a protracted theological struggle against ideological manipulation of the religious sentiments of blacks with the aim of reinforcing the subjugation of black Christians. These two histories (white colonial oppression and exploitation as well as a colonial Christian religion) were nothing but two elements or dimensions of one history. They are one history that takes place at two levels which support and strengthen each other — the ideological level as the level to which religion belongs and the material level of human and social existence.[3] Our forefathers knew this intuitively if not analytically[4] and consequently pursued their struggle of liberation at both levels and left this as a legacy to later generations of black people of this country.[5]

We agree with Rev. I.J. Mosala when he characterized this history and its goal by saying, '...the attempt to implant Christianity among the indigenous black people from the seventeenth century onwards... was an effort to transform African societies by dismantling them...That struggle has been a protracted one. It never ceased'.[6]

Before presenting a detailed description of the evolution of this two-dimensional history of the black struggle or of these two reciprocally related dimensions of this black struggle we need to find a concept of history which is capable of capturing the various and different dynamics and phases of this history in such a manner that its qualitative differences and dialectical unity will be retained.

To my mind this history can only be defined as a dialectical one, as it shall be shown. It is a history that evolved through harmonies and contradictions, a history of setbacks and successes, of apparent defeats and certain victories, a history that makes continual qualitative leaps through these contradictions, temporary setbacks and apparent defeats. It is a history of excruciating pain and one in which a lingering cloud of death accompanies black existence in this country.

Black History: A Dialectical Event

At the dawn of the struggle against colonialism in this country, our forebears fought as separate small nations which were not adequately equipped for the kind of challenge they faced. This made the outcome of their battles against the highly sophisticated weaponry of their enemies a foregone conclusion. They did, however, fight gallantly and win some battles.[7] It was only later in the eighteenth century that they started to realize that it would be more helpful to pool their military and other resources and respond as a united force.[8]

Real awareness of the nature and immensity of oppression and exploitation to which they were subjected and of the necessity of unity of black people came in the nineteenth century when all black people had lost absolute control over their land. They realized then that they were dispossessed as black people by the same white group and that what faced them was an issue of national oppression to which they had to respond as a nation, as one nation. But since African kings and queens (the leaders until then) had been vanquished, black men had to come forward and assume leadership of the black struggle. Since the tribal bases (the only organizational infrastructures until then) were too small for this great challenge, new organizations had to be founded for this purpose. And believe it or not, black pastors of the African Independent Churches were the ones who came forward to provide the leadership. They became the first black people in South Africa to advocate a broad African nationalism and used their church organizations as the first functional bases.[9] But in this case again, the concept of black unity which they upheld and advocated was still too narrow and exclusive of a sizeable section of the black population.[10]

The desired comprehensive concept of black unity was first advocated in 1902 by the African Political Organization, which was headed by Abdullah Abdurahman. It was a unity that included the so-called coloureds. He predicted the impact of this unified force and stated that 'there will one day arise a solid mass of black and coloured humanity whose demands will be irrepressible'.[11] This unity which the African Political Organization advocated was ultimately realized in 1912 with the formation of the African National Congress and displayed in Bloemfontein in 1935 when a wide range of black organizations got together in response to the Hertzog Bills.[12] The unity of that year culminated in the formation of the All African Convention. In the same year, 1935, an organization called the National Liberation League was founded in Cape Town which advocated and achieved the broadest unity among blacks in the struggle against the common oppressor. This unity included all people who were oppressed because they were black and not of the caucasian race, i.e., they were Africans, coloureds and Indians. They were to struggle together against white nationalism under the banner of African nationalism. This was a very radical step during that time because all the (elitist) black organizations had thus far struggled not for national liberation, but for integration in the colonial-settler state.

From the 1940s things changed rapidly. The issue of African nationalism received more emphasis and support. It decided the authenticity of organizations and also became their breaking point. Self-determination became its political 'expression'. There was also insistence on mass mobilization and mass action to achieve this noble goal. The employment of this strategy which had not been used before marked the end of the days of exclusive reliance on deputations and 'gentlemanly' pleas for reforms and inclusion in the white state which had characterized the struggle under the leadership of black elites so far. Regrettably, some amount of moderation in terms of goals as well as strategy persisted. As far as strategy is concerned, while the defiance campaign appeared to be a step forward in the direction of mass action and direct challenge to the white minority government, the African National Congress, which led the defiance campaign, still harboured hopes of liberation coming, in addition to black people's own efforts, through efforts of white liberals. As an example, coloured and Indian voters were called upon to vote United Party which was a white party! This was a strategy of winning white support for black aspirations, a strategy which failed to yield any fruits.

As far as the goal was concerned the Freedom Charter (1955)

represented a clear step of moderation. As E. Harsch puts it, it represented 'a pullback from African nationalist positions'.[13] Both the strategy as well as the goal of the African National Congress were severely criticized by most clear-minded African nationalists. The charter manifested an abandonment of African nationalism as 'the sole ideological basis for the salvation' of black people, these critics argued.[14] This abandonment of African nationalism is proved by emphasizing multi-racialism where ownership of the land of South Africa is concerned.[15] To the African nationalists 'South Africa belonged to the indigenous African population by right...'[16] The strategy of collaboration with white bourgeois liberals as well as that of 'superfluous pacts with insignificant organizations and participation in dummy organizations' was also hammered.[17] When radicalization of goals and strategy was resisted and rejected by the African National Congress young African nationalists left and claimed sole custody of the African nationalist dream of 'Africa for Africans', self-determination and an independent black state. This departure of a small group, while it seemed a defeat, represented a qualitatively higher stage in the black struggle for liberation in terms of goals and strategy and was in line with some past organizations, as analysis would show later.

The immediate effect of this re-emphasis of African nationalism as the ultimate goal of the black struggle lay in drawing the lines very clearly between the oppressor and the oppressed and temporarily halting unprofitable collaboration with elements of the oppressor group, be they liberal or so-called progressive. This emphasis also set the stage for the era of the Black Consciousness Movement. But before we get to that point we have to attend to one other issue.

Released from the grip of preoccupation with fruitless strategies of attracting substantial white support, deputations, petitions and pleas, the African nationalists were free to employ their strategy of mass mobilization and mass action in challenging the white regime. This was actualized in the anti-pass laws campaign of March 1960 which culminated in the Sharpeville massacre and other brutalities by the police of the white state. As we all know the Sharpeville trauma catapulted black political organizations (African National Congress and Pan African Congress) onto the highest stage of the black struggle in terms of strategy. Both organizations decided to launch an armed struggle.

The Labour Front
Colonialism and the settlers' immeasurable greed for land rendered African people landless and therefore without the means of indepen-

dent subsistence. A correlate of this acquisition of land by dispossession on the part of white settlers was a need for cheap labour for their own system of economic production. On the African side the loss of land by the Africans at the Cape initially and right across the country later coupled with new oppressive laws forced them to sell their labour power for a pittance to their conquerors. As a measure of increasing the labour force for the expanding Cape Colony as well as for the growing economic system slaves were imported from the East Indies and the east coast of Africa.

At the earliest stage of the history of black resistance there was apparently no separate responses of labourers as labourers. The only responses were still in the form of political responses by the separate nationalities. There was a continuous flow of black labourers who fled the settler farms in order to join forces with those African nations which were still free and still successfully resisting conquest.

It is in fact the emergence of towns which urbanized Africans as well as the opening of the mining industry (copper mine in Namaqualand opened in 1850, diamond in 1867 and gold in 1886) that introduced African labourers into a new era, the era of labour movements and labour action. They were lumped together irrespective of tribal origin by one common instrument of exploitation. They in turn became aware of their common fate as black people and as black labourers. It became inevitable that they would soon gain a common worker consciousness which would lead to organized, united responses to white exploitation. The innumerable strikes that mark the entire history of South African economic relations bear testimony to the impact of this new area.

It was, however, only in the 1910s that African trade unions were formed and that evidence is found of mass strikes (Kadalie's and others' efforts) right across the entire field of different industries. The upsurge of African industrial actions during that time coincided with an upsurge of political activity by the broad African political parties that transcended the narrow tribal perimeters. Both these responses were triggered by the creation of a union of white nationalism in 1910. As we should be aware, a series of laws which aimed at consolidating white political and economic power by squeezing and crushing African people further were promulgated. (We are here referring to the 1913 Natives Land Act and the 1923 Natives Urban Area Act.) In response to the passing of the Industrial Conciliation Act of 1924, which deprived African workers of the right to unionize and to use the strike weapon, as well as to the 1926 law that reserved skilled jobs in the mining industry for whites, the movement of African unionization rose meteorically.

At the ideological level struggles that emerged in the 1930s among black political parties also reached African trade unions. These ideological struggles pertained to the issue of race and class as well as that of national liberation versus social revolution. There were African political theoreticians who held firmly onto the conviction that 'in South Africa the black liberation struggle (i.e. struggle for national liberation) is the central axis of the class struggle' and those who held and propounded the view that a social revolution which was the ultimate goal of liberation could only be achieved through a class struggle that transcended racial boundaries. There were those who emphasized an agrarian revolution and the role of African peasantry (Workers' Party of S.A. formed in 1934) while others emphasized the leading role of the urban working class (Fourth International Organization of South Africa founded in 1934).

During the Second World War years black people of South Africa were impoverished even further by unemployment that resulted from this war. Black workers and their trade unions were thrown into the debate on whether to support the war efforts of Britain or not. Black workers initiated a strike to support wage claims in 1941 in which sixteen African workers were killed by the police. This strike indicated unambiguously where black workers stood on the issue of support for British imperialism which was threatened by Hitler. (Incidentally, the Communist Party opposed this strike).

Just after the Second World War, in 1946 black workers carried out the largest African strike South Africa had ever seen. It involved 73,000 mine workers who completely paralyzed twenty of the forty-five mines of that time. In spite of the brutal crushing of this strike and the death of thirteen black mine workers this strike convincingly demonstrated the power that African workers wielded once they decided to act. This tradition of workers' mass action has been maintained until today. It also radicalized black thought generally by proving the effectiveness of the strategy of mass action which had been opposed by the largest black political parties until then.

Religion, Theology and Church

We have already stated that the religion of the conqueror — the Christian religion — was, as a social force, to continue the battle of subjugation of Africans at the ideological level and instill in them social norms of a capitalist civilization. It went to work as planned and instilled in African converts 'a belief in the virtues of work, private property and respect for authority',[18] and also incorporated

Africans into 'the mental and cultural universe of the whites'.[19] Paradoxically, this same Christian religion fortunately had the inherent potential of achieving the opposite of the above because as the 'cry of the oppressed creature' it can also serve as an ideological 'protest against real suffering'.

It was therefore inevitable that sooner or later some elements among the materially, physically and culturally subjugated Africans who by now had long been Christianized would gain a new religious consciousness and engage in a new religious praxis, a praxis of ideological and practical resistance to subjugation. This connexion between religion and resistance was there right from the dawn of black religiosity. This was the case in the very first stage of the response to colonialism by black people as separate nationalities. The African kings and queens who led the struggle against dispossession were both religious leaders as well as military commanders. In fact, to them the struggle against dispossession was a religious matter. It was a crusade at the end of which theological reflection and religious cultic practice had to follow.[20]

In the nineteenth century, which is the period during which black people worked towards one national response and established the first political parties, black pastors played a prominent role.[21] Since they had gone through mission schools and acquired a relatively high level of education they naturally assumed leadership in these political organizations. Paradoxically though, while opposing white oppression as perpetrated by the white regime, they remained inside the white church which perpetrated religious oppression and colour and race discrimination. It is difficult, due to the scarcity of documentary evidence, to explain how this could have been possible and to give an informed answer to the question why they remained in these churches. If I may be allowed to speculate, I would be inclined to think that in view of the goals and the strategies of the struggle in the nineteenth and early twentieth centuries, which were mapped out by the black elite and included integration into the colonial-settler state and the capitalist economic system to be achieved through dialogue and pleas, these pastors and other lay Christians probably regarded the situation in the church as a 'first step in the right direction'. This could explain why, while they were painfully aware of contradictions and violations of gospel teaching within the white church, they did not take the most relevant step of moving out. It was not until the second half of the nineteenth century that some black pastors took a step which had already been taken by black Americans who were in a similar situation in the late eighteenth century (Richard Allen left the white Methodist Church in 1787 and founded the African Methodist Episcopal [A.M.E.] Church in 1816), and left some white churches to found the first African Independent Churches.[22] This was a positive translation of their aversion to the white man's Christianity. (We are referring here to Nehemiah Tile who founded the Tembu Church in 1884; Chief Kgantlapane who took part in founding the Native Independent Congregational Church in Taung; Khanyane Napo who founded the African Church in Pretoria in 1889; and Mangena M. Mokone who left the Methodist Church in Pretoria and founded an Ethiopian church in 1892.) Incidentally, through these churches and churchmen a broad African church for Africans and governed by Africans became the rallying point.[23] These churches counted consequently among the greatest bases of the movement for black nationalism until the appearance of the African National Congress, its Youth League and the Pan African Congress.[24]

Black Consciousness Movement

The emergence of the Black Consciousness philosophy and praxis in the 1960s lifted the black struggle ideologically as well as practically to a new height. This does not mean, however, that Black Consciousness was born *ex nihilo*. On the contrary, it has historical links with the ideas of Lembede of the ANC Youth League as well as those of the PAC without being identical with them. We can therefore speak in regard to Black Consciousness of a differentiated continuity with some older movements and ideas. Building on a concept of black unity which was broader than that of the PAC and deeper than that of Lembede of the ANC Youth League the Black Consciousness Movement operated with a two pronged strategy. Functioning with the self-reliance slogan 'Black man you are on your own' this movement gave attention to the psychological dimension of the black man as well as the material dimension where this man lives, where he has to actualize his new self and from where his consciousness is continuously being formed. By doing this the Black Consciousness organizations had laid a basis for an inevitable, radical ideological development as well as a search for an instrument of social analysis which would more adequately unearth the mechanisms of oppression and make social praxis efficacious.

It is another question how long it took for this more radical ideological development to happen. What should be acknowledged is that a basis had been laid for an inevitable historical development which would lift this movement to a higher level enabling it to cope with the pressures of the 1980s and to respond adequately to the challenges of the situation today. From a philosophy which rightly and timely emphasized, among others, the psychological dimension of black people, the Black Consciousness Movement logically developed to a point where it adopted scientific socialism as its ideological instrument. From a praxis the targets of which were identified in terms of visible material oppression, the Black Consciousness organizations naturally developed to a point where the use of a Marxian instrument of social analysis which has been adapted to peculiar South African realities became a normality.

As history shows quite clearly the social praxis of this movement underwent a dialectical development which started with small self-reliance projects and developed qualitatively until the stage of 1976 was reached.[25] This is the stage which Steve Biko had foreseen and described as a collision of steel against steel as the South African car changed gears towards the future.[26] This, however, was not unique with this movement. On the contrary, it is the normal dialectic of history which we observed in the history of the black struggle right through the past three centuries.

What was unique about the Black Consciousness organizations was the deliberate development of a new theology which would be inseparably linked to the Black Consciousness philosophy and based on the Black Consciousness political praxis as it developed dialectically. This link and this basis determined the methodology of this theology, its interlocutor and the authenticity of its subject.

While the other movements also realized the importance of religion and theology in the struggle for liberation to the extent of involving pastors in actual political praxis, not one, to our mind, had made a deliberate effort to stimulate the creation of a new theology.[27] It is our suspicion that they regarded liberal theology of the early twentieth century and the unwritten theology of the Independent Churches as adequate company to the struggle.[28]

Black Consciousness and Black Theology
Among the many projects which the Black Consciousnesss organizations launched to serve as instruments of conscientization was the Black Theology Project. Its launching was a deliberate response to a religious problem which had been positively identified. As Steve Biko put it in 'Black Consciousness and the Quest for True Humanity', the crisis in which blacks find themselves also includes that of a theologial language.[29] The dominant theological language in the churches, especially in the historic churches, functioned as an ideological instrument of oppression and exploitation. It was in response

to that unacceptable situation that Black Theology was developed. Initially it was thought that it would serve as an instrument of conscientization. As we put it elsewhere, 'here too as black pastors and lay people rub shoulders with it they begin to ask questions and we believe that they are going to find answers themselves'.[30] Participation in it succeeded to create new theological subjects out of black lay and professional theologians who had been relegated to a position of theological objects or recipients of a 'ready-made' theology that worked against them and blacks in general.

As these theologians got used to thinking for themselves without asking for permission or approval, theological creativity emerged and grew, the result of which is an accumulation of black theological ideas. Almost invariably the status and role of Black Theology soon changed. In addition to being a project of conscientization it soon became an instrument of theological reflection on the entire evolving liberation praxis which included the self-reliance projects.

This latter role became the major role of Black Theology, i.e., that of critically accompanying the entire struggle as it evolves. This very crucial change, which has eluded the notice of many a student of Black Theology, occurred as a result of the practical involvement of black lay and professional theologians in both the two levels of praxis in the struggle for liberation — the concrete and the theoretical — as well as in the development of a new understanding of biblically witnessed processes. And since this position has not changed, Black Theology continues to be a useful instrument for the continuously evolving struggle for liberation.

Structurally, Black Theology became a theology which, having started as a theoretical reflection on praxis in the light of scripture alone, quickly and inevitably developed into a theology in which the light of the specific praxis of committed blacks falls on the Bible, on the one side, making it comprehensible. On the other side, the transforming light of scripture falls on liberation praxis criticizing it when and where criticism is due, affirming it where credit is due to it, making it qualitatively better as well as driving it forward.

It must be pointed out here that there is no unanimity among black theologians on these methodological issues. Allan Boesak, taking an orthodox Calvinist stand, would like to dispute the legitimacy of the reciprocal meaningfulness between scripture and praxis.[31] To us the praxis of liberation is not totally devoid of effective light because of the presence of Jesus Christ in the struggle of his 'little ones'.[32] Its interlocutor became clearly identifiable as the oppressed and committed black community which is not interchangeable with any other community.[33] It is the concerns, frustrations, puzzles, pains and deaths of this community which form the baggage of questions which inform and reform this theological reflection. It is also the insurrections, the happiness and the hope of this black community-in-praxis which make study of scripture fruitful and a joyful event as this community is enlightened and transformed by what it sees and hears in scripture. The black theologian as the authentic subject of black theologizing is also affected by the link and basis referred to above. This subject, this theologian, can only be a committed black subject who laughs and cries with, for and in the midst of this community, one who deeply shares its fears and frustrations of the present and its hopes for the future. This authentic subject has to be a part of this community itself in order to be able to capture the audible as well as the inaudible voice of suffering as it rises up to heaven from within the valley of death, and the drowning songs of joy as they engulf the small steps of success. He or she must be part of this community in order to be able to capture and register the loneliness and the irrepressible longing for a new day and a new land that abounds in those who are exiled in far away countries.

This subject of reflection together with the entire black community is also the object of transformation and growth. The praxis of liberation in which he or she is involved transforms his or her ideological consciousness, ethical behaviour and personality. If it is a brutalizing praxis, it brutalizes the subject too. If it is a humanizing praxis, it will also humanize him or her. Since it is a communal praxis for a future of communal love and justice it ought to have a healing effect on its subject and all dimensions of his or her existence. This is the internal effect that comes simultaneously with the external impact of the praxis of liberation which Black Theology has to bring out. It has to show that as the new world is created from the ashes of the old the new man is also born from within the womb of the committed through the agency of the Spirit of Jesus Christ who is freely at work in the world of suffering discipleship.

This internal healing effect of the noble project of the creation of a new world of love and justice has to create a new man who will reflect the world he is creating and awaiting. He will be a man who reaches out in love and strives towards internal justice, in that way enlarging his community. Even his ideological, strategic and other discussions have to be permeated by the healing and purifying effects of this historical project. This is the dialectic in the pedagogy of the wilderness journey to the promised land in which we are involved. We have to become better people as the goal of a liberated Azania draws nearer.

It is also the duty of Black Theology to point out that like the situation in the wilderness journey of old all this does not happen mechanically or automatically.

Methodology of Black Theology
How do we go about thinking, talking and writing a Black Theology which will function as a creative, radicalizing and perfecting 'theory of a praxis' in the struggle for the creation of a radically new society and world for black people? How do we go about thinking, talking and writing a Black Theology which will perform a humanizing function in the circles of committed blacks who are actively engaged in the struggle for the creation of the new man for the new world? These are the two questions that embrace two areas of black existence which have to be considered simultaneously all along the desert track to the promised land of a free and just Azania.

The centre of the struggle (in streets, factories, mines, farms, kitchens and gardens of oppressors) as it is waged by blacks — young and old, men and women — where they are individually or collectively located is the starting point and focus of theological reflection. Black Theology does a three-dimensional analysis in which the Marxian tool of social analysis is used. This theology analyzes the material situation today and the position of the community that has opted for the Christian tradition as its source of transformative ideas — logical information for its formation and transformation — in the struggle. The purpose of this analysis is to discover the point at which the struggle is at a given historical moment, as well as to find out whether that acting and reflecting community has also reached that necessary level of radicality which is required for the struggle to be successful. Black Theology further analyzes the material situation in Palestine during the time of Jesus as well as the praxis of this man of Nazareth which is witnessed in scripture as it unfolded and was radicalized by qualitatively and quantitatively increasing opposition. The purpose here is to discover whether Jesus the black Messiah on the one side and the fighting and reflecting black community on the other side are at the same level of engagement and radicality in this identical struggle that develops dialectically from low point to high point, from high point to a higher point. To put it in religious language: the purpose is to find an answer to the question whether Jesus is with us in our struggle and we are with him in his struggle for our liberation. The community then makes the necessary adjustment in its struggle to be with him, side by side, or goes further with him to a higher point of radicality. This entire exercise of reflection holds both for the external as well as the internal aspects of this liberation struggle. It is in doing this that action will be corrected, radicalized and affirmed on the one side and an accumulation of the product of reflection will happen which we call Black Theology.

What elements in the material situation of the acting and reflecting community and of Jesus are analyzed? I would say all elements. When I say all, I think here of the economic, cultural, historical and religious elements. We have to analyze the economic practice of the toiling black masses to find out whether the black worker is a fighting black worker. We have to find out whether the culture of the black community activates the struggle and if it is born in and informs the community. We have to find out whether the history of the black community is a fighting black history that energizes the struggle and whether the religion of this community is an opiate of the community or a black religion of liberation, a black religion that reproduces and stimulates this community in order to go the next mile of the way in answer to the call of the black struggle. This community does all this in order to find out whether there is a correspondence between Jesus as a comprehensive subject of the liberation struggle and ourselves. This should be done to find out whether we are with him in the struggle on the one side and whether he is with us in the struggle on the other side. We have to find out whether our black culture of struggle, black history of struggle, black land of struggle are at the same level of praxis as the corresponding elements of Jesus' struggle, and vice versa. If they are not at the same level on the scale of radicality, then urgent adjustments must be made. The community has to march with him, step by step.

Are we right in looking so comprehensively at the praxis of the community in the light of the praxis of Jesus and vice versa? I would say yes. I say yes because I firmly believe that Jesus who had become the Christ for past generations and still becomes the liberator for present generations, by fighting his way from Bethlehem to Jerusalem, by fighting his way from the manger to the grave, is the event of creation of the black struggling community as a comprehensive subject. He is the event that has embedded itself so deeply and so long in this black community from the beginning of black existence, and right through the painful history of black people, that we have to admit that there is a liberative current that runs through our history, our culture, our economic praxis and our religion. And because it runs through them it continuously makes them liberative and draws them into the liberation struggle that is becoming more and more radical in intensity and goals.

NOTES

1. B. M. Magubane, *The Political Economy of Race and Class in South Africa* (New York: Monthly Review Press, 1979), p. 20: 'The struggle for control of land and labour determined the political and economic status of the African in the settlers' scheme of things'. On page 22 he further argues: 'Colonial imperialism necessitated that Africans be deprived of power, opportunity and reward for their labour . . . '

2. J. C. Adonis in his *Die afgebreekte skeidsmuur weer opgebou* points in this regard at Jan van Riebeeck's prayer in which he dedicated himself to spreading the 'true Reformed Christian doctrine . . . among these wild, cheeky people' (my translation), p. 29. Earlier in his book Adonis characterizes the Reformed teaching of the Gereformeerde Kerk (D.R.C.) in South Africa by saying: ". . . the doctrine of the Reformed Church always demanded intercession for and obedience to the government from its adherents' (my translation), p. 25. Also see J. W. De Gruchy, *Church Struggle in South Africa* (Grand Rapids, Mich.: Eerdmans, 1979): De Gruchy, and C. Villa-Vicencio, eds., *Apartheid Is a Heresy* (Cape Town: David Philip, 1983); G. D. Cloete, and D. J. Smits, eds., *A Moment of Truth* (Grand Rapids, Mich.: Eerdmans, 1984).

3. See Karl Marx, *Selected Writings in Sociology and Philosophy,* trans. Bottomore (London: Watts, 1956), pp. 54, 64, 75. See also chap. 1 in *Selected Writings*; Juan Luis Segundo, *The Liberation of Theology* (Maryknoll, N.Y.: Orbis Books, 1976), pp. 7–38.

4. Many writers on the emergence of the African Independent Churches of the Ethiopian type refer to this. To our mind, E. Roux discusses it most elaborately and systematically. See his *Time Longer Than Rope* (Madison: University of Wisconsin Press, 1964), pp. 77–86.

5. The emergence of Black Theology in our time is a continuation of this tradition.

6. I. J. Mosala, 'Black Theology Revisited', an unpublished paper read at the AZAPO Congress, Jan. 1984, p. 3.

7. E. Harsch, *South Africa: White Rule-Black Revolt* (New York: Monad Press, 1980), p. 180. In 1510 the Khoikhoi defeated F. de Almeida, the Portuguese admiral, and killed him together with 65 of his invading troops, after which the Portuguese avoided the Cape of Makana for nearly one and one half centuries.

8. Moshoeshoe realized this and attempted to forge unity and alliances with other kings in Southern Africa, even as far as Botswana, as a strategy against the European invading settlers.

9. Harsch, *South Africa*. See also Roux, *Time*, pp. 77–86.

10. The coloureds and Indians were excluded from this conception of nationalism.

11. A. Lerumo, *Fifty Fighting Years: The South African Communist Party, 1921–1971* (London: Inkululeko, 1971), p. 32.

12. When in 1934 Prime Minister Hertzog of South Africa introduced into parliament a number of segregationist bills, which included the abolition of the African vote in the Cape of Makana and the establishment of a bogus Natives Representative Council (NRC), more than 400 delegates from various religious, sport, social, civic, political, labour and educational organizations across the country (a forerunner of the UDF?) converged upon Bloemfontein and formed the All African Convention (AAC). The task of this broad umbrella organization was to organize and spearhead rejection of the Hertzog bills. But unfortunately, its leaders, most of whom were also leaders of the African National Congress, ended up co-opted into the NRC. See Harsch, *South Africa*, pp. 211–24.

13. See Harsch, *South Africa*, p. 234. See also M. Motlhabi, *Black Resistance to Apartheid* (Johannesburg: Skotaville, 1984), p. 47.

14. See Harsch, *South Africa*, p. 234.

15. See the Freedom Charter.

16. See Harsch, *South Africa*, p. 234.

17. Ibid., p. 196.

18. Magubane, *Economy*, p. 56.

19. P. Anderson, 'Portugal and the End of Ultra Colonialism', *New Left Review* 16 (1962): 102–3.

20. It is an established fact that all African rulers were also priests. They interceded with the royal ancestors on behalf of the nation and performed all necessary cultic rites before as well as after every war. Makana, for instance, was also a religious leader.

21. See Roux, *Time*; Harsch, *South Africa*; and many other writers on the emergence of the African Independent Churches in South Africa. A little later in 1912 when the ANC was formed black pastors were involved.

22. See Gayraud Wilmore, *Black Religion and Black Radicalism* (Garden City, N.Y.: Anchor Press/Doubleday, 1973).

23. On Ethiopianism, see Roux, *Time*, pp. 77–86; Harsch, *South Africa*; and B. Sundkler, *Bantu Prophets in South Africa* (London: Oxford University Press, 1961).

24. G. M. Gerhart, *Black Power in South Africa* (Berkeley: University of California Press, 1978), pp. 201–4, shows how the PAC in its political campaign in 1960 drew the pastors of the African Independent Churches into its fold.

25. S. Biko, *I Write What I Like* (London: Bowerdean, 1978), p. 30.

26. Ibid., p. 26.

27. See note 24 above. Black pastors were also involved in the leadership of the ANC right from its inception. See Motlhabi, *Black Resistance*.

28. Mr. Madzunya of the PAC called for the establishment of an African national church, but this is not synonymous with a call for a new theology. See Gerhart, *Black Power*, p. 203.

29. Biko, 'Black Consciousness and the Quest for True Humanity', in *I Write*, pp. 22, 23, argues that 'it was the missionaries who confused the people with their new religion. They scared our people with stories of hell. They painted their God as a demanding god who wanted worship or else'.

30. T. A. Mofokeng, *The Crucified among the Crossbearers—Towards a Black Christology* (Kampen, Netherlands: J. H. Kok, 1983), p. 18.

31. See Allan Boesak, *Farewell to Innocence* (Maryknoll, N.Y.: Orbis Books, 1977), p. 16.

32. See Mofokeng, *The Crucified*, chapter 4.

33. The question of the interlocutor in South African Black Theology has raised its head again after it had been answered in the 1970s. The question is raised by the involvement of a handful of whites in the black struggle. Their solidarity has led some blacks to say that this involvement has to have theological consequences at the level of the interlocutor. (This argument reminds us in a way of J. H. Cone's argument with J. Deotis Roberts. See Cone, *God of the Oppressed* [New York: Seabury Press, 1975]; Cone, *My Soul Looks Back* [Maryknoll, N.Y.: Orbis Books, 1985]; and Roberts, *Liberation and Reconciliation* [Philadelphia: Westminster Press, 1971].) In opposition to this assertion we argue that the interlocutor in Black Theology is the black community and not individuals or a collective of individuals who could, in very isolated incidents, include white individuals. Their periodical presence among blacks does not turn the black community into a multi-racial one.

Chapter 8

Black Theology and the Struggle of the Black Woman in Southern Africa
BERNADETTE I. MOSALA

Editors' Abstract

Black Theology, which seeks to be the tool of liberation for black people, has been eloquent by its silence on the oppression of black women. In its opposition to oppressive structures of the church, Black Theology does not include among such structures patriarchalism. The lesson is very clear for black women: the liberation of black women is the responsibility of black women. Neither the church, nor black male theologians, nor white women can be expected to be sensitive to the human needs of black women. This is so because 'liberation does not fall into one's lap. It must be claimed and protected. You cannot give me my liberty and I cannot give you yours'.

> The black church, like all other churches, is a male domi-
> nated church. The difficulty that black male ministers have
> in supporting the equality of women in the church and
> society stems partly from the lack of a clear liberation-
> criterion rooted in the gospel and in the present struggles
> of oppressed peoples...It is truly amazing that many black
> male ministers, young and old, can hear the message of
> liberation in the gospel when related to racism but remain
> deaf to a similar message in the context of sexism
> (J. Jones).

Black Theology, Contextual Theology and Feminist Theology
seem to be underpinned by one origin, viz. experience. For many
centuries western theology offered a particular kind of theology to
non-westerners. Non-westerners have grappled with this form of theology to the point that they resolved the form was not altogether
carved out to suit their experience. Amid all kinds of protestations
black theologians made the statement imperturbably and very firmly
that today, Black Theology had found a place 'in the sun'. Western-
ers and their supporters have come to terms with it and the sky has
not caved in. This is the theological milieu of black women today.

What has been called the objective sources of theology — scripture
and tradition — are themselves codified, collective human experience. Human experience is the starting point and the ending point of
the hermeneutical circle. 'Experience' includes experience of the divine, experience of oneself, and experience of the community and the
world, in an interacting dialectic. Received symbols, formulas, and
laws are either authenticated or not through their ability to illuminate
and interpret experience. The uniqueness of Feminist Theology lies
in its use of women's experience. The use of women's experience in
Feminist Theology explodes as a critical force, exposing classical theology — including its codified traditions, based on male experience
rather than on universal human experience. Feminist Theology
makes the sociology of theological knowledge visible, no longer hid-
den behind mysterious statements about and allusions to objectified
divine and universal authority.

Invisibility of Black Women in Black Theology
It is Jacquelyn Grant who coins the beautiful phrase 'the invisibility
of black women in Black Theology'. As a theologian herself, she no
doubt speaks from *experience*. 'If church is the body of believers, if all
believers have gifts, if all of humanity is created in the image of God,
if Jesus treated all people as persons, if the church is a democratic

body in which no one person is greater than another — then why has the church over the ages assigned its key positions to men? Why have only men played the dominant role in leading the church, spokesmen for God to the assembly of believers? And have these men throughout the history of the church not usually been ordained? Ordination appears to have conferred authority — until recently exclusively on men — to decide for and dictate to the church of God'.

The patriarchal theology that has prevailed throughout most of Christian history in most Christian traditions has rigidly barred women from ministry. The arguments for this exclusion are identical with the arguments of patriarchal anthropology. Women are denied leadership in the churches for the same reasons they are denied leadership in society. Contrary to some recent apologetics, the Christian tradition never affirmed women's inclusion in social leadership while arguing for women's exclusion from ministry based on the special nature of ministry. The arguments for women's exclusion from ministry are applications of the general theology of male headship and female subordination. This subordination, while attributed to women's physiological role in procreation, extends to an inferiority of mind and soul as well. Women are categorized as less capable than men of moral self-control and reason. They can play only a passive role in the giving and receiving of ministry. They should keep silent.

Priestly traditions also define women's 'uncleanness' in religious terms. Female bodiliness is seen as polluting and defiling the sacred. Women must be distanced from the holy. Holiness becomes a male mystery that annuls the finitude and mortality of birth from the female. Women may be baptized, but they cannot represent this process of rebirth and nourishment in the realm of male holiness. The near hysteria that erupted in recent years in the Episcopal Church when women began visibly to use the priestly sacramental symbols reveals the pathology that underlies the exclusion of women from ministry.

The pathology seems to be even more violent when the issue is not just women as preachers but women as priests. This shows the extent to which the rejection of women as maternal flesh adds another dimension beyond simple negation of women as teacher. The most extreme repugnance towards the idea of women in ministry typically is expressed in the question: 'Can you imagine a pregnant women at the altar?'

I have no doubt in my mind that God abhors the subjugation of one person by another. It does not matter who it is. I am sure God is hurt when a German suppresses a Jew, when an Englishman suppresses an

African, when a Canadian or American suppresses a Red Indian, when an Afrikaner suppresses an Englishman — and when they both sit on the African. I am sure God suffers when a man suppresses a women, or when both man and woman domineer and abuse a child.

Challenges for Women

Do women, particularly black women in this country, really want change? Perhaps I cannot be blamed for often suspecting the contrary. Yes, many women are content with the status quo. Why rock the boat? Changing the present circumstances is, in my view, not a matter of choice. Changing from the present circumstances presents a moral imperative to all who care about the Body of Christ. The church which discriminates, which negates the variety of gifts of its body, is missing out on what is authentically and rightfully church. Such negation not only represents missed opportunities and a limited view and scope, it is also dehumanizing.

Women must dismantle clericalism, which is an understanding of leadership as rule that reduces others to subjects to be governed. Clericalism, by definition, disempowers the people and turns them into 'laity' dependent on the clergy. The basic assumption of clericalism is that the people have no direct access to the divine. The clergy monopolize the instruments of mediation between God and the laity. The clergy alone have authorized theological training; they alone are authorized to preach, to teach, to administer the church. They alone possess sacramental power. Ministry in the community of liberation assumes that some people have special gifts and may play particular and different roles. But this specialization is for the sake of empowering the whole community. Teachers teach to overcome the gap between those who know and those who do not. Their teaching gradually creates fellow teachers who can teach others.

The community as a whole becomes empowered to articulate the faith and to speak the word to each other. The sort of teaching that perpetuates the gap between teaching authority and the 'ignorant' is not real teaching, but the clericalization of learning.

It is necessary for the church to realize that if Jesus is the liberator of the oppressed, all of the oppressed must be liberated. But liberation does not fall into one's lap. It must be claimed and protected. You cannot give me my liberty and I cannot give you yours. Unless we are willing to exercise our right to claim power and to do something about bringing about the changes we believe are necessary we will remain the invisible creatures who are always on the outside looking in. Church leaders need to be challenged when they claim 'women do not want women priests', or 'my church is not ready for the ordination of women', or 'we are not ready for church unity'. All the divisive decisions that have been made in the church have been made by men. Women have never been consulted. The church seems to be willing to re-educate people on every issue except the issue of the dignity and equality of women. We must challenge this gap in the search for a new way of being the church.

James Forman has this to say about women:

> The strength of the women overwhelmed me. Here they were in jail, but their spirits seemed to rise each minute. They were yelling at the jailer, cursing, singing, ready to fight if someone came to their cell to mistreat them. Images of other strong black women resisting slavery and servitude flooded my mind. I thought of Georgia Mae Turner and Lecretia Collins and the young girls in the cell block next to me now as the modern-day Harriet Tubmans, Sojourner Truths and all those proud black women who did not allow slavery to break their spirits... As I thought about the women protesting their arrest, I knew that the black liberation movement would escalate, for too many young people were involved. Most of the women in the cells were very young, one of them only fourteen.

Chapter 9

On Violence: A Township Perspective
BUTI TLHAGALE

Editors' Abstract
In this article the author examines the current South African situation of political 'unrest' from a black perspective. He then proceeds to make a critical assessment of the moral principles of a just violent struggle in the light of the South African situation. This assessment is further critically exposed to the gospel imperatives. The conclusion is hardly astounding. Victims of oppression can only remain indifferent at their own peril. This article first appeared in Leadership, *February 1986.*

> Hammer your ploughshares into swords, your sickles into spears (Joel: 3:10)

This essay deliberately deals with a Black Theology of self-defence or self-affirmation in order to distance ourselves consciously from the following two perspectives. The first is the perspective that describes the direct assault (offensive acts) on the state, state institutions, state servants and on the symbols of the capitalist order as 'unrest' or violence without any qualification.

The second distanciation involves the traditional 'Christian' perspective that speaks of non-violence at all costs while institutionalized violence is part of the South African way of life. The crushing might of the police force and the army is periodically employed to stamp out resistance in the black townships or engage in pre-emptive strikes against suspected opponents of the apartheid system in the neighbouring territories.

Different Perspectives on the Current 'Unrest'

The current state of emergency (declared in July 1985) calls to mind the 1961 state of emergency which blacks referred to then as police dictatorship. Today's treason trials recall the mass trials of the early sixties that had been aimed at crushing popular movements of resistance to the tyranny of the state. The black people then resisted the badge of slavery, the 'passes' and the pass laws, with every might. Passes were burnt. Boycotts and strikes were organized. These are comparable to the current school and consumer boycotts.[1] The difference is that today the liberation struggle has become the focal point of young people as never before.

The killings that took place in 1960 and in 1976/77 were mainly the result of police intervention. But so too in 1984/85, when more than 500 people were killed as a result of police intervention. It is usually reported that these people died 'during actions where security forces had to protect property and peaceful communities'.[2] More than 230 black people were killed by other black people during the 1984/85 uprisings.

The intensity of anger and 'violence' that has been seen since September 1984 to today is unparalleled in recent South African history. It all started with the refusal to pay house rentals in the Vaal Triangle and in other areas of the Orange Free State. Members of the community councils were seen as being responsible for the hardships of the black urban people. They therefore became the targets of angry and frustrated people. At any rate these councils were seen as an imposition on the black people by government. It therefore came as no surprise when some of the council members were driven out of their homes and removed mercilessly[3]. But then such a harsh punishment was equally meted out to persons suspected of being informers. Both property and the business premises of people associated directly or indirectly with the local government have been destroyed. Police killings led to more police killings. And so in the East Rand, Transvaal, and in the Eastern Cape, political funerals led to other deaths[4]. Black people turned out by the thousands in an expression of solidarity on these occasions; the anger of the people was palpable. There were other mysterious deaths such as those of the attorney Mrs. Victoria Mxenge of Durban and of the community leader Matthews Goniwe and others of Cradock. In the wake of Mrs. Mxenge's death more than fifty people died in and around Durban.[5]

The situation has been exacerbated by the fact that a significant number of schools came to a standstill and the young people have been pushed irrevocably into the forefront of the political struggle.

During the turmoil of the 1960s African political leaders had little hope that non-violent pressures could bring about radical change in South Africa. The apartheid system has always been understood and felt as an inherently violent system. When the African National Congress and the Pan African Congress openly resorted to violence as a means of bringing about radical political change, a new chapter in black politics had begun.

What the white community perceives as 'unrest', as sheer displays of savagery when persons associated with the apartheid system are burned to death by the application of the 'necklace' — the burning tyre — the black community interprets differently. Indeed the death of persons is to be regretted. But what seems to be a senseless destruction of life and property, of schools and buses and delivery vehicles, is in fact seen by blacks, especially young people, as an aggressive statement of a radical protest, of self-affirmation, a calculated tactic to compel the government to reckon with the frustrated aspirations of the black people.

What is seen as violence by most whites is also experienced as violence by blacks. But then blacks attach a radically different significance to it. It is a protest beyond moral indignation, beyond words. It is a direct assault on the apartheid system.

When blacks destroy community facilities, most whites perceive it as short-sightedness, but blacks on the other hand have virtually no stake in the protection and maintenance of public property in the townships. For years blacks have been referred to as 'temporary sojourners' in the urban areas. The psychological impact of forced homelessness — of 'exile experience' as it were — has now taken its toll. The reversal of this process as a result of the Wiehahn and Riekert reports and the subsequent labour legislation of 1979 have not yet had the desired effect. The inane declaration of a dual citizenship for the black people has had even less effect.[6] The denial of the permanence of the black people in the urban areas has resulted in the direct denial of the development and improvement of the physical environment of the townships.

The litany of denials: of home ownership, of industry, of business premises, of investment in cultural facilities, etc., coupled with the iniquitous influx control system and the extremely limited availability of housing in the urban areas, have all created a deep sense of non-belonging. Besides, blacks have also been denied the right of participating meaningfully in the planning and management of their own local affairs. The establishment of the community councils was a unilateral decision on the part of government. This explains why some councillors have been driven out of their homes, and their property petrol bombed.[7·] Some councils have been dismantled. Community councils are seen as part and parcel of the apartheid system. The series of denials and government highhandedness have led to the reaping of the whirlwind.[8]

The government insists through the media that the current 'unrest' is caused either by the black political organizations, hence the treason trials in Pretoria and Pietermaritzburg, and/or by the 'criminal elements' in the black community.[9] The Congress of South African Students has been banned presumably because it is thought to be responsible for the upheavals. To blame individuals or groups of people for the situation of intense political 'unrest' is to fail to come to grips with the deep-seated discontent of the people. In any situation of political upheaval excesses on the part of the oppressed are to be expected. But this should in no way be confused with the general upsurge of the people in their demand for total freedom.

To blame hooligans or the African National Congress for the so-called unrest is tantamount to burying one's head in the sand and thereby refusing to acknowledge that the apartheid system is the source of the problems. Finally, short of taking up arms like the South African Defence Force or like black political oganizations that have been forced into exile, the present generation — in the complex scenario of consumer boycotts, work stoppages, work stay-aways, school disruptions, protests, the destruction of selected targets, the merciless killings of 'collaborators', etc. — is irrevocably committed to bursting the chains of the apartheid system. The state, through its agencies, has been thrown headlong into the turmoil. And as the dialectical relationship between the enforcers of the unjust laws and those who resist intensifies, the situation ceases to be simply a situation of 'unrest' but becomes a veritable violent struggle between the oppressor and the oppressed.

The heightened level of political awareness pushes blacks further and further into the violent struggle for freedom. Blacks do not want violence anymore than the white electorate — but then this mode of being, of resisting, is highly visible. It demands immediate attention. It confuses the government, destabilizes the country and solicits support from the international community. The violent upheaval therefore, far from being an accidental happening and/or an expression of hostility, is in fact calculated to precipitate an abrupt end to racism and political domination.

This struggle is characterized by a massive upsurge of the black people, especially young people. The so-called peaceful people in the community, even though they are not directly involved in the upheaval, undoubtedly share the sentiments of those who are in the forefront of the liberation struggle. So much for the word 'unrest'. This then brings us to the second distanciation: the traditional Christian perspective on violence.

Christian Perspective on Violence

The Christian discussion on violence tends to revolve around nuclear or bacteriological warfare. The violent struggle of the oppressed people against white domination and against the ruthlessness of capitalism has simply been dismissed as 'terrorism' and therefore immoral. The ambivalence that emerges from the ethical analysis of the violent struggle of the people has simply been shrugged off in favour of the status quo.

The Christian tradition has tended to uphold 'non-violence' as a universal principle while within the very same tradition some speak of non-violence as a strategy rather than a principle. As a strategy it is therefore seen as a Christian attitude that refuses to retaliate:

> You have heard it was said: 'An eye for an eye and a tooth
> for a tooth'. But now I tell you: do not take revenge on
> someone who wrongs you (Mt. 5:38-39).

The ideal of 'peace at all costs' has permeated Christian thinking even though in certain Christian traditions exceptions are made. In expressing the 'peace at all costs' doctrine, Martin Luther King, Jr., has this to say about non-violence:

> ...finally it reaches the opponent and so stirs his consci-
> ence that reconciliation becomes a reality.[10]

The South African black experience denies the above. For almost a century now the inherently violent apartheid system has simply entrenched itself with all the viciousness imaginable. There are no signs of reconciliation on the horizon.

There is of course another tradition. It was articulated by John Paul II in his 1982 'Day of Peace Message':

> Christians have a right and even a duty to protect their
> existence and freedom by proportionate means against an
> unjust aggressor.

The majority of the black people see the white Nationalist Party as having no moral legitimacy to leadership and to government. It has not been elected by the black people but simply imposed itself on the people and denied them basic human rights.

The Christian tradition recognizes the legitimacy of the use of violence to defend the rights of a given state.[11] But then from a township perspective the South African state is essentially a repressive state. The different branches of the state apparatus are seen as executing and maintaining the repression. The army is frequently remembered for its occupation of a foreign territory, Namibia, and for its incursions into Angola. It is equally remembered for its 'pre-emptive strikes' in Lesotho, Mozambique and Botswana — leaving in its wake destroyed human life and property. In the townships where it is currently deployed under the state of emergency, it is said to have succeeded not only in destroying life but also in alienating the black community.[12]

The 'political police' are credited with harassment and even torture. Detainees have died in prisons.[13] The explanations of the causes of death are taken by the township people with a grain of salt. The courts mete out punishment to those who flout the apartheid laws such as the pass laws. The different administrative departments enforce removals of the black people. Finally blacks are excluded from the electoral system. They are precluded from any access to political power and from meaningful participation in the economic system of the country.

In the eyes of the black people, therefore, the state has no legitimacy. Co-optation through the establishment of the homelands has still not lent any meaningful legitimacy to the state. Can a state without any power-base in or even sympathy from the majority of the people have a moral right to rule over the majority or even have a moral right to use violence in order to preserve an intrinsically violent political system?

When blacks resort to violent means of redressing the wrongs of the apartheid system, it is perceived by blacks not only as a right to resist 'in the name of an elementary requirement of justice' but also as a duty to resist the crushing repression of the racist regime.

Military Service
Concerning military service, a document of the Vatican II has this to say:

> All those who enter the military service in loyalty to their country shall look upon themselves as the custodians of

the security and freedom of their fellow countrymen; and
when they carry out their duty properly, they are contributing to the maintenance of peace *(Gaudium et Spes,* no.
79).

In other words some Christian traditions do approve of the maintenance of an army that serves not only as a deterrence but that can
also resort to the use of violence in order to protect the freedom of a
country's citizens. In the South African context, this can only apply in
its fullness to white South Africans. In the first place, blacks have not
been recruited into the army in large numbers, presumably because
they are not the 'real' citizens of South Africa and therefore have no
stake in South Africa.

Secondly, the freedom that is to be safeguarded is the freedom of
whites. Blacks have not experienced the meaning of freedom in
South Africa for centuries. They are denied the freedom of
movement, of association, of choosing their own place of residence.
They lack freedom of speech, etc. The soldiers are therefore 'the
custodians of the security and freedom' of the white people. In the
state of emergency, they have not contributed to the 'maintenance of
peace'; their callous behaviour has indeed strained race relations. In
the eyes of the township people there is no difference between the
security police and the army. They are birds of a feather. Their *raison
d'être* is the protection of whites. Their ruthless killing of black South
Africans, even the innocent people in the neighbouring states, simply
puts the army in the camp of the enemy. Some black people have also
been ruthless in killing those who are seen as enemies and at times
innocent lives have been lost in the process. But then the country is
virtually in a state of civil war.

A significant number of young white people resist conscription.
They see it as morally wrong especially because they know that they
are likely to be sent into the black townships where they are likely to
shoot black people, their neighbours — not so much for the maintenance of 'law and order' but rather for an ideology, for a forced segregation of races, for a status quo that seeks to retain political and
economic power in white hands.

The church, through the appointment of military chaplains, is seen
to give direct moral support and therefore approval to the army
which is an agency of the repressive state apparatus. The army is the
'killing machine' of the state. The enemies of the state are those
blacks who resist the apartheid system and who fight the illegal presence of South Africa in Namibia.

An option for the poor, even though it is undoubtedly a 'spiritual paternalism', would mean a withdrawal from any direct or indirect involvement with the army which is clearly partisan in the South African context. Accusations levelled against the army range through harassment of innocent people, searching the houses of black people, cases of rape, of beating and even shooting people while they run away. The police respond by saying it is only about one percent of the force that is involved in these 'aberrations'. Such accusations cannot go unnoticed. The church that gives moral/spiritual support to such an army cannot remain untainted. The church necessarily finds itself in an ambivalent situation, for both the soldiers and the people they kill belong to the same church. The army is seen by blacks as fighting for the maintenance of white domination while blacks see themselves as fighting for the right to be free in their own country. A choice has to be made. Racial factors play a decisive role concerning loyalties to specific racial groupings or class factions. At times the gospel imperatives play a secondary role. The South African situation can easily be said to be a case in point.

Whilst the black people have a conviction that they have a right to reclaim their fatherland and uphold their dignity and freedom, they do not have the lethal instruments of war which would enable them to protect themselves. As a subjugated people only stones and the ability to destroy and render the country 'ungovernable' remain the immediate instruments of self-assertion. The strategy of ungovernability can be dangerous and costly. But then this is the price blacks will have to pay en route to the land of freedom.

The church therefore holds incompatible and contradictory positions. On the one hand it gives its blessings to the South African military service by allowing its personnel to give spiritual support to the Christian white soldiers and on the other hand it preaches restraint to the black oppressed masses. It participates indirectly in the military might of the state whilst at the same time it decries the repression of the state.

'Jus Ad Bellum'

The nagging question that still needs to be answered is whether a violent struggle by black South Africans can ever be justifiable or indeed whether the violent repression by the apartheid regime is justifiable. Cast in the mould of the classical tradition of the just violent struggle, the township perspective yields the following argument.

The semblance of order and peaceful co-existence has been shattered by the spiral of a violent struggle that has engulfed the black townships. The demand of the black people, especially the youth, is, firstly, the abolition of the present political order and the establishment of a non-racial, democratic political system on the basis of one man, one vote. Secondly, the present exploitative capitalist system ought to give way to a more equitable socialist system that will develop an economic programme with the view to making amends in those areas where the apartheid economic system has simply played havoc and left in its wake human misery.

There is no solution in sight to the present political conflict as the government clings to its racist policies of denying blacks a meaningful citizenship, of upholding the Population Registration Act and the Group Areas Act, of refusing the release of political prisoners, etc. Instead the government has responded to the black violent struggle with the might of the army and the security forces. In the following, that struggle is examined in light of five tenets of the just war doctrine.

Violence as a Last Resort:

There is a rapidly growing belief that violence is virtually the only answer left in the face of the intransigence of the government. The Pharaoh-like ruling Nationalist Party refused to acknowledge the peaceful, non-violent black struggle prior to the establishment of the now banned military wings of the African National Congress and the Pan-African Congress. Even then non-violent, peaceful resistance has continued to this day but to no avail. The current language and practice of violence has come to stay. The violence of blacks is in response to the violence of the apartheid system that has kept blacks in humiliating subjugation. The costs in terms of human suffering and even death are incalculable.

The present violence by blacks is therefore understood as an act of self-defence against a system and a people that practice oppression and exploitation. It is hoped that through violence, justice will eventually be established.

There is no communication between the genuine black leaders and the government. Most black leaders are either in prison or in exile.

Government frowns upon all those who communicate with the African National Congress in search of political solutions.[14] Diplomatic pressures on the government have not achieved the desired effect. So desperate have large sections of the black people become that the present system can no longer continue without disruption. Whereas the older generation of blacks can tolerate injustice and

pain, not so the present young generation. If apartheid has to continue, it will seemingly have to be over their dead bodies.

Disinterested Authority:

There was a time when the just war theorists looked up to a disinterested international authority to intervene in situations of gross injustice. The United Nations has failed dismally to persuade South Africa
to move, for example, out of Namibia. Nor has it succeeded in persuading the Pretoria regime to abandon its racist ways and treat
blacks as equal citizens. White South Africa has become a law unto
itself. South Africa does not recognize the UN as a disinterested
party simply because the UN condemns in unequivocable terms the
intrinsically evil apartheid system.

The major western powers, viz., the U.S., Britain and West Germany, connive at the evils of the apartheid system and therefore fail
to bring any measure of meaningful pressure to bear on South Africa.
America's 'constructive engagement policy' is a classic example of
connivance. This leads to the belief that these powers have vested
interests in South Africa despite the denials. The refusal to apply
meaningful sanctions, claiming that blacks would suffer, is in fact a
refusal to help in the dismantling of the apartheid system. Against the
background of the powerlessness of the United Nations and the connivance of the major western powers, black South Africans are left to
their own limited resources to abolish the unjust political order. It is
therefore against this background that the violent struggle proceeds
apace in·spite of the declaration of the state of emergency.

Competent Authority:

The complexity of the South African situation defies the neatly
worked out moral principles of the classical tradition. If a violent
struggle is to be undertaken at all it should be conducted by a compe-
tent authority. The assumption is that violent struggles are waged by
one state against another. The classical tradition in its moral principles does not envisage an unjust aggressor emerging from within the
boundaries of a single state. Historically, white South Africa could be
viewed as an unjust aggressor for the indigenous black people were
never really seen as forming one single nation with the European
people as they began to settle in South Africa. White South Africans
proceeded to distance themselves from the indigenous people and
even maintained the division by law.

In a situation of oppression recognized leaders of the oppressed
masses constitute the legitimate authority to lead the masses in revolt

against the perpetrators of injustice. In order to prevent this, the government bans or imprisons the credible leadership. The banning of the African National Congress and the Pan African Congress in the early sixties — then the banning of the Black Consciousness oganizations, the Christian Institute and a host of other organizations in 1977 — prevents the black leadership from communicating with the government. If the present violent struggle does not seem to have any distinct leadership, it is because the leadership is not allowed to survive for long in public without running the risk of imprisonment. Nonetheless while violence continues, spokesmen on behalf of the oppressed masses articulate the aspirations of the people and also spell out the conditions that would need to be fulfilled if the true foundations of peace are to be made at all. Positions expressed are generally in line with what the imprisoned leaders would themselves put forward. The conditions laid forth by Bishop Tutu or the churches and other anti-apartheid organizations reflect the aspirations of the masses. If the present violent struggle appears to be leaderless and therefore failing to satisfy the moral principles of the classical tradition, it is simply because the traditional forms of leadership are interferred with by the government, but they do not lose their identity and competence.

Proportionality:

The ethic of force further demands that there be a proportion between the damages suffered in consequence of the perpetration of a grave injustice and the damages that would be inflicted in a violent struggle aimed at repressing an unjust order such as the apartheid system. First, the damages suffered under the repression of the system of racial domination are not always quantifiable. The apartheid machine has forcibly relocated more than 500 000 people in an attempt to streamline the apartheid policy. Thousands have been charged with pass law offences. Thousands of blacks are in exile. The influx control system has generally destroyed family life for those who are denied the freedom of movement and the freedom to sell one's labour where there is a lucrative market. Imprisonment, torture and death in detention still continue on the basis of one's skin colour. The list of the crimes of the apartheid system is endless. That is why this political system is considered to be 'the most vicious since Nazism'.

The violence conducted by the African National Congress in order to blow up installations or government buildings can hardly be comparable to the human suffering caused by the apartheid system.[15]

Lives have indeed been lost in the process. But the South African Defence Force has been swift in retaliating, destroying more lives and destabilizing the neighbouring countries and holding them to ransom.

The current violent struggle since September 1984 has claimed more than 760 lives. More than 500 of these have been reportedly shot by the security force apparently whilst in the line of duty, 'protecting lives and property'. The loss of lives would undoubtedly have been much lower if the troops were kept out of the townships. Whilst any loss of life and property is to be regretted, there is hardly any comparison between the damages caused by the repressive apartheid system and the damages that are currently being incurred in the present political upheaval. The current violence may ebb, but the conviction that violence is the last resort has taken root. This conviction has come to manifest itself in the following way.

Reasonable Prospect of Success:
The current cycle of political upheaval is simply an intense, arresting moment in the cumulative process of resistance since the appearance of the African National Congress on the political scene of South Africa in 1912. This violent struggle has been and continues to be a costly sacrifice as far as human lives and material possessions are concerned. But its outcome, hardly measurable in terms of immediate gains, has altered the course of history for the oppressive classes and the masses of the oppressed people. Whilst on the face of it the violent struggle by blacks appears to have had only a ripple effect on the apartheid arrangements themselves, at the base of it all, it has introduced a serious crack into the granite foundation of the apartheid edifice.

Violent upheavels attract world attention. The display of harsh police behaviour towards blacks on the TV screens hardly endears the apartheid regime to members of the world community in general. The banning of the media coverage of 'unrest' situations is a belated suppression of information[16]. The world response to the South African violent political situation has been that of increasing pressure on the South African government, with foreign governments eventually imposing limited sanctions and sixteen American universities and thirteen American cities abandoning their investments[17]. The effect of sanctions has been interpreted more in terms of a growing repugnance for the apartheid policy. If the present sanctions and the severing of cultural ties have virtually no impact on the economy they nonetheless have a psychological effect on the country. Demands for 'reform' from outside South Africa do not go unheeded by the South

African government:

> The more we reform, the more we are condemned. The further we move away from the era of apartheid, the fiercer the international campaign against us.[18]

In South Africa itself, the corporate community, 'prompted by enlightened self-interest and a broader social responsibility', has also intensified its campaign for reform[19]. Some businessmen have even opened up communication lines with the banned African National Congress.[20]

The government itself has responded to both internal and external pressure. It has extended citizenship to all black people — without granting them political rights. There is a possibility of creating a 'fourth chamber' for the black people. This would be a good excuse to have the country in turmoil. There is also a promise about relaxing the much hated influx control system. So far these are only promises. But the government can no longer go back on its word. It has been said that 'reforms' predate the events of September 1984. For example the labour legislation was changed in 1979. But this change is partly the result of the 1976 upheavals. The inescapable conclusion is that limited violence, costly though it might have been, has undoubtedly attracted the attention of the world community and the local conservative corporate community. Pressure has been exerted on government. Shifts in the apartheid policy have been made and there is no going back.

A Theological Turn

Whilst the logic of the ethic of force when viewed from a township perspective does seem to support at a rational level the justifiability of a violent struggle as a last resort, the gospel imperatives on the other hand seem to challenge the adequacy of the moral principles of a just violent struggle.

Hard-sayings

The criticisms levelled against biblical literalism in scriptural interpretation and against the selective use of biblical texts out of context (proof-texting) notwithstanding, a host of scriptural hard-sayings continue to plague the minds of the oppressed Christians.[21]

— 'If you love those who love you, what reward have you?...' (Mt. 5:46).
— 'You have heard that it was said, "An eye for an eye, and a tooth for a tooth". But now I tell you: Do not take revenge on some-

one who wrongs you' (Mt. 5:38-39).
— 'Father forgive them...' (Lk. 23:24).
— 'Love your enemies and pray for your persecutors' (Mt. 5:44).
— 'Blessed are the peacemakers, for they shall be called the children of God' (Mt. 5:9).

These citations and so too the entire thrust of the Sermon on the Mount (Lk. 6:17-37) not only do not make sense in the face of the continuing repression and the barbarous behaviour of the servants of the state but they also tend to cultivate fatalistic attitudes amongst the oppressed who look forward to the 'fullness of time' that hardly appears on the horizon. The fact of the matter is that for more than two centuries large sections of the white Christian community have continued to treat blacks as 'kaffirs' and as servants and not as friends so that the example set by the Master that all men are equal remains an empty expression (Jn. 15:15). Christians have been commanded to 'love one another just as I love you' (Jn. 15:12). In a South Africa where the Group Areas Act, the Separate Amenities Act, the Population Registration Act, etc., and concepts of 'own affairs' and ethnic identity reign supreme, trust, mutuality and friendship remain foreign and indeed inimical to the official policy of the repressive state.

The black experience therefore appears throughout the last centuries as an experience of the wilderness. Thus South Africa under white domination continues to be a 'Meribah', as it were, a 'Massah' where the black people are exposed to an unending test by fire for no 'apparent reason' while the wicked racists and capitalists thrive and continue to deal treacherously. Like the psalmist, a black living in South Africa would ask:

> Why is it that I came from the womb to behold toil and grief,
> and my days are spent in shame? (Ps. 20:18).

So shattering is the experience of oppression, deprivation and humiliation that the experience of godlessness amongst sections of the black population is here to stay. And so too are the growing convictions of atheism and communism that feed on the devastating scourge of apartheid Christianity.

Man as Centre
Apart from the 'hard-sayings' of the scriptures another dimension of puzzlement derives from the perspective of traditional western ethics. The human-centred strand is said to be dominant in western ethics in spite of the biblical morality that makes God the primary referent and not man. James Gufstafson's recent theological work centres around

this theme.[22] Man has been traditionally seen as the chief end of all creation, thus nature is at the service of man. Rightness or wrongness is determined in relation to the good of man. Man therefore is assumed to be 'ultimate value'.

Even this traditional perspective that has mistakenly established man as the centre of the universe has been unable to burst the apartheid belief that the black people are essentially different from the white people. Arguments have shifted over the years from genetic to cultural differences. In the final analysis the differences are still there — whatever they are, the upshot of this perspective is that it is not man *qua* man who is the measure of things, but a different kind of man, a white man. Thus God is at the service not of all men but some men. The practice of the apartheid system is a ratification of this conviction. The belief held by the universal church, that all men are created in the likeness of God, and the implications of such a belief are completely shut out by the apartheid system of racial segregation and the myth of racial superiority.

Such beliefs and perceptions, rightly or wrongly, propel sections of the black people headlong against the wall. Opting for violence as a strategy to end apartheid therefore derives from a complex set of intermeshing factors, namely: the legacy of pain and bitterness, of repression and alienation and of empty promises of radical political reform; the continuation of racism; the tenacious clinging to the tenets of Christian faith and yet denying them in practice; the ever-increasing cost of living and the growing unemployment — all these factors coalesce and create a desperate situation that cries to heaven for justice.

Signs of the Times

Such a desperate situation, far from crushing the burning desire to be free, has unleashed new energies especially amongst the young black people who have sprung forward to resist injustice. The anger of the weak has confounded the mighty (1 Cor. 1:27). Hundreds of young people have experienced detention without trial. Since the state of emergency, more than 2000 people have been detained.[23]

Some of the young people have laid down their lives for the sake of justice — inexorably pursuing the model of Christ who died at the hands of his persecutors. This supreme sacrifice is in line with the noble tradition of those who have been in prison for more than two decades or those forced into exile for demanding 'simple justice'.

The desire for freedom has been rekindled, hence the relentless effort to subvert the inherently violent socio-political order. The fact that the gospel or the life-history of Christ makes no room for the use of violence to right the wrongs of society remains a massive *scandal* amongst the oppressed. And yet the story of Christ is a story of a series of subversions. He was continually in conflict with the socio-religious and political order of his day.

He touched lepers (the unclean), healed on a Sabbath, cancelled debts, sat at table with debtors. The Gospels are full of instances of radical departure from tradition:

> 'You have heard that it was said...' (Mt. 5:38).
>
> or 'Have you never read...' (Mk. 2:23).
>
> or 'But it is not so among you...' (Mk. 10:43).
>
> or 'Who are my mother and my brothers?' (Mk. 3:33).

Belo in his *A Materialist Reading of the Gospel of Mark* describes this subversion as the 'tearing of the old symbolic order, the bursting of the old order'.[24]

The rekindled desire to be free and the intensive assault on the apartheid institutions are not incompatible with the tradition of subversion modelled on the person of Christ. In fact Christian discipleship demands the subversion of the oppressive socio-political order in order to establish justice and consequently peace.

Conclusion

Unless genuine radical socio-political change is experienced by township and village people, violence is bound to break out intermittently. The meaningful participation in the political process is imperative. Participation must be seen to be real and not a token involvement. But so too the participation in the economy of the country. The apartheid market system favours the retention of privileges of power, wealth and income in the white community. The dispossessed must be seen to have access to the economic resources of the land. If these changes take place, only then can South Africa begin to talk about 'the things that make for peace'. Change in the political arena must be accompanied by change in the economic system. If violence is to be avoided and peace to be established then apartheid must be uprooted completely. Nothing less than the fulfillment of this simple demand will do.

NOTES

1. *Race Relations Survey 1984* (Johannesburg: South African Institute of Race Relations, 1985), pp. 64–80.
2. *The Citizen*, 19 Oct. 1985.
3. *Race Relations*, pp. 82–84.
4. *Race Relations*, p. 73.

5. *The Weekly Mail*, 9 Aug. 1985; *Indicator SA* 3, no. 3 (1985).

6. *The Star*, 2 Sept. 1985.

7. *Indicator SA* 3, no. 2 (1985).

8. Ibid., p. 9.

9. See T. Mazwai, 'Caught in Crossfire', *Indicator SA* 2, no. 2 (1985): 10–11.

10. Martin Luther King, Jr., *The Words of Martin Luther King*, ed. C. King (New York: Newmarket, 1983), p. 79.

11. National Conference of Catholic Bishops, *The Challenge of Peace: God's Promise and Our Response. A Pastoral Letter on War and Peace* (3 May 1983), p. 24.

12. *Race Relations*, pp. 95–101.

13. Ibid., pp. 758–70.

14. *The Citizen*, 5 Nov. 1985.

15. *Race Relations*, 95–101.

16. *The Star*, 5 Nov. 1985.

17. 'Disinvestment: The Myths Examined', *Leadership* 4, no. 3 (1985): 71–79; *The Star*, 12 Sept. 1985; *The Star*, 26 Sept. 1985.

18. State President, quoted in *The Business Day*, 11 Jan. 1985.

19. *The Star*, 26 Sept. 1985; *The Star*, 16 Sept. 1985.

20. *Leadership* 4, no. 3 (1985): 25.

21. S. Schneider, 'New Testament Reflections on Peace and Nuclear Arms', in *Catholics and Nuclear War*, ed. P. Murnion (New York: Crossroad, 1983).

22. J. Gustafson, *Ethics from a Theocentric Perspective*, 2 vols. (Chicago: University of Chicago Press, 1981).

23. *Indicator SA* 3, no. 2 (1985): 3; *The Star*, 4 Nov. 1985.

24. Fernando Belo, *A Materialist Reading of the Gospel of Mark* (Maryknoll, N.Y.: Orbis Books, 1981), p. 111.

Chapter 10

Christianity, Black Theology and Liberating Faith
JULIAN KUNNIE

Editors' Abstract

Black Theology is the fundamental instrument of collective empowerment. In this role Black Theology takes seriously the psychic aspect of the struggle for liberation. Revolutionary consciousness, another name for faith, *is the precondition for a collective awakening of black people in the interests of black liberation from capitalist racist oppression and exploitation. The ideological framework which Black Consciousness provides for Black Theology is a salutary reminder of the need not to neglect this psychic dimension of liberation. For people must believe in the possibility of a successful liberation struggle before they can commit themselves to participating in it. The most obvious modus operandi open to Black Theology for recovering the psychic aspect of liberation is through a historical, hermeneutical connection with the 'African tradition to preserve' the 'authenic Africanity' of Black Theology itself. From the historical resources of African traditions black people have and can continue to draw weapons with which to deal with death. The faith of an embattled African must come to terms with death. The contemporary political scene in Azania where hundreds of black people face up to supremely sophisticated military technology exemplifies this 'will to die' which is possible through a faith whose historical roots go deep.*

Faith in God does not supplant history so that present
conditions become an insignificant matter to believers;
neither should involvement in history so absorb the black
man of faith that he forgets God's place in the current
struggle. Because he can hope in the future, he can best,
under God, oppose the dehumanizing schemes of this
world and the systems of the present to the point of perfecting meaningful change (Major Jones, *Black Awareness: A Theology of Hope*).

Introduction

The majority of black people in Azania is of Christian (up to seventy
percent) affiliation, the remainder being adherents of African traditional religions, Islam or Hinduism. It is now common knowledge
among enlightened people that the religion imported by the missionaries basically functioned in the interests of European economic and
political colonialism to the detriment of the Azanian people. Christianity became *the* major ideological instrument of oppression of the
indigenous people and indoctrinated non-violent resistance and pacifism even in the face of the encroachment of African land by the
European settlers.

We contend that Christianity, as with all world religions, is essentially good for the growth of humankind; it is a particular hermeneutic of Christianity which has been responsible for the legitimation
of racist oppression and peaceful coping with colonialist oppression.
In any prevailing situation religion can be instrumental as a liberating
force or cynically employed to produce alienation.[1] It is the distorted
and superficial interpretation of the biblical revelation which has
been responsible for the subjugation of the minds and bodies of the
Azanian people. Christianity as perpetuated by major, mainline,
western-oriented churches in Azania has been more accommodating
than revolutionary.

In this paper we will argue that Christianity, generically, is indeed a
religion of liberation of humankind, both on a psychic and systemic
level, empowering us to engage in decisive revolutionary struggle in
Azania. Black Theology as a construct of theological systematization
reinforces this contention.

Christianity: A Religion of Liberation

Christianity, as typical of religious faiths, is geared towards upgrading
the quality of human existence on all levels: psychic, social, political,
economic and cultural; it is unique in that God's participation in
human upliftment is revealed in the personhood and event of Jesus
Christ. The account of the Christian revelation as narrated in the

biblical scriptures substantiates a central unequivocal truism: that God is a God of justice and liberation of all humanity for all time whose liberative character was best exemplified in the life, death and resurrection of the person of Jesus Christ. Gibson Winter states:

> The Biblical heritage among others affirms the ultimate power of the divine mystery over every evil force. This is the heart of the Biblical affirmation of the oneness of God.[2]

Juan Segundo, the Latin American theologian, clarifies the essence of the Christian message in his *Liberation of Theology*. In describing the theologies of liberation formulated in the ethos of militarized oppression in Central and South America, Segundo re-evaluates the Christian implication of the gospel. He says:

> They [Christians espousing liberation] would maintain that the longstanding stress on individual salvation in the next world represents a distortion of Jesus' message. He was concerned with man's full and integral liberation, a process which is already at work in history and which makes use of historical means. They would maintain that the church does not possess any sort of magical effectiveness where salvation is concerned but rather liberating factors in its faith and its liturgy ... They would also maintain that there are not two separate orders — one being a supernatural order outside history and the other being a natural order inside history; that instead one and the same grace raises human beings to a supernatural level and provides them with the means they need to achieve their true destiny within one and the same historical process.[3]

This perception of Christianity with God being viscerally and intrinsically involved in the realm of human society is diametrically opposed to the Calvinistic ethic developed by European Christians, which viewed God as totally transcendent and uninvolved in the goings on of human beings. Injustice and exploitation were considered the fate of persons, foreordained by God. In his critique of Protestantism and its legitimation of capitalism, Max Weber wrote:

> It [the traditional Calvinist Christianity] gave me the comforting assurance that the unequal distribution of the goods of this world was a special dispensation of Divine Providence, which in these differences, as in particular grace, pursue secret ends unknown to people. Calvin him-

self had made the much quoted statement that only when
people were poor did they remain obedient to God.[4]

Incidentally, it is the Calvinist interpretation which the white Afrikaner group in South Africa employs to justify its policy of racism
and colonialism. After all, the whites in South Africa adamantly
profess that they are Christians and are acting out the precepts of the
Christian gospel. Sheila Patterson writes:

> And it was the Old Testament and the doctrines of Calvin
> that moulded the Boer (South African of Dutch descent)
> into the Afrikaner of today...the doctrines of sixteenth-
> century Calvinism.[5]

Many of South Africa's dictators are members of the Calvinist
Dutch Reformed Church and sanction policies on 'Christian'
grounds.

The doctrine of white supremacy is not confined to the theology of
the Dutch Reformed Church, however; it subtly manifests itself in
the major ecclesiastical denominations originating in western Europe. It has been western Protestantism and Christendom which have
traditionally propounded a theology of pacifism, one of coping with a
condition of extant oppression, as in Azania, rather than one which is
rooted in African tradition and innovates our uprising against colonial oppression. It is precisely this reason which makes Black Theology in Azania so vitally significant as a model of theological
interpretation and exploration in that situation.

Black Theology: A Paradigm of Psychic Empowerment and Liberation

Black Theology as a theological system makes an incisive break with
oppressive, classical western theology and hence possesses the potential for liberating the mind of the African Christian from all deceptive
and illusory concepts imposed upon him or her by the permeation of
white colonial Christianity. Through this liberative process we become enabled to shoulder our weapons of struggle to decolonize and
re-Africanize our country.

It is unfortunate that James Cone, Allan Boesak and Desmond
Tutu, black theologians central to our study, neglect the stress on the
essential religious component of psychic liberation in their theologies
of black liberation. Black Theology, as a theology of revolution directed against the evils of capitalism and racism, necessitates the
underlying emphasis on psychic liberation and internal transformation, a prerequisite for militant revolutionary change.

In Azania, the Black Consciousness Movement of the late sixties and early seventies was the organ instrumental in conscientizing the African masses in the country. It exposed the anomaly of our oppressed condition and instigated the latent potentialities which we as a collective group wielded for the radical transformation of that condition. It also served to bridge the wedges of division amongst the various 'non-white' ethnic groups in the country and bring those groups together into a more united bloc of black cohesion.

The Black Consciousness Movement, which was essentially religious in nature, was engineered by the cornerstone of the movement, Steve Biko, who had witnessed the destructive effects of the settler colonial system on the minds of Azanian people. Biko concluded that the problem of mental enslavement and powerlessness had to be countered with the doctrine of Black Consciousness. He explained:

> The philosophy of Black Consciousness, therefore, expresses group pride and the determination by the blacks to rise and attain the envisaged self. At the heart of this kind of thinking is the realization by the blacks that the most potent weapon in the hand of the oppressor is the mind of the oppressed. Once the latter has been so effectively manipulated and controlled by the oppressor as to make the oppressed believe that he is a liability to the white man, then there will be nothing the oppressed can do that will really scare the powerful masters. Hence, thinking along the lines of Black Consciousness makes the black man see himself as a being, entire in himself, and not as an extension of a broom or additional leverage to some machine...[6]
>
> Black Consciousness, therefore, takes cognizance of the deliberateness of God's plan in creating people black.[7]

The Black Consciousness Movement, which swept across Azania during the decades of the sixties and seventies, wielded the momentum of a disruptive earthquake as the country became consumed with pockets of resistance and uprisings like that of Durban in 1974 and those that occurred in Soweto in 1976. The latent forces of liberation were being tapped through the elevation of the assertion of African identity. The major causal factor was the surge of the Black Consciousness Movement and its programme of psyshic-cultural liberation. The effects of psychic liberation were clear: mass mobilizations. It is this type of movement which would give momentum to the struggle being waged presently in Azania, and with mass organization it is ensured of success.

The flame of the Black Consciousness Movement sparked the emergence of a new school of theology, Black Theology, which represents the matrix of religious awakening within the Black church sector. Black Theology, like its concomitant in the political arena, sought to reinterpret the biblical narrative in terms of the black experience and placed preponderant emphasis on God's intrinsic nature of freedom and desire for the freedom of the black person and all black people. Ananias Mpunzi, noted black theologian from Azania, asserts:

> Thus Black Theology claims that God affirms my uniqueness and so my blackness. It goes further and says: 'Black person, you are a unique person, and you must express your uniqueness or die, and you must affirm your humanity or become the thing — the object, that others have deluded you into believing yourself to be.' On the one hand, you must tear down every man-made barrier that restricts your freedom to be yourself as a human being no matter what your situation or what others may say or do to you...[8] Black Theology is a powerful call to freedom for black people, calling us to throw off the shackles and structural bonds that hold us in self-denying conformity and bondage to others.[9]

This notion of freedom expressed in Black Theology is based on the freeing character of the human Creator, God, who created all human beings in freedom and as destined to be free. The Genesis account of the creation of human beings affirms this truism. All people have been created in God's image and ought to be free personally and socially, for God is, by nature, a free Being. The divine freedom of God and that of human beings are indissolubly linked together. James Cone posits:

> Divine freedom is the source and content of human freedom. Human freedom, the will to create a new future in history, is grounded in divine freedom, God's will to be for and with us in his future. Because God has created us in freedom and thus wills to be in relation to human beings outside the divine self, freedom is bestowed upon us as a constituent of our created existence...To be content with servitude and oppression is to deny the very ground and intention of our created existence.[10]

Thus, in order to be free beings in conformity to God's intention and plan for human existence, we need to exorcise any force which attempts to abrogate or negate our freedom. In Azania we have realized that in order to be free beings as God has deemed, we need to raise our weapons of struggle to exterminate the powers obstructing our freedom. This process of engagement in the freedom struggle can only materialize through a freedom of our interiorized selves which is reflected in revolutionary praxis on an external level, for both facets of freedom are part of the same continuum.

Black Theology as formulated by the black theologians stands to be enriched and made holistic by adopting this methods of critical analysis, whereby the reflection of society is recognized in its influence on the self and vice versa. This insight is invaluable for comprehending the process of transformation as it occurs within the individual and, in turn, within society. As Peter Berger explains:

> Since society exists as both objective and subjective reality, any adequate theoretical understanding of it must comprehend both aspects...These aspects receive their proper recognition if society is understood in terms of externalization, objectivization and internalization. The same is true of the individual in society who simultaneously externalizes his own being into the social world and internalizes it as an objective reality.[11]

This sociological observation needs to be earnestly considered especially on the level of revolutionary praxis. Theologically speaking, God's activity and power of breaking into the human realm intersects at both levels: God is in direct encounter with the individual on a personal level and is influencing structures towards positive change mediated through collections of persons.

The element of dialectical, intersubjective relations between individuals and the objective reality of society is one which black liberation theologians need to become increasingly sensitized to. Liberation processes never occur in a vacuum or without the conscious activity of individuals; liberation transpires through the active and synchronized co-ordination of the masses of oppressed persons against an alienating and oppressive enemy. It is the self which, as the seat of decisive action, becomes the catalytic agent for revolutionary praxis and hence demands psychic liberation. In this regard Archie Smith's observation on the subjective and objective dimensions of the self is pertinent:

> The objective side of the self, the 'me,' exists in certain

concrete relations to other selves (i.e., as infant with
mother or father), and it occupies a particular position in
the social structure...

On the other hand, the subjective side of the self
emerges through thinking, reflection, and internal conversation. It evolves as the individual stops and thinks about
his or her continuous relationship with others, the environment, and the world. The self is a dynamic process and a
center of consciousness. It not only emerges from its relations with others, but arises in relation to itself and
through the use of language, imagery, and memory. In this
sense the self is a resource for getting hold of its social
origins in the act of reflection. The self that emerges in this
way can construct and reconstruct its own experience.[12]

Of course, this self is perceived only in relation to others, as is
inherent in the biblical understanding of corporate personality of the
individual and in African tradition in which the self exists in organic
and collective terms. Azanian theologian Bonganjalo Goba asserts:

Corporate personality means the embodiment of the community in the individual. The individual represents the
community to which he belongs. What the individual does
affects the community and vice versa...

In Israel the individual was required to act in accordance
with the wishes and demands of his kinship. If he failed to
do this, it affected the community to which he belonged.
So one discovers in this concept of corporate personality, a
unique relation of the individual to the community...

There is a relational cohesion that overrides the wishes
and feelings of the individual. A curse extends to the
whole race and God visits the sins of the fathers on the
children to the fourth generation (Ex. 20). A whole family
is honoured if its head is brave, while the group is pun-
ished for a fault of its leaders (2 Sam. 21). This solidarity is
seen above all in the group's duty to protect its weak and
oppressed members.[13]

Similarly too, in the vein of African tradition, the self is conceived in
relation to his or her membership in the community. The Zulu saying,
'Okwakho okwami' — what belongs to one belongs to all[14] — captures the richness of meaning in the relational self. This illustration
exemplifies just one instance where Black Theology draws upon the
wellspring of African tradition to preserve its authentic Africanity.

It is the conscious self in mutual and cohesive solidarity with the

conscientized Azanian masses which, actualized in revolutionary warfare, would provide the collective empowerment necessary to undermine the illegitimate colonial system imposed upon our country. Our
source of spiritual potency is derived from the Creator of empowerment, Yahweh. As psychically and socially conscious persons
girded with the loincloth of religious inspiration, the now colonized
people of Azania will rise up *en masse* in revolutionary sophistication,
and finally deal the *coup de grâce* to the evil white colonial regime.
Colonized South Africa will be transformed into liberated Azania.
The lingering factor which most people ponder in a situation such as
that in Southern Africa, and it is a legitimate and realistic concern, is
that of fear, the human dimension of fear which paralyzes all people
in the face of seemingly unsurmountable odds. In contexts of repression, this character becomes accentuated and extremely difficult to
circumvent. Fear of reprisal thus becomes an important determinant
in the actualizing of oppression. Gerard Cheliand points out:

> Crushed by the mobilities of routine, we all hesitate to
> engage ourselves in political struggle. We fear energy
> wasted. We fear cutting ourselves off from family and
> friends. One of the most basic mechanisms that sustains
> the status quo is always precisely this pervasive fear of the
> oppressed to break with routine. A revolutionary
> movement is precisely a movement that calls for a break
> with routine, that demands sacrifice for a better world in
> the future.[15]

If one is well acquainted with the South African situation, one can
certainly comprehend the level of fear of uprising from the African
sector of the population. This inclination is understandable, especially in light of the fact that the whites in South Africa are the most
heavily armed population per capita in the world and together possess the most well-equipped military force in Africa.[16]

Once again, we in Azania realize that evil is never unconquerable.
We thus appeal to a higher authority for strength and courage to
eschew our fear: the God of our Christian faith, the God of Africa
and the world who encounters us through the gospel.

The God who is illuminated through the Christian revelation is a
God of justice and freedom, historically substantiated by the central
theme of the Exodus-event sanctioned by Yahweh in the Old Testament,[17] transmitted through the major and minor prophets and cli-
maxing with the event of Jesus Christ. Gustavo Gutierrez, the
renowned Peruvian liberation theologian, postulates:

> The God of Exodus is the God of history and of political
> liberation more than he is the God of nature. Yahweh is
> the Liberator, the *goel* of Israel (Isa. 43:14; 47:4; Jer.
> 50:34)...
> The God who makes the cosmos from chaos is the same
> God who leads Israel from alienation to liberation...The
> work of Christ forms a part of this movement and brings it
> to complete fulfillment.[18]

The biblical narrative palpably indicates that the God of the Christian gospel is indeed a God of holistic liberation over all realms of
life's processes and sides with all oppressed people in their persistent
struggle for freedom. God is the Source and Sustainer of freedom of
all life, actively engaged in initiating and persuading movements of
freedom through concrete events in history. In the Christian faith this
factuality is evidenced by the salvific actions of God in Israel's emancipation from enslavement and oppression in Egypt and Jesus' unequivocal ministry of liberation to all oppressed and marginalized
persons of society. Jesus Christ, the central figure of the Christian
faith, affirms his mission of liberator in his teaching in the temple,
fulfilling God's call to the task of liberation.[19]

> The Spirit of the Lord is upon me because he has anointed
> me to preach good news to the poor.
> He has sent me to proclaim release to the captives and
> recovery of sight to the blind, to set at liberty those who
> are oppressed, to proclaim the acceptable year of the Lord
> (Lk. 4:18).

God is thus never neutral in historical processes engaging humankind. The Brazilian theologian Hugo Assmann argues:

> God has a cause in history, and therefore has enemies.
> God's action in history is not ethereally all-embracing; it is
> specific and precise. It is action on and with the oppressed,
> in the midst of history, on behalf of their liberation.[20]

Hence, the people of Azania are not alone in their state of colonization and struggle for socialistic liberation. God is on our side and
intends that we be free. The divine power of Yahweh is presently
working for freedom in Azania. The God of freedom assures us of a
victory of freedom against the evil principalities and powers which
obstruct our freedom and humanization.

The diabolical structures of colonization and repression prevalent
in South Africa cannot stand up to the force of God's movement of

justice and liberation. Our Christian faith in the God of the Exodus and the resurrection knows no human bounds. As the apostle Paul asserts:

> If God be for us, who can be against us? (Rom. 8:31).

The God of liberation is instrumental in all incidents of just and authentic human emancipation. In the historic struggle of the people of Vietnam, it was God's suasive power of transformation which enabled the Vietnamese to defeat the world's greatest imperialist and colonialist force, the United States of America. The Buddhist faith of the Vietnamese people complemented by their vision for a just and equitable society impelled them to resist every evil tentacle to the point of total self-sacrifice. It was this spirit of determination which won the Vietnamese their freedom. Felix Greene, in describing the Vietnamese revolution, states:

> To the people of Vietnam, the prospect of the French reestablishing their colonial role was unthinkable. They are ready to sacrifice their lives to prevent it. Even with massive US military aid, the French found (as the US was to find ten years later) that to fight a determined peasant population is not easy.[21]

The colonized people of Azania have a faith too, rooted in the Christian tradition and our African heritage, which equips us with the sense of unwavering and fearless determination to extirpate the evil powers besetting our nation. It is our resolve, encompassed by the realization that God is constantly at our side in struggle, and in communication with Her divine transcendence that we can overcome the fear of death and be mobilized to necessary sacrifice.

Faith is that component of human experience in relation to the Transcendent which vivifies the body of religion. It is an inflammatory sense of trust in the Deity, with the full realization and anticipation of Her ability to sustain the stream of creative transformation and liberation regardless of apparently overwhelming indications to the contrary. It is this flame of faith which dispels our inclinations of fear and kindles the notion within us that the finitude of human character and ability is emboldened by God's infinite potentiality. As Paul Tillich elucidates:

> In the religious experience the power of God provokes the feeling of being in the hand of a power which cannot be

conquered by any other power, in ontological terms, which is the infinite resistance against non-being and the eternal victory over it. To participate in this resistance and this victory is felt as the way to overcome the threat of non-being which is the destiny of everything finite.[22]

This faith is not a superficial relationship; it is the medium by which the believer becomes personally and collectively empowered, in conjunction with his or her fellow believers, to engage in reflective action which may entail the inevitability of death. Faith becomes the soulmate of courage and, conversely, this union becomes actualized in dynamic revolutionary praxis. Tillich advances further:

> In a short formulation one could say that courage is that element in faith which is related to the risk of faith. One cannot replace faith by courage but neither can one describe faith without courage. In the complete reunion with the divine ground of being, the element of distance is overcome and with it uncertainity, doubt, courage and risk.[23]

A perusal of the biblical account indicates that the theme of faith of the believer is central to the Judaic-Christian tradition. From the incipient call of Abraham in Genesis 12 to the early Christian community, the element of faith was a primary requisite in the response to God's revelation. In fact, Jesus exemplified this quality of religious faith, par excellence. Jon Sobrino states:

> The content of this faith — what Jesus does in full measure — can be found if we focus on the notion of faith in the Old Testament, which Jesus affirms, and on Jesus' rejection of the Old Testament (Heb. 11); but it is an active faith, a victorious struggle against the difficulties posed by one's situation in real life. It has nothing to do with a victorious struggle against doubts about faith; it is instead a victorious struggle against the conflicts to be found in real-life existence. So faith becomes fidelity (Heb. 3:2; 2:13), not an idealistic fidelity but a fidelity lived in and through suffering (Heb. 2:10,18;12:2).[24]

Through this profound and visceral faith expression, we become empowered through the current of God's creative power to obey God's call to proclaim love, justice and liberation in the world. It is this unshakeable faith which impels us to tangible and reflective praxis mandated by our Christian discipleship. The German ethicist

Dietrich Bonhoeffer reminds us that this demanding faith and obedience is echoed in Jesus' admonition to servanthood on the part of the believer. Bonhoeffer says:

> When Christ calls a person, He bids him come and die.[25]

Bonhoeffer himself attested to this radical cost of discipleship when he participated in an attempt to execute the Nazi dictator, Adolf Hitler, for which he was consequently incarcerated and later executed.

In the Azanian context, it is the type of faith exemplified by the revolutionary action of persons like Dietrich Bonhoeffer that we ought to inculcate. Our faith in the divine, mediated through our perception of the Christian gospel, is the spiritual instrument of empowerment which informs our resolute courage to participate in the liberation struggle. Faith in Yahweh of the scriptures inspires in the hearts of Azanian people fearlessness of the colonizers' militarization, to the point that dying in the battlefield that our streets have become constitutes a religious vocation. James Pike, the Christian ethicist, argues:

> But where the very instruments of orderly protest have been denied, and where evil has entrenched itself and has gained control of the usual organs through which a protest could be registered (either sooner or later), then conspiracy toward a rebellion is not only permissible, but might well be required for fulfillment of Christian vocation.[26]

Canaan Banana, the president of the now liberated Zimbabwe and an active minister of the Zimbabwean liberation movement, describes the dynamism of Christian faith in action effected by the guerrilla freedom fighter:

> Since I have been personally involved in the struggle for our freedom, many passages from the Bible have assumed new and compelling meanings. When Jesus says, 'I have come that they may have life and have it in all its fullness,' to me the implications of this are clear; it means humankind must be free to live in all its fullness. When humankind is denied any part of its life, it must reclaim it. When a young man offers his life to fight for freedom he is following Christ's example. 'Greater love has no man that this, that a man lay down his life for his friends' (John 15:13). What can be more Christian than sacrificing one's life for one's fellow persons? So there is therefore a real

sense in which Christian young people who offer their lives
to fight for their country are bearing their cross. They are
motivated by love of what is dear to them; they sacrifice
their precious lives in order to eliminate the forces of evil,
becoming the martyrs of our freedom and saints of our
time.[27]

Armed with the gospel and all that it leads one to be further armed
with, the Azanian Christian is called to transform his or her religious
faith into liberation praxis. His or her fear of the power of death and
evil is exorcised by the God of Life, symbolized by the paradigm of
Christ's resurrection and triumph over death.

Death, we discover, is not the ultimate determinant, for in every
crucifixion there is a glorious resurrection, a striking analogy for
victory over oppression in society. Likewise in African tradition,
death is not conceived of as the final termination of human existence;
death is viewed as yet another phase in the cycle of life, demonstrated
in the rites of reverence for the dead. This concept is known as the
living-death in African tradition. John Mbiti explains:

> African peoples believe that death is not the end of human
> life. A person continues to exist in the hereafter. This
> continuation of life beyond death is recognized through a
> very widespread practice of remembering the departed,
> which is found throughout Africa. Through rituals,
> dreams, visions, possessions and names they are recalled
> and respected. This does not and cannot mean that they
> are worshipped. The departed are considered to be still
> alive and people show by these practices that they recog-
> nize their presence.[28]

This profound and redoubtable observance has significant implications for revolutionary African situations where Christian fighters
lose their lives in combat and struggle. The figures of Steve Biko,
Bambata, Albert Luthuli and Mangaliso Sobukwe come immediately to mind, titans who have sacrificed their lives for the Azanian
liberation movement. African tradition and the Christian faith inform
the struggling masses of Azania that these valiant and religious martyrs are very far from dead; their spirits live on yearning for a resting
place in a truly free and liberated Azania.

Summary and Conclusion
In the final analysis, we affirm that Christianity is indeed a religion of

liberation, interpreted through the model of Black Theology in Azania. The biblical narrative attests to the gospel's revolutionary character and God's essentially liberative nature, culminating in the personhood of Jesus Christ. As Christians in Azania and fundamentally religious persons, we are called by God to fulfill our responsibility of engaging in revolutionary struggle. We are urged to arm ourselves with the cudgels and necessary weapons of combat, empowered by a dynamic faith in a liberating and supporting God. It is our fervent faith which will remove the mountain of fear of oppression and death to expedite the ushering in of the Kingdom of God in Azania.

NOTES

1. Gregory Baum, *Religion and Alienation* (New York: Paulist Press, 1975), p. 15.
2. Gibson Winter, *Liberating Creation* (New York: Crossroad, 1981), p. 115.
3. Juan Luis Segundo, *The Liberation of Theology* (Maryknoll, N.Y.: Orbis Books, 1976), p. 3.
4. Max Weber, *The Protestant Ethic and the Spirit of Capitalism* (New York: Scribner and Son, 1958), p. 117.
5. Cited in Irving Hexham, *The Irony of Apartheid: The Struggle for National Independence of Afrikaner Calvinism against British Imperialism* (New York: Edwin Mellon Press, 1981), pp. 1-2.
6. Steve Biko, *I Write What I Like* (San Francisco: Harper & Row, 1978), p. 68.
7. Ibid., p. 49.
8. Ananias Mpunzi, 'Black Theology as Liberation Theology', in *The Challenge of Black Theology in South Africa*, ed. Basil Moore (Atlanta: John Knox Press, 1974), p. 137.
9. Ibid., p. 138.
10. James Cone, 'Freedom, History, and Hope', in *Liberation, Revolution and Freedom*, ed. Thomas M. McFadden (New York: Seabury Press, 1975), p. 61.
11. Peter Berger, *The Social Construction of Reality* (New York: Doubleday and Co., 1966), p. 119.
12. Archie Smith, *The Relational Self* (Nashville: Abingdon Press, 1982), pp. 84-85.
13. Bonganjalo Goba, 'Corporate Personality: Ancient Israel and Africa', in *The Challenge of Black Theology in South Africa*, pp. 65-66.
14. Ibid., p. 68.
15. Gerard Cheliand, *Revolution in the Third World* (New York: Penguin Books, 1977), p. x.
16. Patrick Wilmot, *Apartheid and African Liberation*, p. 91.
17. See Jose Miranda, *Marx and the Bible* (Maryknoll, N.Y.: Orbis Books, 1974), pp. 78ff.
18. Gustavo Gutierrez, *A Theology of Liberation* (Maryknoll, N.Y.: Orbis Books, 1973), pp. 157, 158.
19. A good treatment of this theme is found in Leonardo Boff, *Jesus Christ Liberator* (Maryknoll, N.Y.: Orbis Books, 1978), pp. 63ff.
20. Cited by Victorio Araya, 'The God of the Strategic Covenant', in *The Idols of Death and the God of Life*, ed. Pablo Richard et al. (Maryknoll, N.Y.: Orbis Books, 1983), p. 107.
21. Felix Greene, *Vietnam, Vietnam!* (Palo Alto, Calif.: Fulton Publishing Co., 1966), p. 127.
22. Paul Tillich, *Love, Power and Justice* (New York: Oxford University Press, 1954), p. 110.
23. Paul Tillich, *Dynamics of Faith* (New York: Harper and Row, 1957), p. 103.

Chapter 11

A Critique on the Role of Women in the Church

BONITA BENNETT

Editors' Abstract

The oppression of women as women runs across class distinctions. The class-transcending oppression must, however, be situated within its proper context, namely, bourgeois culture which develops from and feeds into capitalist social relations of production, exchange and distribution. Once women's oppression has been properly located in this context, the real nature and magnitude of the oppression and exploitation of black women become evident. In its oppression of women within its own boundaries, the church as a cultural institution within the bourgeois social order reproduces and reinforces the oppression of women that is already inscribed in the very bowels of society. Thus only a return to the Jesus movement and to the latter's perspective on women can offer contemporary women some ideological weapons of struggle for the fight which they are inevitably engaged in. Women can, therefore, not be content with simply fighting for 'some improved status within this present system of capitalism'.

Introduction

The question of the role of women in the church is one which faces the whole of the church in South Africa, not just the female component of it. It is a challenge presented to the whole church as we seek to discover the meaning of total liberation for all of God's people.

Before specifically looking at present types of female involvement in the church, I would like to situate the position of women in a capitalist society.

Economic Exploitation

All women, even those of the ruling class, are oppressed as women in the sense that their worth is linked to their roles as girlfriends, wives or mothers. Women are generally regarded as docile, gentle, amiable and relatively attractive beings. This understanding of women forms part of the bourgeois culture, in which the whole superstructure of ideas serves to explain and reinforce the social relations of capitalism. As mentioned before, this applies to all women, but has very different consequences for women of different classes. For the ruling-class woman it means that she is denied her independence and full dignity as a person. For the working-class woman, too, it means this, but in addition also justifies her material super-exploitation and physical coercion. The black women's position is controlled by a number of forces. The capitalist system needs a right-less group of people who can be controlled and exploited in the labour market. In South Africa, this group is the predominantly black working class. The women of this class of people suffer the most: they are triply exploited. They are exploited because they are black, because they are women, and because they are workers.

Chauvinistic social attitudes hold women as passive and inferior servants of society and of men. They are expected to work for much lower wages than their already low-paid husbands. Most women are forced to work to supplement the family income, and they often don't have much choice but to perform the most menial tasks for the lowest remuneration. They can be used as a reserve labour force when profits depend on extra-low costs, or perhaps when men are needed for military duty. Many people (men and women) do not question this reality of low remuneration for women, because society has so conditioned them into such an expectation.

In a more subtle way, this role assumed by women (passive and submissive) undermines the class consciousness of the working class. Petty dictatorship of the males over their wives and families enables the men to exercise and vent their frustrations and feelings of powerlessness without presenting any sort of serious challenge to the system. The structure of the family with its superior positions of authority for men reinforces aggressive individualism, authoritarianism, and a hierarchical view of social relations — values which are fundamental for the perpetuation of capitalism.

Domestic Exploitation
Women play a vital role in maintaining and reproducing the labour force. With all the odds working against her — of bad living conditions, inadequate health care and educational facilities, low wages, etc. — she is expected to make life liveable for the family. She is often expected to make up for the shortcomings of the system, trying to bridge the gap between week to week subsistence; it is her responsibility to see that the family is fed and clothed. The working woman thus has to work a double shift: at her place of employment, and at home.

Psychological Oppression
The material and psychological oppressions of women reinforce each other. One can go on endlessly looking at the subtle ways in which women are psychologically oppressed and led to believe in their own inferiority. The following are a few examples:

At school, females are encouraged to pursue domestic subjects like home economics and needlework (in preparation for their role), whereas the males are the ones who 'have the head for science and math', etc.; the mass media bombard women with images of 'the woman you'd like to be'; etc...

Now what has all this got to do with Christians? Everything!

The Church's Role
The church has had a particular role in perpetuating myths about the expectations of women. This is just one of the ways in which the church has aided to uphold the system. Tradition has assigned very specific roles to women in the church. They have been labelled as the:
- sinner and temptress;
- childbearer;
- servant;
- subordinate.

The church has limited women to:
- home functions;
- serving children/the old/the sick;
- serving as nurses, nuns, mothers, sisters;
- functioning as fundraisers;
- working as team makers.

These functions are not in themselves necessarily bad, but should they be the sole domain of the woman? And more importantly, is this the only contribution that women are capable of making to the church?

Surely matters such as theological education and debate should not be solely the male domain, but, ideally, should be the sphere of operation of every responsible person. Jesus thought so.

Never can it be asserted that Jesus conformed to a demeaning view of women. It is the church which has conformed to cultural ideas about them. The church has also laid down certain codes of conduct especially for women, being especially concerned about their morality, about their dress, reminding them of their roots in Eve, and the instructions of Paul to be submissive and obedient. Very little is referred to our Lord and liberator — Jesus Christ.

Jesus and Women
Jesus did not only refrain from belittling women: he actually stood up to some of his contemporaries to defend women, which, in the patriarchal society of his time, was a revolutionary act in itself. For example, refer to John 8:3-11, where Jesus defends the woman who had been caught in the act of adultery. (By the way, where was the man?)

The position of women at the time of Jesus was that of second-class citizens. They could hold no position of responsibility except that of mother and wife. They received no education at all, no religious education either. They could not be religious teachers or officials.

Jesus makes a startling pronouncement when he lays down equal standards for both males and females: what is considered to be adultery for the female is as bad for the male.

> Whoever divorces his wife and marries another commits adultery against her: *so too,* if she divorces her husband and marries another, she commits adultery (Mark 10: 11,12).

He reminds his followers of the original will of God, of the equality of the sexes.

When he visited Mary and Martha, he showed a disregard for traditional values (Luke 10:42). He criticized Martha, although she was fulfilling her expected role; he says, '...Mary has chosen what is better' – by choosing to listen to him.

Jesus again broke with traditional practice when he spoke to the Samaritan woman — an unheard of act (John 4:8-30). Jews never spoke to Samaritans, and more especially if they were women.

Jesus was the Messiah: who anointed him? The kings in the Old Testament were anointed by the high priests; Jesus was anointed by a woman (Mark 14:3). He describes her as the first person who recognized the true nature of his messiahship.

Women were very prominent at the time of the crucifixion, and after. The Gospels very specifically point to their presence at the cross (Mark 15:40). The women went with Joseph of Arimethea to bury the body. They prepared the spices and perfumes to anoint the body of our Lord, and they were the first who went to the tomb on Sunday morning and found it empty. The customs and traditions of the time did not allow women to testify and witness. It is significant that women were the first witnesses to the empty tomb, a reversal of the male orientation of the time.

Little acts such as talking to women, calling upon them to testify and witness, allowing women to financially support himself and his disciples — these may seen as small actions to us, but taking place in that society, they were major breaches of tradition.

Jesus' sensitivity and openness to women is striking. He gave women a new status of equality. He saw women as equal partners, and they played a major role in his life. He gave the women he came into contact with a new self-understanding, a new self-worth.

Our role, as women, then, is to live out our full stature in the full character given to us by God; as men, to be aware and careful of chauvinistic attitudes, and to aid in the process of women's liberation; as women and men, to examine whether our own attitudes would be described as Christ-like, or whether they are the result of prejudices.

Women, as well as men, have been equally responsible in perpetuating sexist values. Women have often lived up to the expectations and constraints placed upon them, but this should not be used as an argument for retaining these roles. We have all been part of this process of socialization.

What women are asking for is not a reversal of male-female roles, although this is often taken to be the case. Rather, it is to be recognized as full human beings, with equal intellectual and spiritual worth. Jesus did not glorify women: he acted naturally toward them, accepting them as mature persons who could understand what he was saying and who could respond intelligently to him. He discussed his mission with them, and trusted women to carry out work for him.

Men are affected as much as women by sex-role stereotyping: if women are regarded as being passive, inferior and unintelligent, then men are conditioned to feel aggressive, superior and intellectual. By polarizing the sexes, each is relegated to its 'proper' sphere.

Some people regard the issue of changing sex-roles as a move towards a breakdown of fundamental relationships between the sexes. However, such discussion should rather be regarded as a breakthrough to a non-sexist understanding of human beings who have equal worth, all created in God's image.

Conclusion

Women know that to fight for just some improved status within this present system of capitalism, which needs its present divisions, is useless. Thus black women in South Africa have seen and are continuing to see their role in the struggle for the liberation of *all* people in the country; total liberation cannot be achieved without the liberation of women. This is the challenge facing all Christians in South Africa (and elsewhere): Christ's message is a call for liberation for all people.

Chapter 12

The Use of the Bible in Black Theology
ITUMELENG J. MOSALA

Editors' Abstract

Black Theology, like Liberation Theology in general, has not taken its own criticism of white theology seriously enough. While it has advocated black liberation and the black experience as a focus of its analysis it has continued to draw its biblical hermeneutical assumptions from white theology. Black Theology identifies the Bible with the black experience. This is done irrespective of the class character of the Bible. Aspects of the Bible that can be scientifically shown to derive from the ideological interests of the oppressors of ancient society and that hold together the economic, political and cultural interests of oppressors today are claimed uncritically to be on the side of the oppressed. No wonder the Bible has not yet become a weapon of liberation. Materialist biblical hermeneutics of liberation which see the Bible as the product, the record and the site of class struggles will make possible a liberative appropriation of the Bible. The Book of Micah in the Old Testament is analyzed in this way to point the way to this biblical hermeneutics of liberation.

Introduction
This paper presupposes the contribution of Black Theology to human
knowledge in general and to the black struggle for liberation in particular. No attempt will, therefore, be made to catalogue the virtues
of this theology. Suffice it to recall that among its key contributions is
its insistence on the necessary ideological rootedness of all theology.
This, black theologians may not have pointed to in an explicit way.
The fact, however, that they exposed the cultural assumptions of
white theology and showed their link with white society and white
values exploded the myth of rational objectivity in theology.

The paper will, however, take issue with Black Theology for not
taking its own criticism of white theology seriously enough. It will be
shown that this is particularly the case with regard to the use of the
Bible. The first part of the paper will, therefore, extrapolate features
of Black Theology which, it will be argued, represent an ideological
captivity to the hermeneutical principles of a theology of oppression.
It will further be maintained that it is precisely this slavery to the
hermeneutics of white theology which is responsible for the inability
of Black Theology to become a theoretical weapon of struggle in the
hands of the exploited masses themselves. In this respect we will take
our cue from the words of Marx when he writes:

> The weapon of criticism cannot, of course, replace crit-
> icism of the weapon; material force must be overthrown by
> material force; but theory also becomes a material force as
> soon as it has gripped the masses. Theory is capable of
> gripping the masses as soon as it demonstrates *ad homi-
> nem*, and it demonstrates *ad hominem* as soon as it be-
> comes radical. To be radical is to grasp the root of the
> matter. But for man the root is man himself.[1]

It cannot be contested that although Black Theology has developed
and is well and alive,[2] it has not yet, as a weapon of theory, become
the property of the struggling black masses. To this extent it is a
theory that has not yet become a *material force* because it has not
gripped the masses. It has served its purpose well as a weapon of
criticism against white theology and the white society. That activity,
however, does not replace criticism of the weapon itself. Elsewhere I
have argued that part of the reason why Black Theology has not
become the property of the toiling masses may lie in the class positions and class commitments of its proponents.[3]

The second part of the paper will attempt to set out a programme for biblical hermeneutics of liberation using the Book of Micah as a case study.

Black Theology's Exegetical Starting Point

All major black theological studies in South Africa draw, in some way, from the work of James Cone. While Cone cannot be faulted for the omissions of South African Black Theology, it is nevertheless necessary to trace the trajectory of the biblical hermeneutics of Black Theology back to its first and most outstanding exponent in order to see how it has been uncritically reproduced in this country.

Black Theology's exegetical starting point expresses itself in the notion that the Bible is the revealed 'Word of God'. The task of a black theologian is to recognize 'God's Word' and help illuminate it to those who are oppressed and humiliated in this world. For Cone the 'Word of God', therefore, represents one structuring pole of the biblical hermeneutics of Black Theology while the black experience stands for the other.[4] He summarizes Black Theology's hermeneutical position when he asserts that:

> The Bible is the witness to God's self-disclosure in Jesus Christ. Thus the black experience requires that Scripture be a source of Black Theology. For it was Scripture that enabled slaves to affirm a view of God that differed radically from that of the slave masters. The slave masters' intention was to present a 'Jesus' who would make the slave obedient and docile. Jesus was supposed to make black people better slaves, that is, faithful servants of white masters. But many blacks rejected that view of Jesus, not only because it contradicted their African heritage, but because it contradicted the witness of Scripture.[5]

Thus the black experience of oppression and exploitation provides the epistemological lenses for perceiving the God of the Bible as the God of liberation. This process, however, does not alter Cone's perception of the nature and function of the Bible as the 'Word of God'. Rather, 'scripture', in its status as the 'Word of God', 'established limits to white people's use of Jesus Christ as a confirmation of black oppression'.[6]

Paradoxically, Black Theology's notion of the Bible as the 'Word of God' carries the implication that there is such a thing as a non-ideological appropriation of scripture. Black theologians condemn white people's view of God and Jesus Christ as apolitical and above ideologies on the one hand, but maintain a view of scripture as an absolute, non-ideological 'Word of God' which can be made ideological by being applied to the situation of oppression. This position is taken by even the most theoretically astute of black theologians, Cornel West. He argues:

> An interpretation of the black historical experience and the readings of the biblical texts that emerge out of this experience constitute the raw ingredients for the second step of black theological reflection. By trying to understand the plight of black people in the light of the Bible, black theologians claim to preserve the biblical truth that God sides with the oppressed and acts on their behalf.[7]

To be fair to West it must be added that he goes a step further than Cone and other black theologians by not resting the case at interpreting the black experience in the light of the Bible, but also advocates interpreting the Bible in the light of the black experience. Nevertheless West, like Cone, insists on there being a biblical truth according to which God sides with the oppressed in their struggle for liberation. This is true as far as it goes. But as any hermeneutics that derives from the crucible of class struggle will attest to, the biblical truth that God sides with the oppressed is only one of the biblical truths. The other truth is that the struggle between Yahweh and Baal is not simply an ideological warfare taking place in the minds and hearts of believers, but a struggle between the God of the Israelite landless peasants and subdued slaves and the God of the Israelite royal, noble, landlord and priestly classes. The Bible is as rent apart by the antagonistic struggles of the warring classes of Israelite society as our life is torn asunder by the class divisions of our society.

What then is meant by the Bible as the 'Word of God'? The ideological import of such a theological statement is immense. For the 'Word of God' cannot be the object of criticism. Least of all can the 'Word of God' be critiqued in the light of the black experience. The only appropriate response is *obedience*. At best the black experience can be seen in the light of the 'Word of God', but not vice versa. If the Bible is the 'Word of God', therefore, the implication is that even the 'law and order' God of David and Solomon cannot be the object of criticism in the light of the black experience. The black struggle cannot be hermeneutically connected with the struggles of the oppressed and exploited Israelites against the economic and political domination of the Israelite monarchic state which was undergirded by the ideology of the Davidic-Zionist covenant (2 Samuel 7). Neither can any hermeneutic affinity be established with the landless peasants, exploited workers and destitute underclasses that made up the followers of Jesus. One cannot select one part of the 'Word of God' and neglect the other.

South African black theologians are not free from enslavement to this neo-orthodox theological problematic that regards the notion of the 'Word of God' as a hermeneutical starting point. S. Dwane displays this exegetical bondage when he writes:

> Liberation theology as an aspect of Christian theology cannot play to the gallery of secular expectations. It seeks to understand and to articulate what in the light of his revelation in the past, God is doing now for the redemption of his people. Liberation theology is theocentric and soundly biblical insofar as it points out that God does not luxuriate in his eternal bliss, but reaches out to man and to the world...To say that liberation theology is not a Gospel of liberation is to state the obvious. *The Gospel, it is true, is good news for all men.* And no theology, Western or African, has the right to equate itself with the Gospel. The entire theological enterprise is concerned with the interpretation of *the one Gospel for all sorts of conditions.*[8]

The attempt to claim *the whole* of the Bible in support of black theology is misdirected because it ignores the results of biblical scholarship over the last century and has its roots in ruling-class ideology. By ruling-class ideology we refer to that activity on the part of dominant classes of society by which they seek to establish hegemonic control over other classes through a rationalizing universalization of what are in effect sectional class interests. James Joll makes this point succinctly:

> The hegemony of a political class meant for Gramsci that that class had succeeded in persuading the other classes of society to accept its own moral, political and cultural values. If the ruling class is successful, then this will involve the minimum use of force, as was the case with the successful liberal regimes of the nineteenth century.[9]

Thus the insistence on the Bible as the 'Word of God' must be seen for what it is: an ideological manoeuvre whereby ruling-class interests in the Bible as in our society today are converted into a faith that transcends social, political, racial, sexual and economic divisions. In this way the Bible becomes an ahistorical interclassist document.

Sergio Rostagno has exposed the ideological roots of this line of thinking when he asserts, concerning the church, that:

> Historically speaking, the church has always been a church of the bourgeoisie, even when it claimed to transcend class barriers or labored under the illusion that it pervaded all classes in the same way. Indeed, it has been a truly bourgeois church, if the notion of interclassism is taken as part of bourgeois ideology...The church has been the church of the class which has identified itself with the history of the West, in which Christianity may be considered to have been a major force. Only those members of the working class who accepted this view of history attended church. But most of the working people never accepted this view and only gave the church the kind of formal allegiance subjects give to the claims of their rulers. They could not really belong to the church of another class.[10]

Just as the church has always been the church of the bourgeoisie, theology and biblical exegesis have always been bourgeois theology and exegesis. It is, therefore, a tragedy that rebel theologies like Black Theology and Liberation Theology should adopt uncritically the biblical hermeneutics of bourgeois theology. According to Rostagno bourgeois exegesis shows the sterility of its ahistoricism in that:

> It claims to consider humanity in certain typical existential situations which provide analogies for all historical situations resulting from the human condition. It deals, therefore, with *humanity,* rather than with *workers* as they try to wrest from the dominant class its hold on the means of production and its hold over the vital spheres of human life. In this sense, it could be said that exegesis was an interclass affair...This was an indication that biblical exegesis had been effectively estranged from the labor movement.[11]

The belief in the Bible as the 'Word of God' has had similar effects, that is, *pro-humanity* but anti-black working class and black women. It has, to all intents and purposes, been bourgeois exegesis applied to the working-class situation. The theoretical tragedy of such a state of affairs is that claims in that direction have been made with confidence and pride. Boesak, for instance, states unashamedly that:

> In its focus on the poor and the oppressed, the theology of

liberation is not a new theology; it is simply the proclama-
tion of the age-old gospel, but now liberated from the
deadly hold of the mighty and the powerful and made
relevant to the situation of the oppressed and the poor.[12]

Black Theology needs a new exegetical starting point if it is to
become a material force capable of gripping the black working-class
and peasant masses. Such a starting point needs to be rooted in the
kind of epistemology that underlies the words of Marx and Engels
when they declared: 'The task of history, therefore, once the world
beyond the truth has disappeared, is to establish the truth of this
world'.[13] The social, cultural, political and economic world of the
black working class and peasantry constitutes the only valid hermeneutical starting point for a Black Theology of Liberation.

The Problem of Universality and Particularity in Black Theology
The abstract exegetical starting point of Black Theology leads inevitably to problems about the validity of the particularistic character of
this theology. If the 'Word of God' transcends boundaries of culture,
class, race, sex, etc., how can there be a theology that is concerned
primarily with the issues of a particular race? Conversely, if black
people are right when they claim that in their struggle for liberation
Jesus is on their side, how can the same Jesus remain the supreme
universal disclosure of the 'Word of God'?

This simultaneous concern for a cultureless and culture-bound,
classless and class-based, raceless and race-oriented Jesus manifested
itself fairly early in the development of Black Theology. Thus Gqubule states:

Black Theology is not an attempt to localize Christ in the
black situation, but to make him so universal that the Red
Indian, the Pigmy, the Maori, the Russian, the Hungarian,
the Venda and the American, may each say: 'This man
Jesus is bone of my bone; he speaks in my own accent of
things that are true to me!' Viewed in this way Christianity
can never be a white man's religion although it was
brought to us by a white missionary. It is natural that any
white artist would portray Jesus as a white man.[14]

This line of thinking is corroborated by Mgojo who sees Black
Theology as contextual. By this he seems to understand that it is the
application of universal theological principles to a particular situation. Consequently he traces the development of universal theology

from the Age of Apology through to the period starting in 1720 which he characterizes as the era of evolving theological responses to the technological society. He then concludes:

> In looking at the history of doctrine we can see in every period theology developed in response to challenges from the larger society. This being the case there is nothing strange in a particular segment of the Christian community reflecting on the nature of God in relation to its experience of suffering and oppression. Hence today there is Black Theology.[15]

Thus Mgojo's understanding of the origins and function of Black Theology is rooted in a belief in the fundamental universality of the gospel. This understanding stems from a hermeneutical commitment to the Bible as the 'Word of God'. As a result, he sees the emergence of Black Theology as a logical historical development of Christian theology, not a rebellion against traditional western theology. Indeed Black Theology is simply *contextual* theology, that is, white theology in black clothes. It is little wonder that he applies the following strictures against James Cone:

> Cone's understanding of the theological task in his early work is in conflict with our definition of theology, in fact it is in direct opposition. His focus is on the analysis of the black man's condition, ours is on God as revealed in Jesus Christ and his relationship to the world and man. Cone's approach here could be classified as Christian sociology rather than Christian theology.[16]

This apologetic attitude on the part of black theologians is related to their enslavement to traditional biblical hermeneutics which we discussed above.[17] There are also forms of colonization that are connected to this hermeneutical bondage. In South African Black Theology the debate between African and black theologians exemplifies this crisis of cultural identity. Gqubule, for instance, in addressing one of the points of conflict between Christianity and African religion, locates himself unproblematically in a framework that reflects at once a cultural desertion and a biblical hermeneutical position based in the dominant western culture. He argues:

> There is a widespread belief about the role of the ancestors. One view is that they are an object of worship. Another view is that they are intermediaries who, because

> they know our lot on earth, are better able to mediate to
> God on our behalf. However, for the Christian only the
> Triune God can be the object of worship; moreover the
> Christian Scriptures say: 'There is *one God,* and also *one
> mediator* between God and men, Christ Jesus' (1 Tim.
> 2:5).[18]

The most explicit and often quoted criticism of African Theology
and religion, which feeds on this cultural self-hate, is the one made by
Manas Buthelezi. Buthelezi's strictures are rightly directed against
tendencies to reify the African past, especially African culture. However, the terms of his strictures display an uneasiness about culture
which characterizes the conflict between the universal and the particular in Black Theology. He writes:

> There is a danger that the 'African past' may be romanti-
> cized and conceived in isolation from the realities of the
> present. Yet this 'past' seen as a world view is nothing
> more than a historical abstraction of 'what once was'.
> Rightly or wrongly, one cannot help but sense something
> panicky about the mood which has set the tenor and tempo
> of the current concerns about 'indigenous theology.'[19]

Notwithstanding this rigorously anti-abstractionist stance, Buthelezi proceeds to suggest equally abstractionist solutions to the problem of indigenous theology in South Africa:

> The shift from the 'ideological' to the 'human' expressions
> of ecclesiastical kinship solidarity will serve as a freeing
> factor for indigenous theology. Considerations of *esprit de
> corps* will no longer be a haunting specter for theological
> freedom in Africa, since there will be another way of ex-
> pressing this kinship solidarity.[20]

The abstract universalizing category of the 'human' as opposed to
the concrete particularizing concept of the 'African' helps Buthelezi
to maintain ties with what is 'universal' and, for him, non-ideological,
while at the same time his theology is intended to address the indigenous and, therefore, ideological situation. It may even be argued
that for Buthelezi the 'human' or 'anthropological' is finally given in
the 'Word of God' which he asserts addresses him within the reality
of his blackness.[21] That is why in his view Black Theology is no more
than a methodological technique of theologizing.[22]

Bereft of a theoretical perspective that can locate both the Bible and the black experience within appropriate historical contexts, Buthelezi and other black theologians are unable to explode the myth of the inherent universality of the 'Word of God'. They have been surpassed by the largely illiterate black working class and poor peasantry who have defied the canon of scripture, with its ruling-class ideological basis, by appropriating the Bible in their own way by using the cultural tools emerging out of their struggle for survival.[23] To be able to reopen the canon of scripture in the interests of black liberation, black theologians will need to take the materialist hermeneutical significance of the black experience much more seriously.

The problem of the lack of a black biblical hermeneutics of liberation, however, has its roots in the inherent crisis of the petit bourgeoisie of all shades but especially those of the colonized countries. Amilcar Cabral diagnoses the inherent malaise of this class when he declares:

> As I said, regarding culture there are usually no important modifications at the summit of the indigenous social pyramid or pyramids (groups with a hierarchical structure). Each stratum or class retains its identity, integrated within the larger group, but distinct from the identities of other social categories. By contrast in urban centers and in urban zones of the interior where the colonial power's cultural influence is felt, the problem of identity is more complex. Whereas those at the base of the social pyramid —that is, the majority of the masses of working people from different ethnic groups — and those at the top (the foreign ruling class) keep their identities, *those in the middle range of this pyramid (the native lower middle class) — culturally rootless, alienated or more or less assimilated — flounder* in a social and cultural conflict in quest of their identity.[24]

Cornel West has raised the same question of the cultural crisis of the petit bourgeois class in relation to Latin American Liberation Theology. In the case of this theology the problem expresses itself in terms of the conspicuous absence of blacks and Indians, or the issues related to them, in Liberation Theology. He suggests that when Marxists are preoccupied with an analysis that denigrates the liberating aspects of the culture of oppressed people, the implication is that such Marxists share the ethos — not of the degraded and oppressed minorities — but of the dominant European culture. Seen from the point of view of concern with the hermeneutics of liberation this means that the dominant European culture would constitute their material hermeneutical starting point. West makes the point succinctly when he asserts that:

> Historically, a central feature of this dominant European culture has been its inability to take seriously the culture of colored people and its tendency to degrade and oppress the culture of these people. For oppressed colored people, the central problem is not only repressive capitalist regimes, but also oppressive European civilizing attitudes. And even Marxists who reject oppressive capitalist regimes often display oppressive European civilizing attitudes toward colored peoples. In this sense, such Marxists, though rightly critical of capitalism, remain captives of the worst of European culture.[25]

Thus universal abstract starting points derived presumably from the biblical message will not do for a biblical hermeneutics of liberation. Black Theology for its part will have to rediscover black working-class and poor peasant culture in order to find for itself a materialist hermeneutical starting point. The particularity of the black struggle in its different forms and phases must provide the epistemological lenses with which the Bible can be read. Only such a position seems to us to represent a theoretical break with dominant biblical hermeneutics. Anything else is a tinkering with what in fact must be destroyed.

Biblical Hermeneutics of Liberation: The Case of Micah

Biblical scholars have always been aware of the tendency in biblical literature to use older traditions to address the needs of new situations. The whole question of the reappearance of themes and motifs in different contexts at different times exemplifies this process. This creation of new traditions by means of old ones has in fact been seen as a natural order of things in the internal hermeneutics of the Bible. As Deist puts it, 'It is the primary function of tradition to explain the new in terms of the old and in that way to authorize the new'.[26] G. Von Rad has gone further and drawn attention to the fact that in the biblical literature not only do we have a reapplication of old themes and motifs, but we are confronted with what are matter of fact historical data alongside a 'spiritualising interpretation of these data'.[27] According to him there is a unifying principle that keeps the various traditions together:

> In the process the old disassociated traditions have been
> given a reference and interpretation which in most cases
> was foreign to their original meaning ... Only the reader is
> not aware of the tremendous process of unification lying
> behind the picture given in the source documents.[28]

Until recently, however, biblical scholars seem to have been eluded by the historical-ideological significance of the 'unified diversity' of biblical literature.

By this we mean that although scholars have noticed the disparate character of the material and the manner in which it has been precariously held together by what they have called 'theological interpretative themes' they have nevertheless failed to see the ideological unity that pervades most of the Bible.

In recent times new directions have emerged. N.K. Gottwald's monumental book, *The Tribes of Yahweh,* breaks new ground in a radical way. Amongst other things, Gottwald argues convincingly for the cultic-ideological origins of the texts of the Bible.[29]

This paper intends to set out and to test the use of a materialist method in biblical hermeneutics of liberation. The most basic concept of a materialist approach is the mode of production. By the mode of production is meant the combination of the forces and relations of production. Forces of production refer to the means of production, e.g. land, cattle, trees, raw materials, tools, and factories, plus human labour. In every society human beings use their labour on the means of production in order to set in motion the process of production whereby at least basic human needs are met. The nature or level of development of the forces of production tends to differ in different historical epochs and geographical areas.

The relations of production refer to the places occupied by people in the process of production. The nature of these places is determined by the nature of the division of labour in the society.[30] As to whether there are classes or not in the society depends on whether the process of production is characterized by a social division of labour or not.[31] Relations of production also determine ways of disposing of the social products.

Thus the specific combination of the forces of production (means of production plus labour) with the relations of production (places in the productive process) constitute the mode of production on which societies are based. Modes of production are differentiated from one another by the way in which the surplus social products are appropriated. Hence in a communal mode of production the key characteristic is the communal method of appropriating the surplus products. Tributary modes of production have as their distinguishing feature various forms of exacting tribute. The capitalist mode of production can be differentiated through the appropriation of surplus value which is made up of unrewarded human hours in production extracted by the capitalist class from the labour power of dispossessed workers.

How a society produces and reproduces its life is fundamentally conditioned by its mode of production. The legal, religious, political and philosophical spheres of society develop on the basis of the mode of production and refer back to it.

Any approach, therefore, that seeks to employ a materialist method must inquire into (1) the nature of the mode of production, (2) the constellation of classes necessitated by that mode, (3) the nature of the ideological manifestations arising out of and referring back to that mode of production.

This paper intends, however, to do more than simply apply a materialist method to the biblical text. Rather, it aims at developing a materialist biblical hermeneutics of liberation. For this reason the following points would seem to constitute an adequate programme for such a task:

1. Material conditions of the biblical text — mode of production, class forces and dominant ideology.
2. Ideological conditions of the text — class origins of the text and class interests of the text.
3. Material conditions of the biblical reader — mode of production, classes, dominant ideology.
4. Ideological conditions of the biblical reader — class origins of the reader and class commitments of the reader.
5. Biblical hermeneutics and the class struggle — the Bible as a site of class conflict.
6. The historical-cultural specificity of the class struggle and biblical hermeneutics — towards a Black Theology of Liberation.

Material Conditions of the Book of Micah
The Mode of Production

Given a proper theoretical framework, it does not take much to realise that the Israelite monarchical system was based on a tributary mode of production. Since, however, the concept of a mode of production is a theoretical abstraction, we must give historical specificity to the form of such a mode of production in the Israelite monarchy.

The Forces of Production

The most fundamental means of production in Palestine throughout all ancient historical epochs was the land. People needed land to settle in as families *(bēth 'āvoth)* and as associations of extended families *(mishpahoth)*. But what land they settled in was determined not only by historical factors but also by ecological characteristics. Both agriculture and pastoralism depended for the form they took on the nature of the land as determined by demographical, climatological and topographical factors. The significance of land as a fundamental means of production can be appreciated even more if it is kept in mind that 'environmentally, Palestine is a conglomerate of many different ecological zones of dramatic contrast. These essentially geographical differences in the sub regions of Palestine are reflected in the patterns of settlement, as well as in economic and historical development'.[32] Thus the struggle for the occupation and indeed possession of the more favourable portions of the land of Palestine was one of the key motors of historical development in ancient times.

Both demographical and historical factors, however, led to situations where innumerable communities had to make do with naturally unfavourable parts of the land. Settlements have been uncovered by archaeologists in desert, arid, and hilly areas which are often long distances away from sources of water.

These parts of the land required of necessity particular kinds of technological means to mediate between human labour and the means of production as a way of setting the forces of production in motion. The question of tools, therefore, as part of the means of production, indicates another level at which the historical struggles of ancient Palestine were waged. We are referring here specifically to the struggles of human beings with the natural environment as they attempted to humanize and socialize it.

The Israelite community of the period before the monarchy was forced by circumstance of formidable feudal dictatorships of the city-states of Canaan to retribalize/regroup as an alternative egalitarian society of equals in the hill country of Palestine under extremely adverse natural conditions. The general problem of agriculture, namely, the soil and water, was for them particularly accentuated. C.H.J. De Geus summarizes the situation as follows.

> The tremendous efforts of the terracing of the mountain-slopes were undertaken in order:
>
> a. To transform a continuous slope into a series of level surfaces or terraced planes.

b. To prevent the run-off erosion and enhance the accumulation of soil and water.

c. To get rid of the stones and to form a flat upper layer of cultivatable soil. The stones are used for building the terrace-walls and other structures accompanying the terraces. This third reason is connected with ploughing.

d. To facilitate the transport and distribution of irrigation water in the case of (spring) irrigated terraces.[33]

N.K. Gottwald has recently reconstructed the specific combination of the relations and forces of production, that is the mode of production, of premonarchic Israel. He points among other things to the way in which an egalitarian communal society, arranged in large extended families which were relatively self-contained socio-economic units and political equals, took advantage of the introduction of iron implements for clearing and tilling the land and of slake lime plaster for waterproofing cisterns in order to keep reserve water during the annual dry season.[34.]

Despite the technological breakthrough that the use of iron implements represented for the Israelite communities of the hill country it is well to remember that technical difficulties in the local production of iron imposed a slowness in the general adoption of iron for practical use. There were for instance not yet any local smiths by the time of the beginning of the monarchy (1 Sam. 13:19ff.). As Jane C. Waldbaum has put it:

> In eleventh century contexts agricultural use of iron appears for the first time. Though most tool types continue to be made exclusively in bronze, such objects as a ploughshare from Gibeah, a sickle from Beth Shemesh, and a hafted ax-head from Tell el-Far'ah South — all from occupation levels — testify to the advent of iron for practical use in Palestine, though it is still far less commonly used than bronze.[35]

Archaeological evidence from some Iron Age sites in Palestine indicates that by the tenth century BC there was not only a good supply of iron in Palestine but that some conscious manufacturing of steel was taking place in the area. Stech-Wheeler et al. make the point that:

> The evidence presented by the Tel Qiri axe tends to confirm observations drawn from the Taanach iron. Although

an isolated object from a single site is not sufficient to
permit the characterization of a regional industry, it does
lend support to the contention that steel was being regu-
larly used in the Jezreel Valley by the tenth century B.C.[36]

There is, therefore, no doubt that agricultural production, which
was the basis of the ancient Israelite economy, was optimized by the
generalized use of iron technology. But since 'the seasonal character
of the climate that sets the boundaries of the agricultural year con-
trasts with the aseasonal demand for food which knows no boundaries',[37] it is necessary in a discussion of the forces of production to
identify patterns of labour utilization to get a complete picture of the
nature of the forces of production.

In premonarchic Israel the basic economic unit was the bēth-'av or
father's house. The labour of the family was differentiated on the basis
of age and sex to accomplish the process of producing the basic means
of subsistence. Grain and fruits were grown, and limited animal
husbandry was practiced where the *bēth-'av* owned some sheep and
goats and a few cattle. 'The staple crops were barley and wheat, wine
and olive oil, which were produced alone or in combinations depend-
ing on the variable climate and soil from region to region'.[38] Cooperation between the *bēth-'avs* which made up the *mishpaha* (extended
families networks) (2 Sam. 6:6; 1 Sam. 23:1, Ruth 3:2 and 1 Kings
22:10) helped to spread risk and to increase productivity particularly
in view of the *great diversity* of the agricultural environment created
especially by a variegated landscape overlaid by variations in rainfall,
soil and vegetation.[39]

The forces of production that took shape in the hill country of
Palestine remained fundamentally the same during the period of the
monarchy with differences in the degree of their development. Since,
however, the area occupied by Israelites during the monarchy was far
wider, covering some of the plains and valleys formerly belonging to
the Canaanite city-states, we must refer to the changes brought about
by this expansion in the forces.

Marvin Chaney has suggested that the expansion of the Israelite
land by David's conquest of the alluvial plains and valleys brought
about a change in the relations of production and ideology of premonarchic Israel.[40] We concur with him in this matter. The starting
point, however, for understanding a change in the social relations and
ideology of a social formation is seeing how the alteration in the
forces of production necessitates such a change. The availability of
crown lands in the plains and valleys gave King David the political

power to install a system of land tenure in them which conflicted with the older communally owned and communally tilled land of the hill country. Thus since 'rain agriculture in Palestine was subject to the vicissitudes of periodic drought, blight, and pestilence', the incorporation of the valleys and plains into Israel meant that there were inherent inequalities in the means of production. But however fertile the lands were, wealth was, then as now, a function of human labour. In themselves the crown lands of the plains and valleys could not produce the wealth that the Davidic monarchy required as a material basis of state power. To do this the incipient kingdom required a system of surplus extraction whose presupposition was unrewarded human labour. To be sure the crown lands were tilled and they yielded surpluses, but the mode of integrating human labour into those means of production must be discussed together with the question of the relations of production in the united monarchy of Israel.

The Relations of Production

Although David had incurred debts and obligations to the military mercenaries that fought by his side during the period of his rise to power, it is generally agreed that the capture of the Canaanite lowlands made it possible for him to make grants of land there by way of meeting these obligations rather than from the village lands in the hill country. What is more, the surplus derived from the lowlands helped him to avoid the imposition of heavy demands on the villages in order to finance the new state bureaucracy. Hopkins has isolated four advantages of the economic situation of the period of the monarchy. First, the expansion of the Israelite borders brought about the much needed geopolitical security 'conducive to the smooth operations of agricultural systems'. Second, the monarchic tax-base was expanded thus lightening the burden on village agriculturalists. More importantly the possession of newly acquired lands 'fueled international trade such as that developed with Tyre to supply the court with costly timber'. Third, the expansion of borders helped the agriculturalists to be less vulnerable to the vicissitudes of the Palestinian environment. Fourth, 'the expansion of borders not only meant an increase in sources of income and produce for import/export trade, but also could lead, given propitious geopolitical conditions, to an expansion of transit trade'.[41]

The above notwithstanding, Hopkins rightly argues further that, historically, agrarian states depend more upon surpluses extracted from the agricultural base than on profits from trade. He makes the point aptly that:

Maintaining secure borders and participating in export/
import and transit trade were decisive determinants of the
extent of the burden imposed by the monarchy upon the
village-based agricultural systems. The literary and archaeological record evidences plentitudinous royal-spon-
sored construction relating to these areas of its concern.
The fiscal apparatus which supported these and other activities of the monarchy, with its facilities and personnel ex-
penses, must have required an even greater imposition of
taxes. On top of taxes of agricultural produce, Chaney is
right to emphasize the pernicious effect of royal enterprise
on the availability of tools and labour, both of which it
siphoned away from possible involvement in the agricultural sector.[42]

There are, therefore, three main factors which precipitated
changes in the social relations of production during the monarchy.
Firstly, as Marvin Chaney has stated, the unpredictable nature of the
environment and climate of Palestine on the one hand, and the availability of surplus producing alluvial crown lands on the other created
a situation where people incurred debts through borrowing in times
of crisis.[43] Secondly, as Gottwald argues, the question of military
'call-up on rotation to supplement David's professional army on the
basis of a twelve tribe-system (1 Chron. 27:1-21)' would have had an
impact on the labour needs of the village agricultural systems. This
state of affairs, whatever its extent, would surely have 'contributed to
the neglect of crops and falling of surpluses'.[44] On the basis of exegesis of a number of texts in the books of Samuel and Kings, I have
argued elsewhere that the political murders and rebellions during the
reign of David were a function of the dislocations brought about by
structural changes in the political economy of the monarchy.[45]
Thirdly, Gottwald argues that the imposition of taxes on agriculturalists especially under Solomon marked the dominance of a new mode
of production: the tributary mode of production. Gottwald summa-
rized the fundamental character of this mode expertly when he wrote:

We can identify the quantum leap in pressure on free
agrarians by noting the offices that Solomon added to
those of David's administration:
(1)   a chief administrator over the twelve regional areas
      for the provisioning of an enlarged court establish-
      ment with accelerated taste...

(2)   a large network of officers supervising forced labour operations...

(3)   a head steward who managed the royal household, probably including royal holdings and estates not granted to retainers...

These added officers indicate a more thorough administration of the court proper, and especially a smoother, more regular, and far more abundant flow of resources *from the Israelite cultivators* to the court and royal bureaucracy, both at Jerusalem and wherever officials were installed throughout the land. In this way Solomon 'rationalized', not 'modernized', the agricultural base of the economy, for his basic strategy was not to improve the means of production but to improve the flow of as much agricultural surplus as possible into the control of his regime.[46]

Thus the stage was set for the development of a tributary social formation. The class structure of this formation was characterized by a social division of labour resulting in antagonistic social relations of production, exchange and distribution. At the top of the class structure of the monarchy was the royal aristocracy made up of the king and the nobility, the latter consisting of the king's sons and wives. As R. De Vaux has explained, next to the royal aristocracy but within the ruling class were the *sarim* (chiefs or governors), the *horim* (non-royal nobility), the *nedibim* (members of the houses of assembly by virtue of their wealth and power deriving from their land properties and thus controlling pools of landless labour), the *gibbore hayil* (valiant men, brave warriors, etc.), and the *zeqenim* (heads of influential families that had power most probably on the basis of their property).[47] There can be no doubt that the writer of the Book of Micah has this ruling class in mind when he writes: 'How terrible it will be for those who lie awake and plan evil! When morning comes, as soon as they have the chance, they do the evil they planned. When they want fields, they seize them; when they want houses, they take them. No man's family or property is safe' (Micah 2:1ff.).

Next to the ruling aristocratic and propertied class was the middle class made up of the bureaucratic and state ideologists' sectors, merchants (mainly foreigners), and artisans or craftsmen. The authors of 2 Samuel 20:23ff. describe some of the elements of this class when they state that: 'Joab was in command of the army of Israel; Benaiah son of Jehoiada was in charge of David's bodyguard; Adoniram was in charge of the forced labour; Jehoshaphat son of Ahilud was in charge of the records; Sheva was the court secretary; Zadok and Abiathar were the priests, and Ira from the town of Jair was also one of David's priests'.

Marvin Chaney has estimated that the ruling class together with the middle class made up two percent or less of the population while they controlled half or more of the total goods and services produced in the society.[48] The rest of the Israelite population constituted the oppressed and exploited class. It was made up of poor peasants, debtor slaves, captured slaves, prostitutes and criminals. Micah has them in mind when he declares against the rulers of Israel, 'You skin my people alive and tear the flesh of their bones. You eat my people up. You strip off their skin, break their bones, and chop them up like meat for the pot' (Micah 3:2ff.).

The Book of Micah, therefore, arises out of this tributary mode of production consisting of the class forces we have described. David inaugurated this social formation, Solomon pushed it to its logical conclusion and the rest of the Israelite and Judean rulers took it to its grave. For as Marx writes: 'History is thorough and goes through many phases when taking an old form to the grave'.[49] In the Book of Micah as in other prophetic texts we find some of the evidence about the material conditions out of which these biblical texts came.

Ideological Conditions of the Text
Class Origins and Class Interests of the Text

The route to this point has been a long one. There is no royal road to science. Time and space do not allow us, however, to spell out what remains of this paper in equal detail. Suffice it to indicate in general terms how, having reconstructed the material basis of the text, the biblical hermeneutics of liberation would proceed.

While the text of Micah offers sufficient indications as to the nature of the material conditions, the configuration of class forces, and the effects of class rule, it is nevertheless itself cast within an ideological framework that at the same time creates contradictions within the book and distorts the usefulness of its text for struggling classes today.

Ideology is not a lie. It is rather a harmonization of contradictions in such a way that the class interests of one group are universalized and made acceptable to other classes. Also, ideology is not a selection process or filter through which only certain facts pass. On the contrary it is a process by which the presence of certain facts is constituted by their absence.

Thus making scientific sense of the ideological condition of a text means knowing that text in a way in which it is incapable of knowing itself. Terry Eagleton makes this point expertly when he says:

> The task of criticism, then, is not to situate itself within the same space as the text, allowing it to speak or completing what it necessarily leaves unsaid. On the contrary, its function is to instal itself in the very incompleteness of the work in order to *theorise* it — to explain the ideological necessity of those 'not-saids' which constitute the very principle of its identity. Its object is the unconsciousness of the work — that of which it is not, and cannot be, aware.[50]

The text of Micah is eloquent about certain issues by being silent about them. Biblical scholars have long been puzzled by the literary disjunction between Micah 1 - 3 and Micah 4 - 7, broadly speaking. The first three chapters have been said to be genuinely Micah passages, while the others have been considered later additions. The issue that has not been faced squarely is what kind of additions are they?

Looked at ideologically these chapters fit well into the royal Zion ideology that started during the time of David, was made more sophisticated and began to be the dominant self-consciousness of the nation in the later reigns culminating in the ideological activity of the priestly class during the Babylonian exile. Bourgeois biblical scholarship has long been aware of this development, but has been unwilling or unable to perceive the political significance of such an ideological set-up. Walter Brueggemann was the first biblical scholar to elicit the political importance of ideological development in the Old Testament. He has isolated two different covenant traditions representing two different social, political and ideological tendencies, namely the Mosaic covenant tradition which is revolutionary and the Davidic covenant tradition which is status quo oriented. According to him, the 'Davidic tradition...is situated among the established and secure'.[51] Brueggemann summarizes the tension in the biblical traditions when he says:

> The Davidic-Solomonic tradition with its roots in Abrahamic memory provides an important alternative theological trajectory. We may identify two theological elements which are surely linked to this movement and which are important to the subsequent faith and literature of the Bible. First, it is generally agreed that the emergence of creation faith in Israel has its setting in Jerusalem and its context in the royal consciousness. The shift of social vision is accompanied with a shifted theological method

which embraces more of the imperial myths of the ancient
Near East and breaks with the scandalous historical particularity of the Moses tradition. The result is a universal and
comprehensive world-view which is more inclined toward
social stability than toward social transformation and liberation.[52]

The central themes of this monarchic ideology are stability, grace,
restoration, creation, universal peace, compassion, salvation. They
contrast radically with the ideology of premonarchic Israel which has
themes like justice, solidarity, struggle, vigilance.

The Book of Micah, therefore, is eloquent in its silence about the
ideological struggle waged by the oppressed and exploited class of
monarchic Israel. Apart from making available an otherwise unsuppressable body of information about the material situation of oppression, it simply luxuriates in an elaborate ideological statement of self-
comfort by dwelling on issues like the Lord's universal reign of peace
(Micah 4:1ff.); the promise of return from exile (4:6ff.); God's promise of a ruler from Bethlehem (5:2ff.); the Lord's salvation (7:8ff.)
etc. These are the dominant ideological themes of the book.

It is little wonder that dominant traditional theology has found the
Bible generally politically and ideologically comfortable notwithstanding the unsuppressable evidence of a morally distorted material
situation. The book itself, as indeed most of the Bible, offers no
certain starting point for a theology of liberation. There is simply too
much de-ideologization to be made before it can be hermeneutically
straightforward in terms of the struggle for liberation. In short, it is a
ruling-class document and represents the ideological and political
interests of the ruling class.

Be that as it may there are enough contradictions within the book
to enable eyes that are hermeneutically trained in the struggle for
liberation today to observe the kin struggles of the oppressed and
exploited of the biblical communities in the very absences of those
struggles in the text.

Conclusions: Towards a Black Theology of Liberation
The point that is being made here is that the ideological condition and
commitment of the reader issuing out of the class circumstances of
such a reader are of immense hermeneutical significance. The biblical
hermeneutics of liberation is thoroughly tied up with the political
commitments of the reader. This means that not only is the Bible a
product and a record of class struggles, but it is also a site of similar

struggles acted out by the oppressors and oppressed, exploiters and exploited of our society even as they read the Bible.

Those, therefore, that are committed to the struggles of the black oppressed and exploited people cannot ignore the history, culture, and ideologies of the dominated black people as their primary hermeneutical starting point. There can be no Black Theology of Liberation and no corresponding biblical hermeneutics of liberation outside of the black struggle for both survival and liberation. Such a struggle, however, requires being as clear about issues in the black community as possible. For as Archie Mafeje has observed:

> Despite anthropology, sociology, economics...political science (and, let us add, theology) the oppressed peoples of the world seem to be making their choice and, like them, we shall make our choices according to our vested interests and not according to some contrived professional code...
>
> Be that as it may, very rarely would [commitment to action] take place without being accompanied or preceded by what we have called the problem of intellectual self-consciousness. Therefore clear identification of issues is as important as fighting in the streets or in the mountains.[53]

NOTES

1. Marx and Engels, *On Religion* (Schocken Books, 1964), p. 50.

2. See J. Noko, *The Concept of God in Black Theology*, Ph.D. thesis, McGill University, 1977; Ntshebe, *A Voice of Protest*, M.A. thesis, Rhodes University; S. Mogoba, *The Faith of Urban Blacks*, M.A. thesis, Bristol, 1978; T.A. Mofokeng, *The Crucified among the Crossbearers*, doctoral thesis, Kampen, 1983; and numerous articles in the various issues of the *Journal of Theology for Southern Africa*.

3. 'Black and African Theologies', unpublished paper read at the University of Cape Town (1982). See also the 'Final Statement of the Black Theology Seminar', *ICT News* 1, no. 2 (Sept. 1983), pp. 9ff. S. Nolutshungu, writing on the political interpretation of the so-called 'Black Middle Class', corroborates this contention. He writes: 'As things stand, it is not surprising that attempts to define a modern cultural sensibility for Blacks in the late 1960s and early 1970s were so derivative in idiom and style—deep and authentic though the anguish which they expressed. "Middle class" Blacks remained, even so, firmly attached to the common culture and even in the area of religion where much was written about the need for a black theology, radical dissent was still expressed by separatist churches that were predominantly non-middle-class in following', *Changing South Africa* (Cape Town: David Philip, 1983), p. 125.

4. See J.H. Cone, *God of the Oppressed* (New York: Seabury Press, 1975), p. 8.

5. Ibid., p. 31.

6. Ibid.

7. Cornel West, *Prophesy Deliverance* (Philadelphia: Westminster Press, 1982), p. 109.

8. 'Christology and Liberation', *JTSA* 35 (1981), p. 30. Italics mine.

9. James Joll, *Gramsci* (Fontana Paperbacks, 1977), p. 99.

10. 'The Bible: Is Interclass Reading Legitimate?', in *The Bible and Liberation*, ed. N.K. Gottwald (Maryknoll, N.Y.: Orbis Books, 1983), p. 62.

11. Ibid.

12. A. Boesak, *Farewell to Innocence* (Maryknoll, N.Y.: Orbis Books, 1977), p. 10.

13. Marx and Engels, *Religion*, p. 42.

14. S. Gqubule, 'What is Black Theology', *JTSA* 8 (1974), p. 18.

15. E.K.M. Mgojo, 'Prolegomenon to the Study of Black Theology', *JTSA* 21 (1977), pp. 26f.

16. Ibid.

17. See also E.K. Mosothoane, 'The Use of Scripture in Black Theology', *Scripture and the Use of Scripture* (Pretoria: Unisa, 1979), p. 32.

18. S. Gqubule, *Black Theology*, p. 17.

19. Manas Buthelezi, 'Toward Indigenous Theology in South Africa', in *The Emergent Gospel* (Maryknoll, N.Y.: Orbis Books, 1978), p. 62.

20. Ibid., p. 73.

21. Ibid., p. 74.

22. Ibid.

23. For a helpful study of this process see J.M. Schoffeleer's 'African Christology', unpublished paper, Free University, Amsterdam (1981), passim.

24. Amilcar Cabral, 'The Role of Culture in the Liberation Struggle', *Latin American Research Unit Studies*, Toronto, 1, no. 3 (1977), p. 93.

25. 'The North American Blacks', in *The Challenge of Basic Christian Communities* (Maryknoll, N.Y.: Orbis Books, 1981), p. 256.

26. F. Deist, 'Idealistic *Theologiegeschichte*, Ideology Critique and the Dating of Oracles of Salvation', *OTWSA* 22 and 23 (1980), p. 65.

27. G. Von Rad, *Old Testament Theology* (London: SCM Press, 1975), p. 118.

28. Ibid., p. 118.

29. N.K. Gottwald, *Tribes of Yahweh* (Maryknoll, N.Y.: Orbis Books, and London: SCM Press, 1980), pp. 63ff.

30. M. Clevenot, *Materialist Approaches to the Bible* (Maryknoll, N.Y.: Orbis Books, 1985); F. Belo, *A Materialist Reading of the Gospel of Mark* (Orbis, 1981); W. Brueggemann, *The Prophetic Imagination* (Philadelphia: Fortress, 1978); G. Pixley, *God's Kingdom* (Orbis, 1981); the journals: *Opstand*, Christene v/h Socialisme, Amsterdam; and *Radical Religion*, Community for Religious Research and Education, Berkeley, California.

31. See Donald D. Weiss, 'Marx versus Smith on the Division of Labour,' *Monthly Review* 28, no. 3 (1976), passim.

32. T.L. Thompson, 'The Background of the Patriachs: A Reply to William Dever and Malcolm Clark', *JSOT* 9 (1978), p. 13.

33. C.H.J. De Geus, 'The Importance of Archaeological Research into the Palestinian Agricultural terraces, with an Excursus on the Hebrew Word gbi', *PEQ* 107 (1975), p. 67.

34. N.K. Gottwald, 'Domain Assumptions and Societal Models in the Study of Premonarchic Israel,' *VT Supp.* 28 (1974), p. 95.

35. Jane Waldbaum 'The First Archaeological Appearance of Iron', in *The Coming of the Age of Iron* (New Haven and London: Yale University Press, 1980), p. 86.

36. T. Stech-Wheeler, et al., 'Iron at Taanach and Early Iron Metallurgy in the Eastern Mediterranean', *AJA* 85 (1981), p. 255.

37. David C. Hopkins, 'The Dynamics of Agriculture in Monarchical Israel', *SBL Seminar Papers* (1983), p. 187.

38. N.K. Gottwald, p. 292; Leon Marfoe, 'The Integrative Transformation: Patterns of Sociopolitical Organization in Southern Syria', *BASOR* 234 (1979), p. 5.

39. David C. Hopkins, 'Dynamics', 188.

40. M. Chaney, 'Systematic Study of the Sociology of the Israelite Monarchy', unpublished paper presented to the Society of Biblical Literature seminar on the Sociology of the Monarchy, Annual Meeting, Dec. (1981), p. 12.

41. David C. Hopkins, 'Dynamics', p. 194f.

42. Ibid., p. 195.

43. M. Chaney, 'Study'.

44. N.K. Gottwald, 'Social History of the United Monarchy . . .', paper presented to the SBL seminar on the Sociology of the Monarchy, Annual Meeting, Dec. 20 (1983), p. 5.

45. I.J. Mosala, 'Social Justice in the Early Israelite Monarchy as Illustrated by the Reign of David', M.A. Thesis (unpublished), University of Manchester, 1980, passim.

46. N.K. Gottwald, 'Social History', p. 6.

47. See R. De Vaux, *Ancient Israel* (London: Darton, Longman and Todd, 1961), pp. 68ff.; I.J. Mosala, 'Social Justice', pp. 94ff.

48. M. Chaney, 'Study', p. 7.

49. Marx and Engels, *Religion*.

50. Terry Eagleton, *Criticism and Ideology* (London: Verso, 1980), pp. 89f.

51. W. Brueggemann, 'Trajectories in Old Testament Literature and the Sociology of Ancient Israel,' in *The Bible and Liberation*, ed. Norman Gottwald (Maryknoll, N.Y.: Orbis Books, 1983), p. 308.

52. Ibid., p. 314.

53. Archie Mafeje, 'The Problem of Anthropology in Historical Perspective: An Inquiry into the Growth of the Social Sciences', *Canadian Journal of African Studies* 10, no. 2 (1976), p. 332.

INDEX

Compiled by William H. Schlau